A Passion for Ideas

A Passion for Ideas

how innovators create the new and shape our world

edited by Heinrich v. Pierer
and Bolko v. Oetinger

Purdue University Press
West Lafayette, Indiana

Library of Congress Cataloging-in-Publication Data

Wie kommt das Neue in die Welt? English.
A passion for ideas : how innovators create the new and shape our world / edited by Heinrich von Pierer and Bolko von Oetinger.
p. cm.
Translation of: Wie kommt das Neue in die Welt?
Includes additional material.
Includes bibliographical references.
ISBN 1-55753-209-5 (cloth : alk. paper)
1. Technological innovations. 2. Creative ability. I. Pierer, Heinrich von. II. Oetinger, Bolko von. III. Title.

HC79.T4 W4613 2001
338'.064—dc21   2001044099

Contents

Freedom and Organization

The Individual and the Environment

More and Too Much

Preface

This book, conceived by the Siemens Arts Program and The Boston Consulting Group, was originally published in Germany under the title *Wie kommt das Neue in die Welt?* For the English-language version we have deleted some articles and have commissioned a number of new interviews. Some of the original articles now speak of events that are several years in the past. We have kept them in the book because the occasional dated quality of examples does nothing to decrease the power of the ideas.

The editors appreciate all the work by Ted Buswick, who recreated the book for the English-language edition and managed its development. Thank-you also to our publisher, Tom Bacher, for his belief in this book and his patience and to Dr. Beate Hentschel of the Siemens Arts Program for her contributions. Thank-you to Margaret Hunt and Nancy Macmillan for their copyediting expertise, to Heidi Eckert and Simone Kesten for keeping the communications flowing, and to Matthew Wikswo for editorial insights.

Heinrich v. Pierer
Bolko v. Oetinger

Novitas ante Portas

Bolko v. Oetinger and Heinrich v. Pierer

As indicated by the title of our introduction, the new truly is knocking at the door. As our many authors agree, in many different ways, the new is not hard to find. And the new is often also "unusual," as the original Latin suggests. *Novitas* seeks us out; it lies in the human spirit; it is delivered by all who are creative. It is found abroad and at home; it inheres paradoxically in processes that already exist, finds liberation in innovation, and transforms those who encounter it.

The value of the new is also beyond question. In the final analysis, we really have no choice but to renew ourselves or slide into obscurity. Art must seek new ways to explain the changing world or lose its meaning. Science must answer new questions or surrender its power. Companies must renew themselves or die. Innovation or extinction: there is no alternative to this hard choice.

Or, to put it positively, consider the blessings of the new. If we welcomed innovation in our organizations, businesses, public services, arts organizations, churches, associations, schools, and universities, we could release energy, create jobs, and liberate creative meaning. Why would we do anything but welcome it?

The history of this book and its stories are an instance of creating the new. We, its editors, recognize all too well not only the importance of newness and innovation—it is, after all, our daily bread and butter—but also the difficulty associated with it. With that awareness in mind, we had a simple idea: to understand the new by considering all its facets. Exactly what those facets are, however, turned out to be a difficult question in its own right.

Approached from an institutional perspective (encompassing government, commerce, and higher education), our inquiry threatened to degenerate into a rehashing of timeworn arguments. Hypothetical guidelines such as "More freedom, less order" and "More crisis, less continuity" seemed too deterministic, and seeking the new in "creativity and culture" seemed too amorphous. So to understand the new in new terms, we decided to look in all fields of human endeavor for professionals who have encountered firsthand the new, the unfamiliar, and the unusual.

Who are these innovators? They are a group of visionaries: composers, CEOs, chairmen of the board, philosophers, researchers, managers, writers, choreographers, theater producers, consultants, filmmakers, architects, school directors, Nobel prizewinners, engineers, biochemists, physicists, historians, economists, political scientists, publishers, artists, and citizens of the world from the United States, Holland, Germany, Great Britain, Switzerland, and China.

They tell us that the new is possible, that it requires strength because it involves us in unexpected conflict with what already exists. It has to do with personal commitment to the unknown and accepting speed and consequences. It demands a free spirit in open surroundings. But they also tell us that it takes time. It gives rise to ethical dilemmas and challenges the meaning of our actions. It comes up against organizational and cultural boundaries. It makes its way to us on twisted intellectual, social, technical, psychological, and organizational paths. It needs the helping hand of the obsessed to free itself from the old, and it either breaks through or withers.

As we received and studied these diverse insights, we began to see a common denominator: those who would admit the new must summon extraordinary courage. The barriers can be enormous. A few basic themes emerged as well. Our first two sections (The New and the Known, and Us and Them) highlight the importance of strong individuals. The next two sections (Freedom and Organization, The Individual and the Environment) deal with the role of the social context surrounding innovators. The final section (More and Too Much) asks hard questions about the reasonable limits that innovation must set for itself.

Beyond these overlapping themes, though, we have deliberately chosen to present neither a grand unifying theory of renewal nor a packaged solution ready to take to work on Monday morning. Rather, in the interest of provoking thought, we present a collection of readings whose systematic variations we hope will lead our readers off the beaten track, awaken their senses, and open new perspectives. We aspire to encourage readers in businesses, schools, governments, churches, universities, theaters, and laboratories to express the tension between the old and the new in such a way that the new can enter our lives, broadening the opportunity space and making room for individuals to grow.

The new, in our view, is not meant only in terms of new products, information, or services. It is also meant as renewal. To renew means to recreate oneself, again and again and again, year after year, decade after decade. All organizations have to come out for an encore or become irrelevant. We must never cease to ask ourselves: Will my organization recreate itself again?

The New and the Known

The hardest part in innovating is not the discovery of the great new idea, but freeing oneself from the known—the old familiarities that required such energy, emotion, and dedication when they were created but which now perversely represent the strongest obstacles to change. This was a dilemma for no less a mind than the philosopher Immanuel Kant, who once fired his longtime servant, Martin Lampe, and replaced him with a new one. But on every detail, Kant found that he obsessively compared the new servant's behavior with that of Lampe. Even when he was busy researching arcane scholarly references, Kant heard only the word "Lampe" in his mind. Driven to frustration, he was reduced to writing himself a memo in his notebook: "The name of Lampe must be forgotten." A written re-minder to forget—grotesque, but a testimonial to the real difficulty of making room for the new.

But is the old always a hindrance to the new? Philosophy and rhetoric professor Jürgen Werner, whose article is discussed at greater length elsewhere, claims that the two may be different and inseparable faces of the same coin: "The old is always yesterday's new thing. But that which is new is also always the old of tomor-row." The new is therefore not anything final, but something tran-sitional, because evolution never truly stops, whether it moves in big lurches or tiny steps. Accordingly, as the essays in this section reveal, responses to the tension between new and old vary with cir-cumstances. Sometimes the old can retreat and survive only slightly diminished; there is no need, after all, to overthrow good practices completely if they have not hardened into stifling dogma.

Unfortunately, it is sadly true that those very things that we created with so much effort often do become tyrants: our struc-tures, our customers, our technology, our procedures. By their pure existence they tend to suppress radical alternatives. This phenome-non is well known to artists who literally have their hands on something fundamentally new. It is not an abstract problem; it is the reality of day-to-day work. As filmmaker Peter Greenaway describes the enemy of creativity in the cinema, it is the "tyranny of the text, tyranny of the actor, tyranny of the film format, and, most importantly, tyranny of the camera." If we can't escape them, we can't make a new type of movie.

For ballet maestro William Forsythe, "it isn't possible to create something new within your own four walls, at least the mental ones." We usually do the opposite, only remodeling and repeating the old routines and functions we already know. By preparing ourselves, by letting go of established models, we can rediscover the new within us.

Some artists find that the ability to surrender control rather than exert it is the key to conquering the tyranny of the known. For novelist Harry Mulisch, the new does not come "out of strenuous efforts or intensive thought," but rather through mental disengagement. He speaks of the need to prepare for the moment of creativity and then to wait until it arrives, only at which point one can begin "to 'unlearn,' [to] forget what you know." Unlearning is the hardest part of the innovative work. It might take years to forget. This is not a matter of creating superficial chaos, but of hard work to find the new content. Similarly, Forsythe describes the rhythm and physical energy of dancing as a way to summon "the ability to let go," to "get away from our own thoughts, from our own expertise, which always knows what's right and what's wrong."

The composer Wolfgang Rihm describes the necessary mental predisposition in a similar way. For him the new is always woven into tradition: "Nothing comes into being alone. . . . The new is always here, because it is the old. It is all here only we change our position so that the point of view and what we see is new."

In the results-oriented world of business, it is especially difficult for managers to provide their innovators with the psychological space they require to see the new, including freedom from time constraints and no predetermined answers. But that ability to shield creators from pressure is exactly the role that Rihm sees for mentors and, by extension, for managers: "The only thing that can be taught

[is] the necessity of having your own question. . . . a mentor publicly stands by the student, provides relief, the space that is necessary in order to wait, undisturbed by external compulsions; to wait with *no goal, no result* . . . because the new hesitates to appear where it is expected." Only if we are "being unintentional" and not results-oriented can we find the new. Most managers, scientists, artists, and educators can validate this by pointing to examples of valuable innovations that have appeared serendipitously.

In established businesses, innovation is typically truly welcome only in a time of crisis. Yet it is during the smooth times that we must be preparing for the turbulence to come by planning for the next product or market or customer. To do this requires an ability to openly investigate things not known and things that, to all purposes, appear impossible. The innovative spirit must be liberated—a more difficult, costly, and time-consuming process than might be expected.

Us and Them

As art critic and reporter Katja Blomberg tells us, in 1602 pirates brought the new—in the form of Chinese porcelain—to the courts of Europe, virtually by force. In the years that followed, a dynamic and vigorous interplay occurred between Dutch taste, Chinese manufacturing skills, Japanese suppliers, and Dutch trading networks, resulting in a hybrid Chinese-Dutch-Japanese style that revolutionized the world of European luxury goods. We can imagine no better example for productive relations between "us"—what is known and familiar to our culture, whichever one it is—and "them"—anything that is foreign to us, be it from another culture, race, language, country, city, or company.

Judging from the perspective of today's highly industrialized countries, the routes by which ideas traveled in the seventeenth century seem complicated to us. Even though we have more information to manage, we enjoy global communications of a kind no other generation of humanity has ever had; we have more knowledge, better and faster logistics around the globe, and more technical options to pursue the new than we have had at any other time in history. Yet we feel more comfortable as proud exporters of new products than as intensive recipients of foreign ideas. Perhaps our highly praised globalization is just too new—or we are too conceited, or we increasingly discover that economic issues are not the only ones that matter in our economies. Whatever the case is, we too often persist in an attitude of "not invented here."

But we know that fierce competition is a stimulant. You don't lose by opening yourself up. And there's nothing unworthy about copying. On the contrary, you can gain from openly accepting the unfamiliar and using it. Perhaps we in the Western industrialized countries are at a turning point. Today the path from inside out is still dominant. The richness of content of the opposite path, from outside in, is relatively small. Our mentality continues to be based mainly on an "export-centered world." But in the future we have to admit more inspiration from foreign markets if we want to stay competitive and continue to grow.

Business is moving in that direction. Globalization is not just about organizational structures or building factories in foreign countries or increasing exports; it is about deeply established global networks with suppliers, customers, universities—relationships that thrive on research exchange and daily osmosis between the "other" and "us." Today, multinational companies have established global networks with suppliers, customers, universities, and other research organizations. They easily penetrate national borders and serve their customers worldwide. They have developed important drivers to absorb ideas from the outside, as business consultant Bolko v. Oetinger says. Companies have increasingly invested in their own knowledge networks. There is an enormous global convergence of competences and capabilities. Best practices on a global scale are standard procedures for all modern companies; comparing with the best has become day-to-day business. The initial confusion of physical networks and networking and of systems and people is gone.

Despite the technological thrust of the Internet and the IT revolution, such simple practices as exchanging and rotating people have not only become normal management procedures of successful global companies, their frequency has gone up. A key to success is providing strong roles for outstanding, inspiring individuals, idealists who passionately want to bring, in Bolko v. Oetinger's words, "the foreign organization into their own." In business they play the same important role in innovation as the individual artists in their fields. Even the traditional conflicts in the matrix organization between divisions, countries, and functions can be managed by behavioral approaches, as shown by BP.[1] Today, the average international company is structurally much better prepared to find new ideas and to let them enter than ten years ago. But there is still a long way to go.

The increasing importance of cities and regions as competence centers for certain industries will help foster global exchange processes. For example, Silicon Valley is a center for electronics, Spartanburg for mechanical engineering, and London and New York for finance. Cities and regions are becoming the markets where new ideas are getting exposed, refined, exchanged, and distributed to the world. To be in the most dynamic cities or regions of their field is a must for global companies to attract the best people.

Research on learning points in a similar direction. The more companies become borderless and the more national boundaries disappear, the more organizations and people will look for new identities. The research of Peter Senge and Otto Scharmer of the Society for Organizational Learning indicates that in a learning organization a predetermined structure does not exist; instead participants provide the necessary conditions that allow them to learn. The learning community could be the place where not only the osmosis between new and old takes place, but where a new identity is created. People in large organizations learn well if they agree with the organizational goals and principles, if there is a high degree of self-determination and mutual involvement, and if there are core processes on which practitioners, researchers, and managers who have mastered organizational skills decide together. In such learning communities— sometimes called practice communities because that is where daily professional cooperation takes place—the exchange of ideas materializes in intensive dialogues. Providing this network is the key role of management. Today, in most organizations the various units and layers are too separated from each other, although there are exceptions. In international development teams and on large teams managing major organizational changes, there are very often communities in which know-how can be passed from colleague to colleague. In order to stimulate the osmosis of learning and welcome the unfamiliar, one needs to explicitly manage these communities.

Freedom and Organization

In all the spheres of human behavior (business, education, warfare, religion, politics), a tension invariably exists between freedom and organization—between unconstrained opportunity for the self-determination of creative individuals on the one hand, and, on the other, the rules and protocols which regulate daily practice. This tension is ancient, necessary, and dynamic. It helps us balance the extremes of creative anarchy and uncritically obedient orthodoxy. When little acts of revolution and repression stay within normal bounds, they represent only the healthy effort to optimize the balance between innovation and routine. But in an organization, where should the outer boundaries of that balance be, and how flexible should they be? Directly and indirectly, the articles in "Freedom and Organization" address these questions.

Businesses use the structure of their organizations to institutionalize success. Such rules, often inherited from predecessors, are our own to obey or challenge as we see fit. Since modern business—like warfare and politics—is fundamentally competitive, the new, as a means to strategic advantage, pays a higher dividend than it does in less purely competitive spheres, such as religion and education. With that in mind, business sometimes strives to sacrifice rules on the altar of the new. But this is easier said than done. Are we prepared to grant creative individuals exemptions from our own rules? Are we ready to allow exceptions? And assuming we are, we must then confront the only harder question: How do we do it?

Finding the Right Degree of Order

Some say that innovation and creativity emerge through disorder or disorganization. Innovation expert John Kao's "Virtue of Disorder" takes us to a new economy whose ability to compete is characterized less by efficiency and control than by "speed, originality, intelligence, and agility." This demands creativity. "Creativity in business . . . is subversive to the established order." It leads to the "reperceiving" of existing circumstances and is thereby a catalytic journey of discovery. Strategy and creativity are therefore the two sides of a coin.

Charles Schwab is an example of innovation through a new order. Charles Schwab "began in reaction to almost everything that had been before. And here we are, 25 years later, still thinking of ourselves as an upstart firm," Schwab VP Dan Leemon tells us. Its founders recognized that the old style of financial organization was not sufficiently effective and completely revised it, but they then institutionalized the new way so as to embed creativity. Schwab has been able to build both disruptive and incremental innovation into the corporate culture. Innovation is something that happens in a process between top and bottom, built on intuition and creativity mixed with analysis. The culture and values of highly creative and customer-oriented companies are reflected in employees' feelings of ownership and excitement, financial upsides, and deep convictions about what is good for the customer. Innovation in such companies goes way beyond the obvious. This spirit, generated by the managed culture, can make companies truly innovative.

Maybe what is needed is not so much disorder or a new order but rather a reordering, says Berthold Leibinger, CEO of an industrial firm and veteran of government councils on innovation. He uses the German machine tool industry to show what management can structurally do to increase innovative behavior. Benchmarking showed that German machine tools consistently cost 20–30 percent more than competitors' products, and that two-thirds of that excess was caused by management (products, organizations) and just one-third by the outside environment. Reorganizing TRUMPF GmbH, one of the leading German machine tool companies, into smaller production units of around 100 people who have a lot of freedom to decide increased productivity by 20 percent and processing speed by 50 percent. Revising structures can free up a lot of creativity.

Innovation is a process that can be managed; in some cases, innovation can also be achieved through structure. Regulations can be a help or hindrance to creativity, depending on how you deal with them. Even creative artists have performed well under some rules. Leibinger tells us that Johann Sebastian Bach signed a contract with the city of Leipzig to deliver a cantata every Sunday— and he wrote 300 of them. Friedrich Schiller promised to cover his mortgage payments to the city of Weimar through writing one tragedy per annum for several years.

Nurturing the Individuals

There is no scientifically proven theory of creative action. The late Franz Emanuel Weinert, formerly of the Max Planck Society, speculates, "Perhaps the significant new is invented or discovered just because particularly individual constellations of conditions are in existence." Much innovation comes from a proper nurturing of employees and coworkers. Cross-fertilization of ideas, independence, high expectations, trust, and nonprescriptive leadership come together in scientist Roger Tsien's lab to create a uniquely productive environment.

Watching a biologist at work, we can study *in vivo* how interwoven individual creative strengths, emotional stability, and the processes of learning and research are in finding the new. Tsien, using a theatrical analogy, describes his breakthrough research in biochemistry as a situation in which somebody had already written the novel, but not yet the play. Tsien discovered the work, picked it up, and turned it into a production: he found the key application to the idea. The scientific education that allowed him to do this was one where he was not taught, but rather enabled, to execute his own creative designs. The proper atmosphere, as Tsien shows, can be critical in enabling innovation in students or coworkers.

Business executive Michael Hilti offers more ideas about nurturing individuals. Much is said nowadays about how we can revolutionize our rigid company structures. On closer examination, this rapidly translates into liberation of the individual, whom we have tied up, like Gulliver, with hundreds of little rules. We have to loosen the ties—for example, by enlarging individual responsibility and self-control, trusting others more, and allowing for experimentation and multiple or alternative playing fields. How do we create an environment in the business, Hilti asks, "in which people feel comfortable and let their creativity unfold"? By using a human touch, encouraging people to take care of others—the beginner, the weaker person, the colleague on the same team—and to promote not just their own ideas, but also those of others and "incorporate [them] into the business." Because innovation comes from people, it's especially important to nurture the middle-rank talent. There are always limits and decisions that have to be accepted, but the status quo can be substantially improved when seen from a different perspective, by having employees (or yourself) working more in different areas, in different countries, and on different tasks. Instead of defining new rules, we should "keep the business in motion," says Hilti, by giving people freedom to move.

Nurturing the Organizational Forces

Similarly, business executive Ron Sommer tells how innovation requires "a microclimate which is fertile and encourages the flow of ideas." This "fluidity of ideas must be combined with high levels of motivation and the willingness to work hard." Paradoxically, he believes that innovation also needs laziness. Ketchup, for example, was invented because "people were too lazy to press tomatoes," bicycles and cars "because they were too lazy to walk."

Widening the space of creativity by encouraging the flow of ideas does not imply abandoning organizational rules. However, creativity and spontaneity can only flourish with substantial liberation from rules, be they governmental, societal, or organizational, because "the influence of what is old and established is persistent, so a considerable expenditure of energy is needed to think up something new, get a new idea off the ground, and make it work, " explains Siemens president and chief executive officer Heinrich v. Pierer. Indeed, the modern corporation is able to provide a fruitful context for innovations to blossom. As innovation rarely emerges in isolation nowadays, the creative personality also needs the organization, its knowledge, means, and skills, its targets and motivation, its team and its other creative people.

As individuals must be nurtured, so must the larger organizational forces. The new is always hidden in the old; it is part of the old. One needs to deal with the old. Only if we systematically research our existing products, services, processes, customers, competitive offerings, and markets will avenues for innovation appear, sometimes as tacit compromises, hidden weaknesses, or possible gaps. Once we have discovered them, we need to look for new solutions. We also must reexperience failures and setbacks that need to be acknowledged and understood for further learning. How the corporate culture deals with failures and how it helps the organization deal with them are key for encouraging the new. By systematically sharing failures, best practices, and the knowledge of universities, research organizations, and suppliers, the learning of the organization can be substantially improved.

Disruptive innovations, such as those engineered at Charles Schwab & Company, are the result of their culture's allowing for an open dialogue among and between the top and the bottom; of strong leadership on the one hand and strong ownership of the employees on the other hand; and a strong culture and values shared by both. It is a constant, productive, managed cultural tension that creates new things.

The Individual and the Environment

Since the nineteenth century, creativity has been the province of the genius, understood as a solitary individual, working alone to express—at great personal cost—the insights afforded by pure imagination. In theory, adverse environments only increased the value of his effort. In retrospect, it seems as if the geniuses of each era suffered the greatest personal hardships: social, economic, romantic, or medical.

But the model of the romantic genius is only one possible relationship between creative individuals and their environments, albeit a remarkably persuasive and enduring one. Now newer models of genius are emerging: models with new understandings of what geniuses are, of how they work, about how they function within complex environments, even about how one can shape their environments to help them.

Current psychological research no longer believes in the rare "genius as the creator of the significant new," Weinert tells us. Besides, in our modern world, the new frequently results from the cooperation of many individuals, not from just one person.

Weinert fruitfully complicates our idea of what it means to be a creative human being. For the conventional image of the solitary romantic genius, driven by flashes of unpredictable insight, Weinert substitutes a new notion of a creative person: someone who is not characterized only by high cognitive qualities, but rather an individual endowed with a "wealth of imaginative thought, the ability to draw analogies, and for metaphoric, associative and playful thought, as well as the competence in analytical and constructive intellectual thought." This standard is certainly very high, and who among us could claim to meet it entirely? Creativity is not only dependent upon cognitive skills, but also on the acquisition and exploitation of fertile scientific realms, a strong curiousity, the desire to create things anew, to experiment playfully in one's environment, not succumbing to contradictions, and to pursue one's goals compulsively.

Forging the Right Environment

Is it sufficient to simply put the best and the brightest at the critical decision points of our organizations to ensure the most innovative solutions? Of course, creative individuals or groups of talented people are always present at the birth of anything new. As we explore to what extent an individual creates the innovation solely by himself or is supported by a cultural environment, we start again with the individual: We hear how a theatrical producer/director (Harold Prince) and a composer and multimedia artist (Todd Winkler) view their own creativity, and what a Far Eastern Gropius scholar (Tao Ho) has to say about how the creative mind works.

Sometimes the force of a dominant creative personality can

yield innovative results. How can a Broadway producer stay creative and remain financially viable? Harold Prince points to three things. First, he has a deep conviction about his "artistic idea" that overrules everything else, such as customers, profits, marketing—what he characterizes as Wall Street. Second, he has the flexibility to rapidly change the program if it is not successful, not venturing too far out on an "artistic limb" or dwelling on failures. Third, he encourages entrepreneurs to stick with him for the long haul. (In this, he has an advantage over most CEOs.) Creative freedom and rules are not mutually exclusive; they can live in a healthy symbiosis. One just has to find that proper balance between market forces and artistic expression and have the force of personality and/or past success to convince others to agree.

Creativity does not lie in the binary "either/or"; it rests in the frequent "maybe," in fuzzy logic, in the intersections of different disciplines. Todd Winkler uses digital technology to bridge artistic disciplines and thereby widen his creative horizon. Whether he designs his computerized music to interact with musicians or with dancers, Winkler's goal is "a good conversation" or "a jazz ensemble, especially a free jazz band, in which the way each player plays is affected by, and affects, the others. It's the same feeling of engagement as in conversation." He's not there yet, but his software does interact with other sounds or with human motion to create improvisational duets, and the musicians and dancers are frequently inspired by this strange partner. Winkler is careful in how he uses technology as a creative tool. He believes that technology has made life more difficult, not easier, and that technology should be used in his creative arena only when it is essential.

Tao Ho says that unchecked technology, driven by anxiety, could "alienate the human heart from the hand," and the architect could lose his creative prerogative to the computer or to standardized production. He sees "inspiration, emotion, or intuition" as the driving elements that link the left and right halves of the brain. This link forges the balance between the yin and yang, function and beauty, knowledge and wisdom. The creative mind has the ability to create relationships between completely unrelated parts, to see inspiring connections between discrete phenomena. The computer can read a series of notes and play Chopin's Nocturnes, but it will never sound like Rubinstein. Only the interpreter is able to transform these notes into a sensitive flow of musical expression.

Prince warns against the pressures of Wall Street. Winkler and Ho are concerned with our reaction to the pressures of technology. Publisher, essayist, and poet John Barnie advises writers to avoid the attractions offered by politics, academia, and the media. He tells us not to suffocate the writer—the writer often needs to be isolated to be creative. Weinert gives us an alternative view by seeing the benefits of group environments, explaining how innovations usually emerge from a specific cultural context. Physicist Gerd Binnig combines aspects of these views, first presenting a perspective of multiple layers, giving us an image of creative environments embedded one in another. Within this structure, the individual, must be willing to be vulnerable and foolish as long as creativity and intelligence are being served. Binnig concludes by emphasizing the importance of isolation, of "differentiating yourself from other things."

These views collectively tell us that different individuals and occupations require different environments for maximum creativity, and that the relationships between individuals and their environments are crucial. The previous section indicated that some organizational structures are more likely to enhance creativity than others. Organizations can be manipulated to be more stimulating or less stimulating, and this is where we can really help the new break through. When such organizations generate a "high level of demands, strong task-orientation, shared attentiveness towards new ideas, an open atmosphere for discussions and a balanced relationship between individual competition and social common ground," as Weinert describes it, new ideas may take root and flourish.

Can we change monotonous environments and repetitive activity so as to encourage creativity? Jürgen Werner explains how the Benedictine monks long ago found ways to conquer spiritual inertia and rediscover the new in a world that on the surface changed little from day to day. "Nothing is as tiring as always having to look at the same thing." Their solution, according to Werner, was to make room for the necessary, creative stillness. Leisure requires undisturbed reflection and time, or else it does not generate anything new. The new is mentally painful, because it separates us from old values and attitudes that we have come to cherish. The new, a tender blossom, needs "space for leisure, thereby providing space for creative rest," just as extinction-threatened nature requires nature reserves. If inquiry is "threatened by extinction," then so is the new. Here lies the connection to free association, to the very human source of doubt, the searching for and closing of gaps, that are the properties of creative people.

We need such a permanent spiritual pendulum swinging between our environment and us, creating momentum instead of inertia. In the face of the hectic habits of our daily lives, we must consciously make room for the necessary stillness and purposeless musings that are the origin of creativity. We must intentionally disturb ourselves through the careful management of leisure.

We must live with contradictions. They are the sources of the new. Our thoughts should sometimes alter their course like a dialectic pendulum. In business, market anomalies are known to be a strong signal for an imminent breakthrough. In the midst of such a tension, the real voyage of discovery begins; and the back-and-forth motion between opposing ideas, which we hope makes us more receptive to innovation, sustains it. As Werner observes, "Creativity is more than individual ability. It grows from the systematic interplay of psychological readiness, social demands, economic incentives, intellectual talents, and a series of conditions that promote attentiveness."

Mary Frates, taking the perspective of a director of an educational and cultural organization, knows that isolation is not even a possibility. For her, a constant productive and managed cultural tension creates new things. To keep her organization afloat and growing, Frates learned the important role of the political environment it had to adapt to and nurture and the sponsor environment it had to look for in order to keep innovating. Her story is an inspiration to those in the public sector who often feel overwhelmed by all the forces bearing down from outside.

The Business Environment

The businesspeople play a prominent role in this creative game. Their managerial ability to introduce new products or services on a global level and quickly adapt concepts at a moment's notice cannot be valued highly enough. Businesses are particularly well suited to lead the revolution in new creative environments because they have well thought-out structures and managers responsible for the different units. Therefore, every business should have a sufficient number of supervised creative units in which working conditions can be created so that people can react in an innovative, mobile, and rapid manner.

Leaders are changing their approaches to the relationship between workers and their environment:

- freeing minds from corporate baggage so they can make high-quality decisions;
- experimenting with new group and organizational structures;
- designing workspace to increase openness, tolerance, and a supportive atmosphere;
- finding the creative potential in constraints; and
- building cultures of creativity.

Weinert talks about the creative nature of extraordinary people. Being cognizant of the environments in which they act, we can then better observe individuals, both extraordinary and typical, reacting to their environments. The more their working conditions are stress-free and supportive—thereby encouraging the individual to be creative—the more likely it is that the new can gain a foothold.

More and Too Much

Our standard model of progress contains a very important premise. As long as we believe in growth and evolution, we must have innovation. Innovation is the engine of growth, and we all know that growth is what keeps companies alive, quantitatively and qualitatively. But what would happen if innovation reached the end of its natural lifetime—and, with it, growth? Is this theoretically impossible?

Suppose for a moment that we really have achieved the high point of innovation, that the capacity for innovation is nearly exhausted. What if only the smallest improvements remained to be made? What if growth rested "on finite information resources," as sociology professor Gerhard Schulze asks us? Is there "an anthropologically limited supply of goals that appear to be reasonable, at least in regard to products that should have a specific use?" And who determines what is reasonable?

Is there more than just profits to be considered in running a business? Where is self-control and responsibility? Who thinks about future generations? No one wants to allow our world to be ecologically out of control, but who will take care of it, when the achievments of the nation-states continue to fade away? The "personal responsibility" of the economic participants is becoming an "indispensable instrument of control," says international business advisor Stephan Schmidheiny. Taking responsibility means creating, restructuring, limiting, but also extracting initiative. It is about creating our world so as to conserve energy and protect the environment. Couldn't sustainability provide the impetus for the new? Is there a new category of the new that comes from resource-conserving progress?

Schmidheiny's sense of personal and global responsibility is further developed by architect William McDonough. He sees the status quo as ecologically destructive and believes we have to look at problems in new ways. But rather than take an extreme position that could unintentionally destroy business while saving the environment, McDonough recognizes that short-term profitability must remain. Through high-profile work, such as that at Ford's River Rouge plant, he's demonstrating his principles to the business world.

Technology consultant and author Christoph-Friedrich v. Braun raises such interesting questions as how we determine the difference between what we can change and what we should change. The power of the idea conflicts with the anxiety that the growth spiral will reach a natural limit, that our ideas will be extinguished. Economists believe dearly in the power of new ideas. Even they know the ethical limits and the discussions that we must all face: does the next "more" still make economic or social sense? And what does "sense" mean? Who determines sense? The thought that the new could also be a wasted effort has always stirred entrepreneurs and it always will. Are there ecological limits (Schmidheiny and McDonough)? Is continued growth simply achieved by "more" speed, quantity, newness, improvement (v. Braun)?

Forty years after *Sputnik* triggered the biggest technology race ever known, we claim that next to technical innovation itself, time is the main driver and competitive weapon of innovation-based growth. Indeed, the "escalation of acceleration," as v. Braun calls it, has become a symbol of our society. But what happens when the acceleration reaches its natural limits? Won't we then have to return to the real innovation if we are to offer more to consumers?

But what is real innovation? Who sets the standard? In asking what progress really means, we find answers about the new. Could it be that the new is hiding some place else, where one didn't expect it—in sustained growth? How can we reconcile the need for speed with the importance of those protected spaces for unrestricted inquiry?

We conclude with core questions regarding the new: Why? To what purpose?

Will we leave a better world behind with the new than when we first encountered it? We have questions but no answers. Everyone must proceed through these doubts and tensions, or else the new cannot gain a foothold.

We have seen the new in its incredible diversity and seen the forces with which it must wrestle. We know that the new must pass through an exciting, multilayered psychological, economic, organizational, and technical process if it is to come to us. We can help. Therein lies the appeal.

The new is like the seed of a plant in the springtime that must painfully break through the hard soil of what already exists. The ideas of experts on various facets of innovation lead us to five basic principles that could help us make way for the new.

First, we must loosen the hardened ground for the seedling with a quick and powerful scoop of a virtual spade. This requires a lot from us because we will have to say good-bye to the conventional just when it appears to be most successful. Courage and risk-taking are required.

Second, so many exceptional but strange seeds will be offered to us. Why not be bold and mix in a few unknown ones with our own and see what happens? We only have to set up a net so that we can catch it all when it blossoms and bears fruit.

Third, we need a healthy environment: a macroclimate that keeps government and society out of the sanctuary where questioning can take place and requires that we engage ourselves publicly;

and a microclimate that provides enormous creative possibilities. Plowing our own ground and removing the weeds—that shouldn't be too difficult.

Fourth, we need the strongest seeds—those with the greatest potential for creativity—and we must develop the most appropriate soil for them. Working together, we stand the best chance for seeing that our hope is fulfilled: the seeds sprout.

Fifth and last, our efforts to let in the new must persist so that we don't allow a deceptive equilibrium or inertia to settle in and cause us to fall down again. We must till each furrow ceaselessly but in a disciplined way, until we see the tender young shoots in the ground.

We can already accomplish these five activities. Even if we need all of them at the same place at the same time, that doesn't seem so difficult. Yet the process is deceptively hard. Innovation is Herculean work, an unbelievably demanding task that affects all of us. It is rarely a harmonious process; it is hard work by great people. When it works, it offers a moment of transcendence. As Mary Frates comments on her work on art education of children: "All say we've changed their lives."

Note

1.   See Morten T. Hansen and Bolko von Oetinger, Introducing T-Shaped Managers: Knowledge Management's Next Generation, *Harvard Business Review*, March 2001, 107–116.

the New
and the
Known

Real Movies Are Yet to Come
An Interview with Peter Greenaway
Hannah Hurtzig

In the film *The Cook, the Thief, His Wife and Her Lover,* Spica, the boorish thief, finds an ex-libris note in a book that leads him to the address of the librarian who is his wife's lover, whom he then cruelly tortures with a book and then murders. The address is clearly recognizable: Falconberg Court—Greenaway's business address. I had hoped to meet him there, the site of one of his best portrait photos as well. A properly dressed gentleman, looking his viewers straight in the eye, meters of film reels stacked on shelves in the background, and across his knees, a large, valuable old book, an edition by Flavius Josephus, the late-classical historian of Jewish culture. Greenaway's didactically outstretched index finger points at an illustration in the book. There he is: the educated British gentleman, experimental filmmaker, and avid reader, savior of literary culture in film, archivist, and scholar. However, I met him in his King Street office in an unspectacular rear courtyard, a totally unglamorous office. We had one hour, and I managed to coax an additional half-hour conversational encore from him. I have interviewed several artists in the past, but this case was different in one regard: every single sentence Greenaway uttered during this time was at once statement, reference, and information, combined and articulated with sophistication, in perfect Oxford English.

The following statement, which came out of the interview, would fit under any portrait: "We must first hold a mirror up to art before we hold a mirror up to nature."

Jean Renoir said that an artist only has one idea in his lifetime, which he then repeats over and over again.

I believe he said that the artist has two ideas. Since my two ideas encompass sexuality and death, they are fortunately big enough to keep me busy my whole life. But I had most of my ideas by the age of 25, and they continue to sustain me.

When one encounters your early films, it is clear that the figures and names, and even the types of animals, that appear once are carried throughout your entire work. Is one never again free of the spirits one invokes?

Why should one want to be free of them? It is a beautiful thing always to sleep with the same woman and always to eat strawberries in June. Some of our most important life experiences are based on repetition.

Can one then say that the themes in your films are repetitious, but that your innovation, your inventions in the technological realm, can be considered a new film language in the making?

I believe so. I am not particularly interested in the traditional significance of cinema, which is another story altogether. I don't think we have actually seen real movies yet. What we have been shown up to now are merely illustrated texts. Real movies will develop for the first time in the next hundred years. Take Scorsese, Spielberg, and even Godard. The text always comes first, then the image. Motion pictures are not yet much more than a busy bookstore, a truly wretched way to discover cinema. Right now we are in the prologue to filmmaking. But the new technologies springing up all over the world out of nowhere will help us along. As far as motion pictures are concerned, we must first free ourselves from tyranny, and there are four types: tyranny of the text, tyranny of the actor, tyranny of the film format, and, most importantly, tyranny of the camera. Filmmaking must separate itself from the camera to free itself from slavery. I am quite sure of one thing: the camera gets in the way of the film.

Picasso said: "I don't paint what I see; I paint what I think." So far we have only made films of things we can see. New technologies will give us the freedom to make films about what we think.

With films such as Prospero's Books *and* The Pillow Book, *in which you test the technical possibilities of the medium, you were closer to a movie of ideas. And it is these films that seem to have met with great misunderstanding.*

My mentor, John Cage, said: "If you put 20 percent innovation into a work of art, you immediately lose 80 percent of the viewers for the next 15 years." I think that is a ridiculously optimistic view. The understanding that the general public has for artistic form, for example, has currently evolved as far as impressionism, which has been around for 150 years.

As one who is attempting to reinvigorate the film medium, how do you avoid commercial suicide? What survival tactics do you use to maintain your innovative spirit?

In the beginning, I had no idea of this, but we—naturally you can't make a film by yourself—produce our films in an "A-B, A-B" rhythm. Film A is not necessarily commercial, but is set in a public domain, and "B" is a more experimental film. *The Draughtsman's*

Contract was an A-film. *A Zed & Two Noughts* is a much more interesting film but received much less publicity. *Prospero's Books* and *The Baby of Mâcon* were B-films, and it appears that my last film, *The Pillow Book,* has become an A-film again. It has recently been discovered by a new generation of young people who are familiar with the new technologies but who have never before seen a Greenaway film.

I don't want to become the type of filmmaker Ivory is, but I also don't want to remain trapped under the ice. I want to be a mainstream filmmaker, but on my own terms.

Your films feature Jewish-Cabalistic traditions and Christian iconography, they draw on Jacobean drama and ancient miracle plays, they examine the saturnine world of the Renaissance and the architecture of the Revolution. Boullées—there are mysterious archives and encyclopedias of almost-forgotten worlds of images. And yet at the same time, you challenge the viewer with completely new images . . .

We are in danger of losing the old languages of forms. But—and this is probably typically postmodern—we must be able to recapitulate and re-record these old languages in order to remain conscious of their historical continuity. In my films, one can see that I am a dyed-in-the-wool atheist, but I always had the best grades in theology.

In all other arts except for film, there were profound revolutions in the twentieth century. Music was freed from melody, painting was freed from figures, and even literature was able to be partially freed from content. This allowed music, painting, and literature to be occupied with what they could actually do. But the dogma of storytelling has beaten film into unconsciousness. People today go to a movie theater exclusively to see a story.

The concept of storytelling in film is just as dreadful as the introduction of the immaculate conception in Roman Catholic beliefs: if you want to be Catholic today, you must believe in the immaculate conception, and if you want to be a filmmaker today, you must believe in cinematic storytelling.

In addition to classic cinematic storytelling, you also don't seem to be particularly satisfied with the current technical limitations of filmmaking.

A painter chooses the format for a picture based on the content. Theoretically, there is always a symbiosis of content and form. But for filmmakers at the end of the twentieth century, only three formats of pictures are available: I.33:I, the television format; I.66:I, the academy format; and 2.35:I, Cinemascope. I cannot make the aspect ratios for movies, the relationship of image width and image height in traditional cinematography, match my content. With *The Pillow Book,* we had just begun to change the software in cooperation with the production company. A change in the aspect ratios was possible for the first time through the new computer interface technology. I made suggestions to the technicians and programmers, and together we opened a window for new film manipulations. We have dipped a toe into an ocean of possibilities, to put it metaphorically. But one must be very careful with such claims of having discovered something new. As Borges said: "Every new idea gives birth to its predecessors." A classic example of this would be the embracing of Heironymus Bosch by the Surrealists. And the idea of a fragmented screen is credited to Abel Gance in the film *Napoleon,* back in 1929.

In my new project, *Tulse Luper Suitcase,* I will examine the various methods of adapting a film. The film for the big screen will hopefully be made to be seen in an 8-hour time continuum. We will film 16 television episodes, there will be two CD-ROMs, and we will be on the Internet. There are several reasons for this. My "art films" survive in a large city theater around three weeks and then vanish altogether for a long time. In a provincial city, they never appear at all. Even if 26 million people have seen *The Cook, the Thief,*

His Wife and Her Lover, it is nothing in comparison to *Mission Impossible* or *Jurassic Park.* With these new technologies, I can turn to another public.

How does the use of new media influence your "message"?

Tulse Luper Suitcase is a huge encyclopedia-like film, in which we invent the entire world of my hero. The public receives all the information, a bit like receiving the genetic design along with the ready-made baby, which you can then put diapers on. I turn my material over to the viewers so they can watch it and think about it according to their own timing and rhythm, as often as they like.

For example, I have reworked the story of Scheherazade from *1001 Nights* for the end of the twentieth century. Even in an 8-hour film, I have no room for the 371 characters that are in the story, but there is space on the CD-ROM and on the Internet. *Tulse Luper Suitcase* is the story of uranium. Its number in the periodic table is 92. We therefore have 92 suitcases, all the size of a logbook, found in the airplane that dropped the bomb on Hiroshima. I won't be able to unpack all the suitcases in the film, but on the CD, I will pack and unpack the cases so carefully that the dust on the bottom is visible. So the ideal viewer goes to the theater, watches the TV series at home, views the CD-ROM on another screen, and draws his cross-references. These are footnotes. I love books with footnotes. Actually, all I really want to do is write many, many footnotes.

The artist as an eternal annotation . . . This is evocative of the two tragicomic copyists Bouvard and Pécuchet . . .

I have written a 300-page screenplay on this wonderful last novel by Flaubert. But it will probably never become a film, since one of the two ideal actors has already died. John Gielgud is still living, but unfortunately Redgrave is gone.

What is the artist to us? What is his or her place in society?

We venerate subjectivity. Politically and socially, we have organized ourselves more or less democratically, but we still cling to the concept of the Renaissance artist. Some day we need to get rid of our Corbusiers and Stravinskys, our fetish Michelangelo. But that would require a great sacrifice on the part of artists. I, too, want to keep my subjectivity; I am fascinated by people precisely because of their subjectivity. Interactivity is an interesting subject in this context in that it supposedly destroys subjectivity. But that has yet to be determined. I still don't know what interactivity actually is. The most interactive activity I know is reading, and that has been going on for 5,000 years.

In most of your films, the first few minutes contain a complete introduction of content and style of what we will see. A type of didactic prologue, thematic instructions for viewing.

This is true. The film is offered for immediate consumption at the very beginning—before the film, actually. Because I am not as interested in *what* happens as I am in *how* it happens, I furnish all the necessary information right at the start, so that the viewer can then concentrate on what is most important.

I cultivate a "theater of ideas." The moment of awakening is always an idea. In *The Belly of an Architect,* for example, I discuss the responsibility of architecture in the 1980s and 90s; that was the predominant phenomenon I wanted to explore.

Can you say what motivates your creativity?

I don't really know very much about that. Actually, I would love to be an architect. But I can no longer become an architect because I have no time for it. And I work in a two-dimensional medium, which is a deep disappointment for somebody who actually wants to be an architect. So I made a film about it. The impulse for creativity therefore comes from disappointment. I think this is the way most of us are motivated.

2
Unlearning
An Interview with Harry Mulisch
Peter Saalbach

The writer Harry Mulisch was 32 when he left his strongest competition in the dust. He beat Cees Nooteboom and Hugo Claus in a caramel pudding–eating contest, eating more than a hundred servings. That was in 1959.

Well-wishers can now greet the victor daily between 9 A.M. and 6 P.M. in the literature museum of The Hague, in the form of a bust. Besides the arts of writing and enjoying life, the thin man with the huge nose is characterized by one other striking tendency: the inclination to plant new ideas in the world. Like the theory of architecture in his extensive novel *The Discovery of Heaven,* which charts a daring course from the dome of the Pantheon to the domes of atomic power plants. Or like his notion of personality, according to which every person has an absolute age, which they maintain as their fundamental state of being. His own numeric age over the past 70 years has been 17, because at that age, you feel like a genius and never would be one without dreams. Success is all right with Mulisch; with a touch of self-irony, he says: "In Holland, I'm world-famous."

Mulisch, who was once voted best-dressed writer of the year, shows up for the interview in neat cowboy clothes: jeans, checked shirt, leather vest. But he comes across more as an aristocrat. His head is the dominant feature of his overall appearance, with a long, aristocratically narrow face rising up to an unusually large skull. He wears his grayish-white, wavy hair carefully combed back. His body is boyishly slim, his stride purposefully erect.

Before the interview begins over by his desk, with a sphinx on the wall to the left and Moses with the Ten Commandments on the cabinet to the right, his 39-year-old partner, Kitty, says hello; then their son, Menso, bursts in, and finally, the dachshund, Isa, who intimately explores the writer's famous nose for about two minutes. Afterwards, in tones of utter conviction, Mulisch reveals the essentials of a new theory: "That won't do any harm because dogs have a germ-killing substance in their saliva. Otherwise they'd be sick all the time."

In addition to fun and games, the dark and sinister also have a place in the life and work of the author, who has published more than 60 titles in 40 years of literary activity. His mother was a Jew who narrowly escaped deportation to the concentration camps following the occupation of Holland by the Germans. His grandmother and great-grandmother were killed in the gas chambers. His father, Kurt, a former officer of the Austro-Hungarian Empire, was employed in Antwerp during the war as a personnel director for Lippmann-Rosenthal & Co., a bank for confiscated Jewish property. In 1945, he had to serve three years in an internment camp for collaboration.

The question of how evil develops in the world and how one can suddenly find oneself entangled in it is a topic Mulisch has never let go of. "I never fantasize," he writes in his "Self Portrait with Turban." "I remember things that never happened."

Mulisch's work combines things that don't appear to belong together; even the process by which his books emerge combines a meticulous preparation of objective details with pure intuition. Anyone who has read his novels, full of surprising twists and turns, and closely followed the free flow of his thoughts would wonder about the scrupulous order in the work studio of his Amsterdam townhouse. This is the home of a prolific conceptionalist, a systematic person who organizes and sorts his material before giving himself over to poetry.

He is an alchemist of words. A man who carries a secret: his inner experience reveals that art is created there. Can he also provide information on how it is created?

You write from the middle of the European drug metropolis. Do you smoke pot?

Drugs are not really my thing. I smoked a cigarette once about 25 years ago. Everyone else laughed like idiots, but I had to lie down and thought, that's it, I'm done for. Maybe I'm just high by nature. If you try to add something to that, then you die.

Is there some other type of intoxication that's necessary for Mr. Mulisch to become Harry Mulisch, the writer?

Yes, there is a kind of intoxication. But how does it work with writing? It isn't that I go around here and suddenly know or see something, which I then sit down and write about. In other words, I couldn't really do that if I tried. But I have to do it. It comes more from the paper to me than the other way around, do you see?

No.

Well, I have a hard time understanding it, too. At any rate, it doesn't have much to do with rationality or with thinking at all. If you *think*, it's like you're going through a jungle full of vines and hacking your way free with a knife. This is how many people imagine writing. But the opposite is true. You must not imagine the man with the knife, but instead, a 90-year-old gently sliding down into a warm bath.

Mulisch as an old man in a bathtub? Isn't your absolute age 17?

The 17-year-old stands for being curious about life and for the self-awareness of knowing you want to do—and can do—something quite extraordinary. I'll give you another example of a type of person: I had a very good friend who was a chess grand master . . .

. . . the Giant and the Nose—wasn't that how the two of you were known around the city?

Yes, and he is also the model for the character of Ono in my novel *The Discovery of Heaven*. When I played chess with him, he would always give me his queen, and then look as though he were sound asleep. I remember exactly how he once plunked his knight down almost at random. I was puzzled and asked him: "Why did you just do that?" He said: "Because it looks prettier that way." See? Great achievements that exceed what already exists and what has already been prepared don't come out of strenuous efforts or intensive thought, or even from a field that seems to be as rational as a chess game.

Something new that first comes from the tepid water, then from the dozing state of half-sleep. Isn't this a contradiction to the creative act as it is experienced in the Mulisch house, where every novel is decidedly preplanned?

Of course, I think through the characters and the plot very thoroughly in advance. But the preparation also has to do with not wanting to begin. Because once the first sentence is written, the tone for the whole thing is set. You have to wait for this moment and know exactly when it comes: now! Then if you begin, you quickly notice that all the things you prepared develop in a completely different way. You have to "unlearn," you have to forget what you know. You have to be able to separate yourself from it.

Have you ever separated yourself so far that you ultimately lost sight of the book?

I worked nearly three years on one book that went completely wrong. Also a part of "unlearning."

Does this formula apply to other creative endeavors as well?

It's the same everywhere. In economics, politics, science, and of course in all the arts. This paradoxical mix of rationality and intuitive irrationality is part of it. You have to keep your eye on the form very rationally, and whatever happens must then be allowed to develop freely. Otherwise, it's all a bust and the scientific theory turns out to be hogwash.

What is at the beginning of the creative process: the plan or the idea?

Einstein himself once explained how it happens. He was 14 or 15 and thought, How would the world look if I were sitting on a beam of light? That was the beginning of the theory of relativity—the absurd thought of a young boy.

Do you write every day?

That would be nice. But writing doesn't just mean sitting at the computer or with a pen and paper. You have to stay close to the manuscript, like a babysitter. You must not leave the child alone. And if the child falls asleep, you still can't do anything.

Do you worry that the child will never wake up again?

Not anymore—not for a long time now. I know that it will awaken again all at once. The fear of not being able to write anymore is in itself what causes paralysis. When it doesn't work, then I don't write. That can last a week, a month, even a year.

No sympathy for the poor publisher who is waiting for you to slide into the warm bath again or for your baby to awaken from a coma?

The publisher naturally is forever asking when the new book will be ready. I'm writing a new novel right now that is supposed to be ready in the fall. This kind of tension is bad for me. Maybe it won't be ready for two or three years. It doesn't matter to me. Deadline pressure is only useful for making sure small tasks get done. You end up getting into bathwater that is too hot or too cold, or you drag the baby out of his sweet dreams, kicking and screaming.

Being a writer is a solitary process. Are you ever lonely in your work?

The work of writers is similar to the work of God. This is why they usually have an unpleasant character. The only world there is for them is their own. I am hopelessly locked in this cage. But I am loneliest when I don't work. You live in two worlds—in reality and in the world you create. The workroom here is a no-man's land, the dead zone between the two worlds.

Is there one emotional state that is more productive than any other?

That question is based on the assumption that creativity is actually in me. But as I said, creativity is in what I make. I live when I write, not the other way around.

The darkness of World War II had a deep effect on your family and also plays a dominant role in your books. The question is almost obscene: Do these kinds of horrible experiences promote artistic production?

Yes, they do. Many of my younger colleagues are jealous of the war experience. What do they have? Vietnam from afar, a little bit of student uproar. And they are already past 50. It is worse still for the very young, who have absolutely nothing except their everyday life. It is possible that this young generation might start a war—not the intellectuals, but the more primitive people. A fresh, happy war—there are actually historical examples of this.

You personally followed the Eichmann trial in Israel. It was the inspiration for your book Criminal Case 40/61 *more than 30 years ago. In it, you provokingly name Eichmann as a "symbol of progress." Would you write this the same way today?*

Without a single cut. I describe him as a mechanical man. If he had received the opposite command, to bring all Jews to Israel and found a Jewish state there, he would have carried it out, too.

A German characteristic?

No, a police mentality that's the same everywhere. What is interesting is that he wasn't a Nazi; he wasn't an ideologue like Hitler and Himmler, who really believed that the Jews were our misfortune. And then, Hitler himself never hurt a fly. But he did shoot himself, acting of his own accord.

What predestines people to exercise power? You developed the theory that this ability goes back to "physical constitution." Do you mean something like a big nose instead of charisma?

The Greek word "charisma" simply means talent, or gift. But it's more than that. Someone who has power thinks that it's because of his personality or his appearance. The real changers of the world are physical phenomena that make people fall in love with them, willingly and blindly. People love their physique, their voice, their gestures, even as they cheer on and follow their words. I compare Hitler to a dancer who mastered his movements down to the smallest detail. Dali once said about Hitler: "I love his back." Heidegger mentioned "his beautiful hands." Without such physical manifestations, Hitler, an uneducated person with such demented ideas, would have run into someone who would have silenced him long before the catastrophe.

Is there a comparable person living today?

I asked that same question to Albert Speer, Hitler's architect, when I visited him as part of my research for the book *The Future of Yesterday*. First he told me that for him, Hitler was still very much alive, very physically present—in the flesh, not spiritually! Speer was also one of those people who was not a Nazi, but in love. Not sexually, but it was love. He thought for a long time about whom he could name as being comparable to Hitler. All at once, he said: "Rudi Dutschke." The Anti-Hitler, the boogie-man of the middle classes. But he had these eyes. Speer was in love with Führer-flesh.

Why is there no Führer-flesh in sight at present?

Because it isn't needed. There are such people, and they're currently filling other positions. But if everything goes wrong tomorrow, then they will all suddenly be there again, the good and the evil controllers of the world.

Mr. Mulisch, you started with the slow slide into the bathtub and now end with the love of Führer-flesh. Is there not a relevant theory to be developed from this?

That's the kind of thing you'll find in my books.

3

That's the Nature of All Changeable Things
An Interview with William Forsythe

Arnd Wesemann

Tight Roaring Circle stands in the middle of London, a peculiar installation of the renowned Frankfurt choreographer William Forsythe. The white rubber castle-in-the-air occupying the Roundhouse, an old Victorian railway depot in Camden, heated up London critics earlier this year, when we met in Forsythe's small apartment in Covent Garden. William Forsythe, his partner, dancer Dana Caspersen, and the composer Joel Ryan had once again given a demonstration of what choreography is capable of—in this case, a completely out-of-balance apparatus of dancers on an elastic rubber snow-white castle in the air, which made for huge fun after the performance, especially for the children romping around. For Forsythe, dancing is a special kind of philosophizing: it touches all areas, not only the body, but also the media and even the economy.

What does it mean for you to experience something new? Can you encounter uncharted territory especially when you completely forget yourself for a time?

At the very least, it means, if we're talking about innovation, that you have to move to the other side of what you already know. It isn't possible to create something new within your own four walls, at least the mental ones. I think we usually do the opposite. We constantly remodel functionality, designing it according to our own expertise. And we repeat only the old routines and the functions we know. If our actions are functional, then it should be about using this functionality to separate ourselves from personal affects and habits.

How does that work with dance?

The more you try to shake off control over yourself, to prescribe a kind of physical transparency, a feeling of disappearing, the more it is possible to gain a different dynamic and differentiated forms. You can move with phenomenal speed, which tells you exactly where you lose your own movement—where you cease to move consciously; instead, you are no longer even producing the movement yourself.

In *Eidos : Telos,* we use the timing of the film, the film take, as structure for the dance. A take structures the dance. In each take, we changed the direction of the dance. This helped us move away from the subjective decision about when there should be changes in the tempo of the dance. We oriented ourselves to the take, which more than anything helped us get away from our own thoughts, from our own expertise, which always knows what's right and what's wrong. That's what I mean by a different dynamic, the ability to let go. If you look at the global economy, it's exactly the same thing. We understand its mechanisms, at least to a certain degree. We see how to make the mechanisms useful and what we can still add to them. But we also see how much more difficult it is to make an innovation possible in a system and to forget established things than it is to deal with an innovation once it has appeared.

Isn't there a basic fear in entrusting oneself to something different, something strange?

The only way in our case to abandon ourselves to the film is to enter into the cinematic. You have to be able to give in sometimes. You can be wrong and make mistakes, and the result can be miserable. But it is one thing to make mistakes, and something entirely different to simply deliver a bad film. Trial and error is the only way we have to change something. What we are attempting is to regard choreography as an event, a happening; that's the nature of all changeable things in life: that they can be altered. We don't create anything lasting; on the contrary, we produce things that are extremely ephemeral. We don't try to establish anything; we try instead to disestablish.

You studied with George Balanchine in New York and then became quite well-known for innovation in that you overextended Balanchine's technique and took it to its limit . . .

But that's on account of the technique itself. Balanchine once said you can't invent new steps. Just as it does an economist very little good to discover a new form of economy. What is much more interesting in the development, whether of choreographic or economic traditions, is what sets these symbols—steps or money—into motion in the first place. What ensures that mass—material goods and physical bodies—will move? It's interesting to me how things are set into motion, and when and why structures are laid down and take root. It's the same in economics as in the history of dance. You can't define why specific movements are characteristically Balanchine, even if I believe I understand it. In regard to Balanchine's technique, you can basically always continue to develop it and take it to the point at which it naturally results in distortions and deformities. But Balanchine was not "pure" then; only today he is relatively "pure." In his own day he wasn't pure, however. He developed the techniques of Petipa—that is to say, what counted for pure at that time. Marius Petipa invented the idea of a "pure" dance—complex formations, symmetries, and kaleidoscopic paths of movement. George Balanchine simply twisted them a little, I think out of curiosity or boredom. He began to shape them less symmetrically, and the longer he was in America, the more informal his work became. He used the same principles of ballet, but he interpreted them in new ways.

Which you did in 1983 with Gänge, *which revolutionized the well-known* Swan Lake . . .

That was also only an interpretation. You can read certain things in every possible way you can think of. It merely depends on which level you look at things. *Swan Lake* is a relatively conventional, bourgeois domestic drama; the young prince falls in love with the young woman—what would otherwise be a subject suitable only for daytime TV, if you take away all the imperial scenery with the castle and the nobility. The actual content is unbelievably banal. So we took away the surface and departed from the narrative. This had something to do at the time with my reading of Roland Barthes.

And from it you produced a ballet innovation just the same . . .

Because you have to leave tradition to be able to see something lasting from a somewhat different viewpoint. Innovation implies nothing more than a letting go of a specific standpoint. If your foundation is something as undefined as a dance event, it's not hard at all to distance yourself from *any* foundation. Even the body seems undefined. There are a great many criteria for how you can work with the body and how you can view it. A body is not just a body, aside from all the historical criteria about how and when the body was regarded at all, whether in dance or in society. The personal relationship to your own body, the infinite number of movements to or away from the historical paradigms that constitute the body, do not form a single criterion for dance. Why someone dances in the first place, and what effect the dancing brings about, whom it speaks to, whether it speaks at all, whom it communicates with—these are the important questions. But are they historical or comparative questions if you consider that myriad possibilities exist for physical movements? Nobody else can do with his or her body what I can do with mine, and vice versa.

Does that mean that the body is potentially conservative, because it always has far too many possibilities, or is it potentially innovative because it can never exhaust all the possibilities?

I think that the body is like a gigantic inner space, comparable to the Internet. And yes, it has an infinite number of possibilities. But this concept of "infinite" touches on a specific physical experience. If I am not mistaken, Leibniz once accordingly said that it is the body that has shown us infinity, which allows us continuously to experience again and again, and to be aware of our bodies in new ways. We permanently experience new physical configurations of our bodies, but on a time axis. The body exists on a temporal arrow, through which it changes itself; this is what makes it so enormously complex. The dance, the body, exist only in a form of time. This experience of the endless complexity of a body on a temporal arrow, the body's changes over the course of time—this is what dance is about. It gives the body a place in time.

Can this body be continuously developed, also in the sense of innovation?

No. Of course, you can work very hard on innovations. But you barely manage to leave your house through the back door searching for something new, and you run and run, one whole time around the world, and then one day, you come home again through the long-open front door of your own work field. This is exactly what I said in the beginning, why it's so hard to leave your own work area. There are any number of modern, contemporary choreographers, who try like crazy to be abstract or innovative as they reflect on their bodies and try out different things, only to land again with nothing more than a poorly executed *jeté*. They run two risks: not knowing enough about the body, or knowing too much. You need usable knowledge about the body, but you also need to know the limitations within which it moves, and the limitations that have been drawn around it.

Your own work area means understanding the body more as an interface than as a connecting piece to other disciplines?

Of course. It's always been like that. The thing about the interface is a body metaphor. Today we associate the interface with something virtual, something that seems to me to be a metaphor for the presence of everything that's absent, for what religion has been. The virtual is the hope that one won't ever have to completely disappear. The virtual always says, here is something where there is actually nothing. I think virtuality is an important metaphysical moment that very simply belongs to the body, so that the body loses its fear. Virtuality is an additive to life, an interface to life. That's why virtuality always seems so material to me. It belongs to the body, to the establishment of reality, and not to anything unreal or immaterial, which it's credited with.

Based on this, wouldn't dance be something thoroughly virtual, as well?

You could say it that way. Choreographies always have only the tendency to exist. But they don't exist the way a glass exists on a table. They are mere events. Choreographies should be grouped with particle physics, which is actively involved with the event in an area that, although not virtual, lacks the tactile realm. It also has to do with faith. Physicists must simply have faith that an event that they consider theoretically possible actually exists. They can only prove it by participating in the particle event. They cannot physically grasp it. From this point of view, the dance is more similar to natural science than to the electronic media.

Hence, dance as physical research?

Everything you do appears in a historical context, in the flow of history, which you have to reevaluate time and time again. As in physics, you don't discover anything brand-new. You can only uncover what already exists. The body exists, and the possibility to continue to develop the body "innovatively" has existed exactly the same length of time. It's a matter of *wanting* to find something. For an expression to surface in the body of a dancer, the will of the choreographer is required, as in particle physics, to make this expression at all possible. In a certain way, the choreographer is not so far removed from the particle physicist, who continues to engage in research because of obsession or intellectual curiosity, or whatever motivates him or her. When seen this way, innovation is merely the wish to transfer something into being.

You mention "expression." Is there such a thing as a "new expression"?

The body contains so much potential, with so many possibilities to help or hurt someone with pen and paper and a simple mechanical gesture—writing. The body offers so many possibilities that I don't want to ask "What is innovative?" but rather "What is logical?" The body is an instrument used to describe a possible space in an architectonic sense. But at the same time, it can't establish a space. The body, even when it isn't moving and is apparently only in one certain condition, describes a paradox in that basically there is no condition; rather, everything is constantly moving. Business people know this; they focus on capital, and their entire cause, their motivation, is to increase capital. They aren't thinking of standing still or of an "anti-innovation" attitude. They have to move capital. I recently had a conversation with one of our sponsors from J. P. Morgan, and we reached several agreements in this area. They want the capital to move, they want dynamic capital—not the kind that is locked in somewhere and has reached a static condition. It's the same with information. What doesn't move is actually lost. Innovation is just another expression for movement.

4

Trust Gravity!
An Interview with Wolfgang Rihm
Margarete Zander

What are the foundations of your work as a composer?
Is it that you are an heir of the musical tradition you continue to
develop, or is it more the network of contemporary influences that
affects you as part of a global system of relationships?

I see and experience myself as a person who composes music.
Whether I am an heir, a "continuing developer" of music history, networked in terms of influence, globally systemized or whatever else,
any person whose life depends on the answer to this burning question
can explore it, even if it is only to find out *how* my work "must" be
heard. Is it the work of an heir or a "continuing developer"? Or is it
more network-influenced or more systematically global? For this
knowledge should for the most part only relieve one: listening, viewing, occupation. An artist who undertakes historic research on himself has already become an artistically commercial figure by that act
alone. But maybe this is a consolation: *everyone* is an heir, *everyone*
is a "continuing developer," everyone comes from a network of influences, everyone exists in a global system.

Can innovation in music come about from the relation to musical tradition alone, or is it fed from a diversity of inspirations?

In principle, the tradition of a phenomenon can't be separated from the whole to which it owes its existence. "Tradition" is always the present that's just unfolding. In other words: *we* are the tradition of our past; not "the past is our tradition." Schönberg is the tradition of Brahms, Brahms is the tradition of Beethoven—tradition *is* already innovation. It cannot originate "alone," since it is made by people who have a "present." Again and again a new present: now—now—now—and again—now . . . And in each now-time, everything works together. Nothing comes into being alone. Many things *remain* alone, after they have been acknowledged as new. But it only seems that way, since they really are "in the world."

What role can a teacher or a mentor play?

A teacher or mentor can only be someone who expects everything and can never be disappointed. Ideally, he creates an undertow or current by means of the space he offers; and through this undertow, the student arrives at *his own question*. Because that's it, the only thing that can be taught: the necessity of having your own question. A teacher who threatens a student with answers kills the student. A teacher who offers tricks, systems, functions, and overviews thereby confesses, at least openly, that he is no master. What's more, a mentor publicly stands by the student, provides relief, the space that is necessary in order to wait, undisturbed by external compulsions; to wait with *no goal, no result* . . . because the new hesitates to appear where it is expected.

Can the ability to work innovatively be passed on to others?

The ability to work is an individual thing, and must not be measured in terms of supposed efficiency. By experience I know that a basically industrious person with a good work ethic will have a hard time with a job that threatens to open an area that is foreign to him. Being unintentional is the highest luxury we can afford ourselves. But only we can provide it for ourselves. Being unintentional can never be inherited and has nothing to do with the ridiculous illusions of leisure with which we cover our deep bondage, which forces us to "structure" our free time. Being unintentional can be a bit hopeless temporarily, a state of extremely unhappy melancholy, absolutely nothing "positive," no "off-to-new-shores!" mentality. But if we stick it out and survive through the apparently wasted time, it can be that we suddenly find ourselves facing something new and know that all the lamentation over "innovation" is just occupational therapy. We don't even know *what* we want to make new, because we don't know the thing at all that we're saying is in need of innovation. This recognition wakes us up and we can finally devote ourselves to actual learning: the learning about what's already here. Something new inevitably comes out of this, whether we want it or not.

As a composer, do you feel you are a part of society, a social "player"?

Yes. But I don't see anything in that which distinguishes me. No one really has any other choice. Because even if I say of myself: "No, I don't feel I am a part of society!" that is still a social action because society, such as it is, is something my behavior helps create. Society is always *we*.

It is often said that the development of innovations depends on a fertile breeding ground. Where do you find this breeding ground? How do you keep making it new?

New things can also arise in confined and barren places. It depends on your criteria. The breeding ground starts out as an internal one. But if you have found something new and take it outside where it is barren and confined, it can deteriorate. Need is another relative term: a well-situated society that doesn't recognize its own art is naturally needier than a relatively poor society that has learned that the only thing that will be worth remembering in the distant future is its art.

For me, the best breeding ground for the development of those things that I don't know—and these things are the only ones that can really be called "new"—the freedom from time constraints. I try to create the economic basis for this undisturbed state through confusion. I compose works that hardly resemble one another; I correct and criticize myself through each of my works, each new piece criticizes the previous ones. I therefore—at least, I hope so—am not producing anything that could be recognized as artistic commercialism; instead, I produce contradictory objects in a confusing oeuvre. But not to worry: I didn't decide to do it this way, I just *am* this way. A prerequisite of the breeding ground is therefore identity—even if it is formed controversially. The first controversy of course comes up immediately if I, through this confusion that is supposed to guarantee me an undisturbed state, run into enormous time constraints . . . and that is usually the case.

Do you think in terms of "economics"?

Probably not. I don't haggle over fees or that sort of thing, and any other income that comes my way I spew out very quickly. I think my allusion to digestive processes here is a propos. For the most part, the spending principle reigns. With no payment, there is no art. I mean, no "real" art, because the mass quantities of art that appear in sound, image, and word hardly owe anything to spending, as sparse as it is.

You compose a great deal. Being able to manage such a quantity of work usually requires some sort of economic division of time— "time management" is the buzzword. What are your strategies for dealing with time?

It may look to you as though I compose a lot. I don't see it that way. I have a phlegmatic and melancholic predisposition. Only an occasional spurt from a more sanguine part of myself gives the impression of ceaseless work. Mostly I just hang around. At least that's my impression. I find the idea of "time management" as a consciously organized classification system absolutely grotesque in my case. I am an artist, not the Three Tenors. I know that everything will work out. And if it doesn't, then so be it, it doesn't. Of course, I keep a scheduling calendar—which means that when I see a deadline looming over me in three days, I don't even start the work, but let the three days go by more or less hopelessly. Everyone tells me to hire a secretary. However, in the time it takes to tell the secretary what to do, I have already taken care of it with paper and ink. It is so ridiculous when you get these letters or faxes from totally insignificant people who ply you with strings of numbers and symbols to ensure some sort of accessibility. All this self-organization is only an expression of emptiness. I treasure my hopeless, washed-out days.

The philosopher Peter Sloterdijk once said, "Invent yourself," and then went on to write that we haven't discovered in ourselves any regulatory scale in the final analysis but rather an energetic groundlessness. Is that in line with the way you look at things?

Yes, Sloterdijk writes: "If reasonable subjects examine themselves reasonably, they will discover in themselves not a regulatory scale for the final analysis, but an energetic groundlessness." Actually, a fitting reaction would be a healthy panic. Then Sloterdijk quotes René Char: "Only one privilege is given to us with death: to create art before death comes." That is indeed a consolation. Look at it this way: without this energetic groundlessness, which we must experience, there would be no art before death, hence death would be the victor. Now it comes down to finding reasonable subjects who will get involved in this experience. Given the poor condition of reason today—it is completely enslaved as the servant of utility—it may be difficult to find contemporaries who are reasonable and capable, who can endure the view into the abyss, this groundlessness, if they even find it to be reasonable. My advice: Clarify reason into death, which gives us the chance to have a life before it appears. We will devote ourselves to life all on our own if we also devote ourselves to death.

"Remain in a state of becoming"—you formulated this dialectic principle as an appeal to yourself. Is consciousness alone enough to create this tension?

This paradoxically formulated wish is absolutely worthless if we try to apply it to ourselves in terms of innovation efficiency. What I mean is: remain fruitful, but don't trust your fruits. They are not the goal. The becoming that they enclose—break it out! Begin again! Knowing all the time that there isn't any beginning. Everything is already here. Be in contradiction, but not in the officially recognized position of the contradictor. Avoid being result-oriented; that desiccates, makes things brittle. But create as though the act of creation were possible. Trust in the inherent dynamic of things, in inclinations and gravity—and for God's sake keep your paws off recipes for the effective maximization of innovation. The more we want the new, the more familiar we become with its form. But then it becomes that much less new.

Do you need challenges?

Yes. The Latin word *innovare* means to make new, but it also means "to give yourself entirely to something all over again." That makes me think. Something I give myself to all over again can't be new; I would already know it. And it can't mean that I only seek the surprise, the thrill of novelty. So it comes down to the question: Is innovation an absolute value? What place does it have in this society of ours, which hardly differentiates between innovation leading to a new laundry detergent or to a changed attitude toward life? Do the concepts of "new" and "innovation" characterize what is actually sought? Does "innovation" merely distract us from the overall picture?

When I received the outline for this book on the new, I first thought, "Oh, good, here is that great essay by Boris Groys, 'Regarding the New: Concerning a Culture Economy'—they should read that." And then I made a few notes. Maybe you can use them in closing:

The new is always here, because it is the old. It is all here, only we change our position so that the point of view and what we see is new.

If we don't move, nothing is new for us.

For us, "new" happens *only* through movement.

Us
and
Them

5

Original, Copy, and Coffee Cup

Katja Blomberg

Fine porcelain first arrived in Europe from China at the beginning of the seventeenth century. In 1602, over one hundred years before the "discovery" of this white gold by Friedrich Böttger at the Dresden Court of August the Strong, a group of Dutch sailors seized the exotic cargo of a Portuguese ship. Their booty contained a large number of everyday objects from a material that was at that time unknown in the West. At an auction in the large trading metropolis of Amsterdam, dealers from the four corners of the world provided a quick distribution of this high-quality, first-class product. The brittle porcelain quite obviously exceeded the faience used in Europe in hardness, lightness, transparency, and delicacy of form. Demand for the rare pieces skyrocketed, and suddenly a new market developed for the import of other porcelain.

With the establishment of the Dutch East India Company on the southern Japanese island of Kyushu in 1609, official trade between Europe and Japan began, and within a short time, one of the main items included was Chinese Ming porcelain. At first, the traditional Chinese forms and decor were sufficient in the West. In 1635, however, the Dutch customers began to send to East Asia wooden models that were more in line with the European taste in form, and porcelain was to be manufactured there in accordance with these guidelines. So around 1640, the first Chinese tea and coffee services based on Western patterns appeared. Again because of the changing tastes of the European nobility, which by the middle of the seventeenth century included exotic drinks such as coffee, tea, and hot chocolate, the priceless service ensembles containing Chinese porcelain cups with handles were soon especially coveted.

When the production and export of Chinese goods dwindled with the downfall of the Ming Dynasty around 1657, European importers shifted their business to manufacturers in Japan. This was where the goods introduced on the European market would continue to be produced, based on Chinese decor according to Dutch forms. However, Japanese motifs were soon mixed in among the established models, which gave birth to Chinese-Japanese products in the Western style. In addition, the Dutch East India Company also acquired the original Japanese porcelain, which was in high demand for accessorizing countless magnificent rooms in European castles and palaces, and was also prized as a gift for European royalty. As trade picked up again with the middle class at the beginning of the eighteenth century, the production of Asian porcelain for export was again moved to China. Since the European importers could have porcelain produced more cheaply there, Chinese manufacturers began to produce in what was now a mixed Chinese-Dutch-Japanese style. At the same time, Dutch painters began decorating unpainted East Asian porcelain in the "Japanese" style. This new hybrid was even sold in some places as the original Japanese ware. Only a thorough stylistic analysis can disclose whether the pieces are misunderstood reproductions of Asian plants—i.e., Dutch forgeries.

In 1708, the Europeans finally succeeded in manufacturing the white, translucent porcelain in Europe itself. Shortly after, the

Meissen porcelain manufactury of August the Strong began producing its own designs of the European-modified Japanese Kakiemon style. The Saxon king preferred collecting original Japanese porcelain, and now his painters could copy those pieces. The entire range of variations of European-Asian mixed porcelain, as it was manufactured in the seventeenth and early eighteenth centuries, was displayed by August the Strong in 1729 in his Dresden palace. He had Japanese export models in the Western style as well as the original pieces; he had pieces from Meissen that were patterned after the East Asian models. Purely European designs with no vestiges of the Chinese-Japanese motifs did not appear until the following decades.

The last chapter up to now in the long history of the mutual influence of European and Asian styles began in the last third of the nineteenth century. During the Japanese Meiji reforms of 1867, because of the extensive importation of Western science, technology, medicine, forms of government, military structures, law, and pedagogy, there was first an introduction, followed by an imitation, of Western ways of serving food and coffee. In its consumer culture as well, Japan has been integrating Western forms and presentations ever since. For example, the enjoyment of coffee from Western cups and saucers is just as well-established as the traditional tea culture. The 1980s and 1990s were ultimately witness to the Western discovery of modern Japanese designs for industrial and consumer goods, including table porcelain. The trading game continues . . .

6

East Is West and West Is East
The World as a Unit
Bolko v. Oetinger

The time has come: Rudyard Kipling's often misunderstood verse "East is East and West is West, and never the twain shall meet . . ." is being turned around. Although Kipling was well aware of the deep cultural tensions between his beloved India and the civilizing mission of the British Empire, he nevertheless recognized that the individual can also absorb the unfamiliar, which is always paramount to the new:

> Oh, East is East, and West is West, and never the twain shall meet,
> Till Earth and Sky stand presently at God's great Judgement Seat.
> But there is neither East nor West, Border nor Breed, nor Birth,
> When two strong men stand face to face, tho' they come from
> the ends of the earth.
> (from "The Ballad of East and West")

The individual's desire to experience the unfamiliar is the door through which the new can enter. Today, we refer to this process, which is occurring on a massive scale, as "globalization." The extent of the phenomenon is new, but an extensive exchange between individual merchants and traders has, of course, always been commonplace.

The door will only open if it is unlocked from both sides. The unfamiliar will only come and go if it can adapt to both rooms. If the new can combine with the old, then the presence of the unfamiliar results in enrichment: innovation is continuity and continuity is innovation.

It is, therefore, deceptive to believe that globalization can be attributed to organizational structures. Globalization requires exchange. Structures can only be a test tube for this osmosis.

Exchange has become easier for us: in cultural terms we are no more similar today than in Kipling's day. Nor does a world culture exist, but we have become incomparably more cosmopolitan. Led by an international managerial elite, we see our world as a single unit in terms of economics—despite all the cultural differences, which have not only remained in place but are becoming even more pronounced.

Around the globe the market is tearing down national borders; cities and regions are becoming the new economic governors. The world economy is increasingly dominated by multinational companies. Although they make no claim to global power, they do enjoy unfettered freedom to use the world markets for their own ends. Trained in time-based management, launching their new products everywhere almost simultaneously, they move at high speed through an open world, increasingly adapting their structures in real time. They bring the new to the farthest-flung corners of the globe.

Operating in friction-free markets with falling transaction costs, they are forced to pursue the most advantageous solution because costs, services, and goods can be compared worldwide: production plants are becoming as mobile as the goods they produce, and manufacturing locations as ephemeral as capital and knowledge. The inevitable consequence is increasing "factor cost hopping." Those who control capital can be choosy and seek investment opportunities where the greatest returns are generated for shareholders. Investors value internationally competitive companies more than those centered on a specific country. For the first time in history we are living in a genuine world economy on both sides of the balance sheet.

The tensions this brings in its wake make it appear as if the world economy is accelerating, but they also express something far more basic: every economic revolution begins with a radical invention, and every radical invention leads to the worldwide migration of capital and production. To this extent, globalization is driven by technology. The information revolution together with the worldwide dissemination of the free-market philosophy have brought previously isolated sectors and regions and their workforces into direct competition with each other. "The world is in the process of becoming a global sourcing cell in which ideas and products are available simultaneously everywhere" (Rosabeth Moss Kanter, *World Class,* p. 37). The amalgamating impact of technology on individual cultures is becoming the historically most important question in this process.

This is most apparent in the Internet. As a network of networks, it is based on a deep-seated human need which was already felt in the ancient world. The agora as a place of assembly was a square without walls and without restrictions on access where citizens gathered to communicate. As the first global agora, the Internet offers free access to the global dialogue. The global marketplace is in the process of creation!

Thus, today, the new can be disseminated incomparably more rapidly and more efficiently than ever before. "The alienation of one's own experience" (Thomas Knoblauch, p. 155) is becoming commonplace because as companies, consumers, and employees we have greater and more intensive possibilities for dialogue with the unfamiliar. Doors are being opened, the "spatial opening up of the world" (Joachim Starbatty, p. 17) is the consequence. Globalization allows all companies the grandiose opportunity to experience more of the new from outside and thus become more productive.

Companies as Catalysts

Advantages from Skills

Because of the "gradual convergence of skills" (Kanter, *World Class,* p. 88)—today one can manufacture most products anywhere at the same costs and with the same quality—global advantages are geared less to physical assets than to intangible differences such as brand, network coordination, and proprietary skills such as the speed and quality of development and the dominance of individual strata of value added (so-called "stratified competition"), often combined with dominance over technical standards—today led in exemplary manner by the Wintel dynasty.

This knowledge-based competition is conducted not only over expert skills, but also increasingly over organizational skills—the knowledge of *how* one does something. Proprietary skills—understood as institutionalized processes—define the true advantages of global companies: Intel outsmarts clones and competitors by faster development times, Dell is the master of a logistically determined segment-of-one competition trimmed to attaining absolute top speeds, Microsoft dominates technical standards. Retailing revolutionaries such as Toys "R" Us, Disney, The Gap, Benetton, and The Body Shop have used capabilities-based competition as catalysts of global growth. They have implied knowledge, which can't be bought or sold. Developed and assimilated internally, these skills belong to the company.

Advantages lie in the better and faster coordination of a cross-border network in which knowledge from widely different sources (inventors, customers, competitors, suppliers, research institutes) and the process skills of all those involved globally are better managed in terms of costs and performance than they are in the competitor's network.

The Force of Networks

Companies push innovation both within the company and further afield. Their advantages are rooted in their home countries, but major markets are waiting abroad. There is no doubt about the way into these markets; one exports and invests directly in the foreign country. Only a handful of companies, however, have dedicated real consideration to the return route. This is mostly blocked by the traditional strength of a domestic industry. The German automobile industry, for example, long neglected transferring ideas back from abroad, and new ideas from the United States and Japan were accepted too late, such as the van, off-road vehicles, and kanban. German growth sectors were molded by others: the van market by Chrysler and Renault, the jeep market by the Japanese and AMC.

The peripheries of global companies can, however, prove to be the source of innovation, "hothouses of entrepreneurship and innovation" (C. A. Barlett and S. Ghoshal, p. 128). At Philips a large number of product ideas were born outside the Netherlands and disseminated worldwide, such as color television in Canada, stereo in Australia, and teletext in Great Britain. Similarly, Unilever's foreign subsidiaries have developed new products or marketing and distribution ideas, for example, Timotei in Finland, Impulse in South Africa, and the marketing ideas for Snuggle in Germany.

The more ideas wander back and forth, the greater the importance of a network. Networks are tissues of dialogue consisting of functions, national organizations, business units, value added strata, and indeed the independent networks of customers, suppliers, and cooperation partners—however they may be spread around the globe. Within these networks, exchange takes place in an almost osmotic manner. Here, as Kipling said, East and West meet, and as in his verses, "strong men" meet to pass on the new "face to face." Network is dialogue work. An NEC manager put his finger on it: "Networking is among people." Organizational skills are created by way of reciprocal inter-penetration. The companies which are most highly networked are more open and innovative.

The number of networks today is massive: one estimates that 256,000 subsidiaries of international companies are introducing the latest technology and management methods throughout the world. And they are growing. Since the beginning of the 1980s direct investment abroad has grown faster than world trade and world aggregate economic output. And what is roaming osmotically through these networks?

The new enters through a dialogue network of strong employees and independent units working together informally. In the words of the former CEO of Unilever NV, Floris A. Maljers: "Thinking transnationally means an informal type of worldwide cooperation among self-sufficient units" (p. 46). This exchange is supported by a shared organizational culture, in the case of Unilever a kind of "Unileverization" of all managers, and naturally by outstanding management personalities. The object is ambitious. David Whitwam, the CEO of Whirlpool, who wants to transform his American-based company into a global enterprise as quickly as possible, seeks out staff who are prepared to exchange ideas, processes, and systems across all organizational boundaries and who are not concerned with the "not invented here" concept. Is this really possible?

In order to work in an international network one needs strong nodes, a healthy localization. All manufacturers of consumer goods who had to adapt their products to national variations in taste have discovered this. The CEO of Unilever, Michael Perry, has expressed this succinctly: "A global brand is simply a local brand reproduced many times" (N. O'Leary, p. 25). All world strategies must be implemented locally, and the better and faster presumed and genuine differences are recognized, the faster the new can establish itself.

NEC refers to this procedure—local anchoring and its networking—as "mesh globalization," whereby NEC attempts to balance out the key technical skills in the different countries. For example, software development is based in the United States because of its greater creativity and entrepreneurship, hardware is based in Japan because of its highly developed sense of team work and quality assurance, while at the same time these countries are more closely linked with each other, and thus central control is withdrawn from Tokyo.

In order to ensure cross-border cooperation—and this is the purpose of a global network—the global processes, i.e., research, product development, and marketing processes, must be molded osmotically. In contrast, it is fruitless to seek to resolve definitively the never-ending dispute between matrix, divisionalization, and strong or weak country heads.

Network Configurations

The work of The Boston Consulting Group has developed a process configuration consisting of rings, stars, and centers: in ring processes important information can be exchanged between countries (learning), in star configurations exchange takes place via a center (not necessarily identical with headquarters), so it can be highly coordinated. If there is only one center, then all power is naturally focused there.

In practice, all three concepts mix at the horizontal and vertical levels: Procter & Gamble follows the ring approach for product development (strong country influences, "world category teams"), similar to Electrolux (Council of Country Heads, "The 1992 Council," and "product-line boards"). Hewlett Packard follows the star approach (several central business unit development centers, three large laboratories for basic research), Honda a star concept with a strong Japanese center, while Gillette controls everything from a single center (after all, shaving is the same everywhere) and absorbs just as much from outside via world benchmarking, world sourcing, and world production as would be possible in ring or star configurations. In these three configurations, processes, human resources, and information systems are geared to exchange: rotation, visits, training, evaluations, common methods, teams, meetings and all information technologies (e-mail, voice mail, video, business TV). The dialogue of highly qualified managers determines the success of the network.

Staff work together in rings in so-called "communities of practice," groups working together closely, as was described in detail by the Institute for Research and Learning (IRL) in Palo Alto. At GM the new Saturn was developed by American and German engineers in Germany based on the Opel Vauxhall Vectra, the Cadillac Catera is based on the Opel Omega, and German developers were sent to Detroit to adapt American cars to European standards for the German market.

The connection between the national and the international company plays a significant role in the exchange process. If this fails to function properly, then the new will have difficulty in moving from the center of the company outwards to the periphery and back to the center or into other parts of the periphery. The new must find its way through these critical bottlenecks of global organizations. In most companies too much consideration is given to competences and far too little to how people work together and deal with each other, i.e., how they give and take and learn together in the process: whether the central office understands local circumstances, whether communication is occurring in both directions, whether the country manager is becoming a local prince, whether mutual respect and reciprocal trust prevail. Only in this way can a "community of practice" function properly in which osmotic learning takes place. A manager at the periphery will be adequately motivated to accept the new and pass it on only if he is involved in decision-making. However, developing trust also involves cultivating long-term personal relationships. This contradicts ideas of fast-moving staff rotation.

Customers as Source

The new thrives on "customers." Customer needs are an important —though not the only—source of the new, which emerges from intense dialogue between the inside and the outside.

Hilti attaches great importance to key international customers who are closely linked to their own product innovation. The process is designed in such a way that users, experts, and planning engineers from the most important markets of the world are actively involved in development. Through lead-user workshops, concept testing, and ongoing surveys they influence the development process, while technical potential is reserved for the research process. Erich von Hippel's analyses of the sources of innovation have clearly identified how greatly the new is determined by customers. This can occur in a direct and global manner, as at Hilti, or indirectly, by general adaptation to market needs.

When NEC was developing its business for large telephone switching systems in the United States at the end of the 1980s, the American branch pushed through, in a long-drawn-out process, far-reaching software changes in the NEAX 61 in Japan for the American market. The U.S. manager of NEC did not "merely" implement the U.S. strategy, he was decisively involved in its creation (Barlett and Ghoshal, p. 128f).

Procter & Gamble's success with Vicks VapoRub in India not only shows the value of localization—a Western product for the treatment of colds (in winter) had to be adapted to the situation in India (colds caught during the monsoon season in summer)—but the local P&G, starting from the active ingredients of Vicks

VapoRub and old Indian pharmacological traditions, also developed an independent herbal substance for India. P&G's worldwide research not only accepted the procedure, but institutionalized it with its own large research center in India. Thus the Western product triggered in the East a process of innovation for customers in India.

Barmag AG, based in Remscheid-Lennep, has been conducting a lively business in machinery for synthetic fibers with China for the past 20 years. Technical ideas flow in both directions, innovations flow back to Germany from China, the result of customer requirements. The Chinese technicians come to Germany regularly for several weeks to give concrete technical form to their ideas. This applies to questions relating not only to products, but also to manufacture and assembly. Initially, this procedure affects only Chinese customers, but further dissemination in other parts of the world is conceivable. The exchange between the international subsidiaries and headquarters via meetings, training, trade fairs, personal contacts, and written media is an important procedure in disseminating information and knowledge.

After heavy losses of market shares to Unicharm and Kao in the Japanese market for disposable diapers, Procter & Gamble developed the product qualities demanded by Japanese customers (increased absorption, smaller sizes) in Japan and then disseminated these innovations via a rapid international rollout throughout the entire world. It was P&G's experience in Japan that helped the company secure world market-leadership.

The new appears not only in the form of ideas for new products and improvements of old ones, but also in the form of process and specialized knowledge, two essential elements in revitalizing intangible assets.

As a result of the introduction of Japanese automobile transplants in Great Britain (Honda, Nissan, and Toyota), British supplier-manufacturer relationships were completely changed along

Japanese lines. The previous relationship of animosity between manufacturer and supplier and the "multi-supplier" policy this entailed were replaced in Great Britain by "open books" and the "single-supplier" policy. Management principles such as kaizen, kanban, and simultaneous engineering followed. In turn German suppliers to the automobile industry in Great Britain, such as Kostal, were forced to accept Toyota's production system because the Japanese/British customers demanded it. And so the new spread further afield.

"Do your research where the markets are" is an apt summary of Japanese research policy in the United States (Martin Beise and Heike Belitz, p. 226). In 1993 Japanese companies were represented in the USA by 174 independent research institutes. Their most important motive to conduct research in the USA is the proximity to the customer, which helps familiarize the parent company with the needs of American customers, followed by access to highly qualified researchers and closeness to their own off-shore manufacturing plants. In California alone, there are eleven Japanese design studios, including those of Mazda, Mitsubishi, Toyota, Subaru, Honda, and Nissan. These already existed in the 1970s, before the Japanese had managed to penetrate the U.S. market. The intention was to incorporate future customer needs in designs. To enable the individual engineer to take customer needs into account, the Japanese developers of the Lexus lived in the same districts as the potential customers for BMW and Mercedes.

Although the greater part of the Japanese research institutes in the United States carries out product adaptations for the U.S. market and supports manufacturing processes at nearby production plants, a somewhat smaller number has settled down where knowledge is concentrated, near the leading American research institutes and zones (Princeton, Palo Alto, Silicon Valley, Los Angeles). Their objective is to obtain access to scientific and technological talent as

a source of new knowledge in order to enrich their own technological skills. Japanese electronics research in the USA has concentrated on areas for which the Japanese were unable to find their
own researchers at home: parallel computing, software, artificial intelligence.

So globalization does not simply mean exporting, buying companies, and opening factories in Asia; it also involves the organizational skill of collecting and employing know-how worldwide.
Innovation and the ability to transfer and integrate, with global
managers leading the way, are becoming the most important elements in the migration of knowledge.

Idealists as Conveyors

The term "network" is abstract and conceals the fact that the new is
exchanged by strong personalities. They explain the unfamiliar to
their own organization, they lead the foreign organization up to
their own. Passionately and gradually they increasingly foster trust.
If one looks more closely at this global osmosis, one discovers the
important role played by the individual.

The software adaptation at NEC described above was intended
to enable the company to compete in the American market for large
telephone switching stations and was the work of a local U.S. manager, Howard Gottlieb, who was almost obsessed with pushing
through in Tokyo the software changes required by the American
market. The Indian Vicks VapoRub success of Procter & Gamble
would have been inconceivable without the personality of the Indian manager Guicharan Das. The history of the development of
liquid crystals at Hoffmann-La Roche with its international rami-
fications shows the strong commitment of two researchers, Schadt
and Helfrich.

These events and a recent study of the research institutes of 32

American, Japanese, and European companies show that their leaders must be not only excellent scientists, but also highly prudent managers able to integrate the foreign R&D facilities into the existing network thanks to their good knowledge of the domestic centers as well as of the foreign R&D establishments. They are global coordinators of technical knowledge and not local administrators. They must know where to find the door through which they can transport the new to the center and bring it back from there.

The stronger an individual's basis of trust with the unfamiliar is, the more impact he or she can have. What impact this trust can have can be seen in the case of Barmag AG, where Hans-Joachim Becker, a member of the board with long-standing experience of China, was invited by the Chinese government to collaborate on the development of the five-year plan for synthetic fiber production. In the American-European symbiosis of Spartanburg, which is described below, trust was achieved when the Europeans settled there.

One remarkable example of the role of the individual on both the giving and taking side is the development of the Japanese and American quality movement.

In 1955 Japanese industry started introducing Western methods of quality control, as they were having great difficulty selling Japanese products in America and Europe. Two American experts, W. Edwards Deming and Joseph M. Juran, taught the Japanese to regard quality as a strategic weapon, which was thus placed in the hands of the relevant CEOs. The Japanese did not simply count defective parts, they were interested in cross-functional processes and continuous improvements—from the customer's point of view.

As American managers regarded quality as the norm and not as a competitive weapon, they delegated the work to quality assurance departments. Although Juran alerted American industry at the beginning of the 1960s to the progress made by the Japanese in the field of quality, it did not react until the Japanese had caught up in terms of quality in the 1970s. So then American managers traveled to Japan to find out on the spot how high quality could be produced at low cost. However, it was not until the 1980s that quality became a board-level issue when the Malcolm Baldridge Award was introduced. The originally American philosophy of quality, developed into a strategic tool in Japan, now penetrated—in its reimported form—American companies again.

Will one have to wait another twenty years for the exchange of a revolutionary idea? This is scarcely likely. The waves of time-based management and reengineering traveled around the globe in just a few years. This was the work of a world management elite, which cultivates an international management culture and a shared code, which follows similar concepts throughout the world, and whose members—as in all elites—feel closely bound to each other.

Cities as Ports of Entry

"The world came to Spartanburg." This sentence describes the industrial history of a town in South Carolina in which innovative local managers imported European manufacturing skills and which was analyzed in an exemplary fashion by Rosabeth Kanter (Kanter, p. 273). The example of Spartanburg is so important because it shows how the strategic import of European manufacturing skills carried out by a handful of top managers and municipal politicians improved the city's manufacturing know-how so dramatically that today it is the center for highly skilled, medium-sized mechanical engineering companies in America. Today in the Spartanburg region, along Interstate 85, one can find the highest per capita density of engineers anywhere in the United States, the lowest downtimes due to strikes, and a low unemployment rate. It was no wonder that BMW was drawn to Spartanburg in 1992.

Once again, individuals played an outstanding role: personalities

such as Roger Milliken, CEO of Milliken & Company; Richard Tur-
key, president of the Chamber of Commerce; and Paul Forster, the
head of Hoechst-Celanese, who brought European companies to
Spartanburg. Milliken attracted German and Swiss textile-machinery
makers such as Rieter, first their marketing and service units, later
their manufacturing units. They brought know-how in specialized
mechanical engineering with them. Training programs were created
for workers; the qualifications of the workforce rose to world level
and attracted companies beyond the textile industry and its suppliers.
Initially, the companies transferred technologies and skills to Spartanburg, and in time the companies became so innovative that the
parent companies were inspired in turn by them. German medium-
sized companies emerged in Spartanburg. The printing company R. R.
Donnelley developed an apprenticeship system along German lines.
Higher tax revenues allowed a basic improvement in the quality of
local schooling, and SAT (Scholastic Aptitude Test) scores rose by
128 points.

Spartanburg has not become a kind of foreign colony; it is
rather the case that the locals have become more cosmopolitan by
acquiring world standards. Spartanburg was the place where American and European companies could exchange the new.

In a world of knowledge in which the old national state is losing
importance, cities or regions have to take over a more important
role in order to improve international competitiveness locally. The
large number of Asian free-enterprise zones are such centers of osmosis where East meets West, where both sides discover the other
and themselves, just as Spartanburg is an ideal place of exchange
for sophisticated manufacturing and Boston for the most modern
management concepts. Cities have to become better at attracting
talented people, acquiring skills, enlarging horizons, and matching
up to world standards. They must maintain contacts with the world
economy, or they will disappear. Companies have to understand

that cities where exchange can take place can also help them to become internationally competitive. Skill centers for the entire world can then be located there. Siemens, for example, has concentrated its nuclear medicine activities in Chicago and hydroelectric plants in Brazil, and an important software center in Bangalore in India. Cities should not be satisfied with merely developing sector strengths, they must make every effort to become places where new ideas are exchanged. In this respect, cities will have to conduct foreign (economic) policy.

Knowledge is stored in the minds of people. The nearer they are physically to each other, the more nest-warmth they generate, the better they can communicate and the more innovative and effective they become. Thus the innovation-agglomerations of Silicon Valley and Seattle, the extremely high specialization productivity of New York, and the concentration of electronics and space-travel experts in Munich are bound up with the geographical location. The physical availability of experts and free knowledge are bound up together. Although the Internet and company networks allow knowledge to be made available everywhere for the first time in history, the question remains, "Where will knowledge settle down physically?" Only where it is most beautiful, or where the infrastructure is the best, or where industrial skills are available to turn knowledge into products? A location must attract talent: freedom (few rules), a cultural environment, and other talented persons are just as important, because talented persons attract more of the same.

Culture as a Growing Medium

How can the global company master this exchange despite all national cultural differences? To achieve this, a clear difference must be made between national culture and organizational culture. Kipling was thinking of the first; managers are concerned with the second.

Studies conducted within IBM have shown that although national differences are preserved in a global company, the organizational culture, which is based on common practices, can easily mitigate these national dimensions. For this reason, strong organizations with their own practices are in a position to operate in many different cultures; we can therefore become more cosmopolitan without abandoning our national culture. This parallel approach has enabled Malaysia to join the semiconductor elite and is allowing the Chinese to preserve their culture and simultaneously to adopt Western business practices. Kipling was right: East and West are culturally very different, but Eastern and Western companies can nevertheless work together closely.

We have been accustomed to this cooperation meaning that Western cultures give and developing countries accept. If one is really to use globalization to foster the new, however, we must also be willing to receive. Germany, though, is viewed from outside as poor at receiving. This includes inadequate closeness to customers and services, the belief that it always has the right know-how, the tendency to conceal small changes with debates of principle, and being weak at cooperation and afraid of risk. Peter F. Drucker has also reproached German industry for serious "provincialism," with not wanting to absorb from outside and of acting according to the principle: "If we've always done it this way, then we can afford to leave it like that. After all, we are perfect" (Peter F. Drucker, p. 17).

Osmosis as Management Responsibility

Importing inspiration instead of exporting German engineering know-how: we come from an export-centered world and exist in a world in which inspiration from foreign countries is joining up with ideas generated at home to a greater extent than ever before. For this reason, exchange will become a matter of survival for us.

Learning is a route to osmosis, and the familiar and the foreign meet only in individuals willing to host such an exchange. The new is brought to one's own organization via in-company networks, a global elite, cities, and international customers. Strong personalities are then needed, and there must be an open environment in the company.

World ideas wander from the outside to the inside of the company and from inside the company back out again. Guiding this circuit of inspiration is a primary management responsibility, because those who are too inward-looking today (i.e., Europe) have already lost half of their customers (Asia). Those companies who see the way to Asia but overlook the way back are merely relocating and are not renewing themselves. We need the global manager who keeps this exchange going like a natural process of osmosis.

The more intense the dialogue, the greater the chance that the new will be let in. Globalization provides more points of dialogue and more communities of practice, which we failed to notice before.

In the process of globalization the new can enrich us significantly, not by sending a physically packed invention from one place to another, but by the "emergence of a possibility" (Knoblauch, p. 3) that crystallizes during the process of exchange. This search for the new possibility is a human yearning, which Ernst Bloch has described wonderfully: "The objective-real possibility encompasses existing reality like an infinitely greater sea which contains feasibilities which are, so to speak, just waiting for us to grasp it. . . . The Not-Yet is that which is pending, which is not yet realized, but which is therefore not impossible. In this world, the category of the Not-Yet is possible, as in a world in which the designable, the modifiable can still happen, as in a world which is still open to itself, unfinished, process-like, and thus fragmentary—in brief, a world whose horizon stretches beyond it" (E. Bloch, p. 107f).

In the process of mutual exchange we expose our company, our division, our marketing organization, our R&D to the unfamiliar. We open up the horizon; and perhaps a talk, a visit, an experience, an experiment suffices to make possible the Not-Yet. Everything is already in place:

- We already have a world market for products, ideas, work, and locations.
- Now that manufacturing has followed marketing to distant places and that designers have followed manufacturing, development now follows as the last link in the value-added chain.
- Knowledge and intelligence have replaced labor as the primary source of added value, and the local areas of innovation are becoming places of exchange.
- Companies have every conceivable opportunity to discover the new: they learn from their international customers and suppliers, they maintain listening posts in Japan and Silicon Valley, they are learning from joint ventures, they are recruiting global managers, they regard economic areas independently of their frontiers.
- The speed at which the new is absorbed and implemented has increased significantly. Time-to-market has still not come to an end.
- The possibilities of combination are increasing: today, value-added structures are being broken up and recombined to a far greater extent and far more frequently than ever before.

Most companies acknowledge the importance of the exchange process, but we are only at the very beginnings of a systematic approach to it. Thought is only just beginning to be dedicated to it; only a few organizations are truly global in this sense. Products are still conceived too much for Germany and then exported, not developed for the world and then adapted for Germany. Inspiration from outside still accounts for only a small part of innovation. Skill centers outside Germany are still the exception rather than the equally weighted rule. Does our giver-mentality impair our readiness to absorb and thus prevent genuine exchange? Is copying degrading for us?

Resistance to the new is fueled by fear of the unfamiliar. As the unfamiliar only becomes visible in the reflection of oneself, the fear of the unfamiliar is based on the fear of having to change oneself. Fear locks doors. Here we find the worry of the medium-sized company that it might give away knowledge and thus rationalize itself away. But in the long term it is precisely those companies that have built up jobs abroad that have also flourished at home. It is the fear of the zero-sum game. But this is the real error, for it is in the osmosis of exchange—and not giving know-how away unilaterally—that new possibilities arise. As long as we ourselves do not believe that exchange creates new value, then exchange does not take place.

Companies play the decisive role here. They are like artists; they see possibilities before others discover them. Surprise is their métier. They will disrupt existing markets with the new, and that is their job as companies. They have to explain the new to their employees, because the unfamiliar needs to be explained, otherwise it fuels fears and is rejected. The companies must lead their employees firmly through this change and will enjoy creative pleasure in the process because . . .

. . . there is neither East nor West, Border nor Breed, nor Birth,
When two strong men stand face to face, tho' they come from
the ends of the earth.

Bibliography

Barlett, Christopher A., and Sumantra Ghoshal. What is a Global Manager? *Harvard Business Review,* September–October 1992, pp. 124–132.

Beise, Martin, and Heike Belitz. Internationalisierung von F&E multinationaler Unternehmen in Deutschland (International-ization of the R&D of multinational companies in Germany). In *Internationales Innovationsmanagement: Gestaltung von Innovationsprozessen im globalen Wettbewerb* (Molding Inno-vation Processes in Global Competition), ed. Oliver Gassmann and Maximilian von Zedtwitz. Munich: Verlag Franz Vahlen, 1966, pp. 215–229.

Bloch, Ernst. *Abschied von der Utopie?* (Good-by to Utopia?) Lec-tures, edited and with a postscript epilogue by Hanna Gekle. Frankfurt/Main: Suhrkamp, 1980.

In Complexity Lies Opportunity, Global Competition Operating in a Regional World: The International Industrial Conference in San Francisco (Panel Discussion). *Across the Board,* 31, 1 (January 1994).

Das, Gurcharan. Local Memoirs of a Global Manager. *Harvard Business Review,* March–April 1993, pp. 38–47.

Drucker, Peter F. Die deutsche Provinzialität kann teuer werden: Ein Gespräch über die Zukunft Deutschlands mit dem Manage-ment-Theoretiker Peter F. Drucker (German Provincialism Could Get Expensive: A Talk on Germany's Future with the Management Theoretician Peter F. Drucker). *Frankfurter All-gemeine Zeitung,* June 9, 1992, p. 17.

Florida, R., and M. Kenney. The Globalization of Japanese R&D: The Economic Geography of Japanese R&D Investment in the United States. *Economic Geography,* 70, 4 (October 1994), pp. 344–370.

Hippel, Eric von. *The Sources of Innovation.* New York, Oxford: Oxford University Press, 1988.

Hofstede, Geert. *Cultures and Organizations, Software of the Mind. Intercultural Cooperation and its Importance for Sur-vival.* New York: McGraw-Hill, 1997.

Kanter, Rosabeth Moss. Thriving Locally in the Global Economy. *Harvard Business Review,* September–October 1995, pp. 151–160.

Kanter, Rosabeth Moss. Transcending Business Boundaries: 12,000 World Managers View Change. *Harvard Business Review,* May–June 1991, pp. 151–164.

Kanter, Rosabeth Moss. *World Class: Thriving Locally in the Global Economy.* New York: Touchstone, Simon & Schuster, 1997.

Knoblauch, Thomas. *Die Möglichkeit des Neuen—Innovation in einer lernenden Unternehmung* (The Possibility of the New—Innovation in a Learning Enterprise). Stuttgart: M&P, Verlag für Wissenschaft und Forschung, 1996.

Kuemmerle, Walter. Building Effective R&D Capabilities Abroad. *Harvard Business Review,* March–April 1997, pp. 61–70.

Maljers, Floris A. Inside Unilever: The Evolving Transnational Company. *Harvard Business Review,* September–October 1992, pp. 46–52.

Maruca, Regina Fazio. The Right Way to Go Global: An Interview with Whirlpool CEO David Whitwam. *Harvard Business Review,* March–April 1994, pp. 134–145.

Meil, Pamela. "Der Blick von Aussen" or the "View from Outside." In *Zukunftsperspektiven industrieller Produktion: Ergebnisse des Expertenkreises "Zukunftsstrategien."* Ed. B. Lutz, vol. 4. Frankfurt a.M.: Campus, 1997.

O'Leary, Noreen. The Hand on the Lever. *Adweek,* December 14, 1992, pp. 22–27.

Starbatty, Joachim. Ohne Angst vor einer offenen Welt (Free of Fear of an Open World). *Frankfurter Allgemeine Zeitung,* January 25, 1997, p. 17.

7

Learning Communities
Toward a Triadic Differentiation of Learning Networks

Peter M. Senge and Claus Otto Scharmer

Leaders in organizations around the world are confronted with a world where boundaries are blurring, old certainties are crumbling, and where they must continually help people redefine their focus and direction without losing their sense of identity and purposefulness. The world is growing increasingly complex and traditional organizations are becoming increasingly confused.

This is a hopeless task for isolated hero leaders. Organizations of individual leaders, each seeking to fill their own needs and "optimize their own part of the system," will continue to produce increasing fragmentation and suboptimization. The deep problems afflicting our organizations and our societies will not be resolved.

The leadership challenges ahead will only be met by communities of people who collectively can build knowledge and continually adapt in the face of increasing complexity and change. The key strategic questions concern the nature of such communities and how they can be fostered. In this essay, we attempt to develop some basic ideas about the sources of organizational confusion and share the journey of one group of companies, the MIT Center for Organizational Learning, seeking a new way to lead and learn for the twenty-first century.

Rising Complexity and Blurring Boundaries

Reflecting on the recent merger of Shell Oil (U.S.) and Texaco's "downstream" oil production activities, CEO Phil Carroll commented, "We are entering an era of blurring organizational boundaries. As individuals this means a world of multiple institutional relationships of increasingly ambiguous identity."

Leaders and managers around the world find themselves increasingly dealing with the following three types of blurring boundaries:

- between and within organizations
- between research, consulting, and practice,
- and between knowledge, self, and reality.

The blurring boundaries between and within organizations are widely discussed in the business and popular press. Articles abound on networked organizations, boundaryless organizations, multiple strategic alliances, and virtual or imaginary organizations. All convey the increasing ambiguity of organizational identity, and the increasingly diverse and dynamic ways of getting work done.

The blurring boundaries between research, consulting, and practice are less widely discussed but no less important in our judgment, especially when one considers how management innovation takes place. Examples for this kind of blurring boundaries are industrial companies that offer consultancy services through their former internal consultants, consulting companies that actively participate in the field of management research, and business schools that heavily engage in executive education where they more or less directly compete with large consulting firms.

The blurring boundaries between knowledge, self, and reality receive even less attention, but they are at the heart of concerns such as that expressed by Shell's Carroll. In the industrial age, "who I am" became inseparable from "what I do" and "whom I work for." Reality was often the world as defined in my place of work. The more strongly I identified with my company, the more I was likely to see the world as defined by my company. All of this is changing in today's unstable labor marketplace. Interestingly, when asked what might hold these increasingly complex strategic alliances together, Carroll suggested that managers must become increasingly focused on the intangible realms of identity and culture. In their recent study on multinational companies as differentiated networks, Nohria and Ghoshal (1997) argue that "normative integration is the glue that holds differentiated networks together as entities called firms." Put differently, the more knowledge about self and identity becomes critical for corporate action, the more leaders find themselves wrestling with the blurring boundaries of knowledge, self, and reality, trying to help their organizations' members and affiliates develop knowledge about who they are and who they want to be (self-knowledge).

The New Leadership Challenge: Coping with Three Types of Rising Complexities

But these three types of blurring boundaries are being driven by three types of rising complexity, which seems to be growing inexorably as we pass from the industrial age to the "systems age." (This is the term coined by Russell Ackoff, which we prefer to more popular terms like "information age"). It is imperative for leaders to understand these three types of complexity. Only then can they begin to move beyond reacting to blurring boundaries and begin to work with, and perhaps even shape, the forces generating the blurring boundaries.

These three types of increasing complexity redefine the day-today work of corporate leaders around the world. They are dynamic complexity, behavioral complexity, and generative complexity.

Dynamic complexity characterizes the extent to which cause and effect are distant in space and time. In situations of high dynamic complexity the causes of problems cannot be readily determined by firsthand experience, and few, if any, of the actors in the system may have a sound understanding of the causes of the problems. An example of this type of complexity is a drop in sales, to which management responds with additional expenditure on marketing, without realizing that the real cause for the drop in sales may not be a lack of marketing activities but a lack of service quality (Forrester 1969, 1971; Senge 1990; Roth & Senge 1995).

Both dynamic complexity and the blurring boundaries of organizations are expressions of an ever-increasing interdependency. One key driver that underlies this process is the long-term trend of globalization. As a consequence, managers and leaders operate in increasingly interdependent settings that do not allow simple coordination through hierarchical chains of command. Moveover, with more people involved in decision making, managers and leaders are simultaneously confronted with the second type of complexity: behavioral complexity.

Behavioral complexity characterizes the extent of diversity in mental models, values (Roth & Senge 1995), and political interests. Situations of low behavioral complexity are characterized by shared assumptions, world views, and interests by the respective players. Situations of high behavioral complexity are characterized by deep conflicts in assumptions, beliefs, world views, and political interests. An example for this type of complexity would be if the product manager came to believe that the cause of a sales decline was falling service quality, but she failed to implement any plan for improving service quality because she got mired in conflicting political agendas and distrust between the marketing, sales, and corporate quality departments. Thus, even if she succeeded in understanding the dynamic complexity (identifying the root causes) she faced, she failed in terms of resolving the behavioral complexity, which was equally a part of her problem.

The key driving force that underlies behavioral complexity is the long-term trend toward localization, increasing distribution of power and authority, bringing more and more different people into decision-making processes. Behavioral complexity is not about global unity but about local differences, about different mental models and distinct cultural assumptions and perspectives. Both localization and globalization drive not only the reconfiguration of corporate structures but also the way these corporate bodies link to consulting- and research-based organizations within the process of corporate knowledge creation. With the notion of knowledge creation, the third type of complexity enters the picture.

Generative complexity characterizes the extent of tight coupling between knowledge, self, and reality (Scharmer 1997). In situations of low generative complexity we are dealing with problems and alternatives we by and large know about. For example, wage negotiations between employers and unions may be high in behavioral complexity but low in generative complexity (different interests, given alternatives). In situations of high generative complexity we are dealing with problems and alternatives we do not know because they are yet to be determined (different views, not-yet-defined alternatives). For example, if the product manager finds out that maybe the "real" problem for the drop in sales is not the poor quality of service but rather the poor quality of the product, then she might try to involve the lead customers in co-creating the next generation of products (Hippel 1986). However, nobody know what the new product will be, who should participate in the co-creation process, and how the process should be structured for engaging various key players. In short, generative complexity is about how to involve multiple players in processes of collaborative co-creation.

Neither purpose, nor players, nor processes are given in typical situations of generative complexity.

Generative complexity seems to be the least understood of the three types of complexity. It clearly links to the blurring boundaries between self, knowledge, and reality. Generative complexity inheres in all processes that deal with emergent and not-yet-enacted realities. Tight coupling between knowledge, self, and reality means that the way new knowledge is brought forth into reality is closely linked and interwoven with evolving selves. Increasing generative complexity arises from a third underlying driving force, a trend that could be labeled individualization. From this point of view, Phil Carroll's remark on "increasingly ambiguous identity" reveals an additional subtlety. As the ability to "identify" self with corporation declines, creating identity becomes a more challenging issue. People must start to know themselves better because they cannot take their professional identity for granted. Conversely, work environments that foster genuine reflection and active collective "meaning making" may become more and more important. Mort Meyerson, CEO of Perot Systems, describing his role as CEO, says, "I couldn't get us into businesses or out of businesses. I couldn't set the company's strategy, delineate the company's tactics, or write the field orders for our competitive battles. I couldn't decide what products to launch. The way to be a leader today is different. I no longer call the shots. I'm not the decision maker. . . . The essence of leadership today," says Meyerson, "is to make sure that the organization knows itself."

How can leaders cope with problems characterized by increasing dynamic, behavioral, and generative complexity? Put differently: How can leaders cope with problems that have causes difficult to determine, that involve numerous players with different agendas and mental models, and that are related to not-yet-defined purposes, emerging realities, and evolving self-knowledge?

Such questions are difficult, perhaps pointless, to answer in the abstract. Rather than trying, we offer only our own experiences, as members of one community of people who have wrestled with these questions. Hopefully, our tentative conclusions and preliminary efforts will be helpful to others as well.

The Learning Consortium at MIT

Starting in 1991, a group of large, primarily U.S.-based corporations came together to found the MIT Center for Organizational Learning. Our intent was to foster collaboration in exploring how companies could learn faster and better. One of the key premises underlying the founding of the MIT consortium was that in order to bring about significant organization-wide change, it takes more than focusing on organizations individually—it takes a group of organizations willing to work together, providing examples, help, and inspiration to one another (Senge 1993; Schein 1995).

The First Six Years: What Has Worked and What Hasn't
Since then, there have been some significant accomplishments. For example, many member companies have created practice fields, such as learning laboratories, to facilitate learning in the context of real work settings. The focus on certain "core learning capabilities"—understanding interdependency, inquiring effectively into complex issues, fostering personal and shared vision, and learning what it means to continually learn—has produced significant business results and significant personal change (e.g., Roth 1996). Especially powerful changes have occurred when teams start to see together the systemic structures they enact, and how their problems arise from their own ways of thinking, conversing, and acting together, rather than from outside forces beyond their control.

There have also been significant setbacks, including both the failure to sustain time and energy for learning in the midst of increasing day-to-day pressures and the failure to leverage local successes for the benefit of the larger organization. Sustaining learning appears to require a healthy "leadership ecology" (Senge 1996) that is rare in contemporary corporations. This includes local line leaders who put new ideas into business practice, "internal networkers" who carry the seeds of new ideas and practices to different parts of a large organization, and executive leaders who can nurture a culture of inquiry and openness and create effective learning infrastructures. If this leadership ecology is deficient, deep changes fail to spread. Grand ideas promulgated by visionary chief executives never achieve broad implementation. And successful local innovators can easily find themselves at the mercy of a hostile "corporate immune system" (Senge 1996, 1997).

Shift of Focus: From Learning Organizations to Learning Communities

Perhaps the most significant outcome during the first six years may be that we have seen the gradual emergence of a learning community. This learning community is evident in interorganizational learning infrastructures like the Practitioner Conference or the Liaison Officer Group or the Annual Conference, in which practitioners, researchers, and consultants throughout the whole community engage in cross-organizational reflections, help one another, and share in the management of the consortium. It is evident in the willingness to share openly developments that contribute to competitive advantage—for example, Phil Carroll's quote above is taken from his address at the November 1996 Practitioner's Conference, hosted by Shell in Houston. And it is becoming increasingly evident in the development of learning communities within several of the member organizations, where in some cases there are literally thousands of people engaged in "organizational learning" experiments. We are becoming convinced that learning communities, once created, are very difficult to destroy. They appear to represent a natural pattern of organizing—perhaps *the* natural way to organize for learning.

This realization of the power of learning communities has developed gradually over several years. In part the awakening was semantic. Many years ago, Chris Argyris and Donald Schön posed the simple question, "What is an organization that It can learn?" (Argyris & Schön 1996). In some sense the process of generating knowledge and embedding that knowledge in new skills, capabilities, and practices can only occur in a human community, regardless of whether or not the members of that community are conscious of themselves as a collective. In other words, all "organizational learning" is in fact community learning.

More recently, our appreciation of the role of learning communities has deepened as a result of a two-year period of reflection and self-inquiry among the members of the MIT Learning Center. This redesign process has involved representatives from Ford, Chrysler, Hewlett-Packard, Shell Oil, EDS, and Harley-Davidson, along with a group of senior consultants working in these companies and MIT faculty and research staff. In particular, this team gradually uncovered a central question that seems to lie at the heart of our challenges going forward: "How do you organize a learning community?" or, perhaps better, "How does a learning community organize itself and what can enable that organizing?"

Organizing Continually Evolving Learning Communities

Early on in our period of reflection, we concluded that the essence of a learning community was a group of people committed to the integration of theory and practice, concept and capability, the world of research and the world of action. The members of a learning community are stewards of a knowledge-creating process, both helping one another enhance their capacity for effective action and reflecting on and conceptualizing their evolving understanding. More specifically, there are three core activities which operationally define a learning community:

- research: a disciplined approach to discovery and understanding, with a commitment to share what's learned,
- capacity building: enhancing people's capabilities, individually and collectively, to produce results they truly care about, and
- practice: people working together to achieve practical outcomes.

Core Activities: Interweaving of Research, Capacity Building, and Practice

Conceived of in this way, a learning community links and interweaves the following three subcommunities: a community of practitioners, such as line managers, product development teams, teachers, or executives; a community of researchers, who may come from universities, independent research institutions, or from within practice institutions; and a community of consultants or facilitators and others involved in various forms of capacity building. Thus the core task of a learning community is to interweave and cross-fertilize researching, capacity building, and practice between and within individuals, institutions, and communities.

With that, a defining property of a learning community is to enable each member to participate in all three core activities of knowledge creation. Some of the deepest insights invariably come from practitioners, just as some of the most gifted researchers are masterful teachers, and many of the best consultants in our community are also extremely accomplished practitioners and/or researchers.

To see why each of the three core activities is integral to institutional learning, imagine each perspective's advocate arguing for why that perspective is what matters most. The practitioner says, "Nothing matters unless a practical result is achieved. The only valid way to gauge real learning is through evidence that people accomplish something they couldn't accomplish before." The capacity builder says, "There is no learning unless people have new capabilities. You haven't 'learned' to ride a bicycle when you've done it one time, but only when you can demonstrate a capability to ride again and again." The researcher on the other hand says, "None of this ultimately matters very much unless those who have not been involved directly in a learning process can benefit from it. Unless there is a diffusion of knowledge beyond a particular learning group, no generalizable knowledge has been produced."

What truly characterizes a learning community is the willingness to embrace all three of these perspectives as equally true and as equally important in creating knowledge.

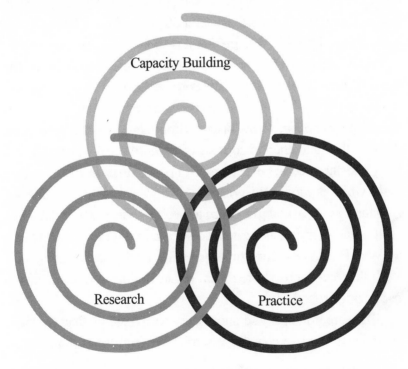

Figure 1. The three core activities in the community of learning

Over our two-year period of reflection and re-creation of the MIT Learning Center, the simple picture above has emerged as an icon for our group. It represents each of the three domains—

research, capacity building, and practice—as spirals of activity and energy, interacting in a larger knowledge-creating process. A learning community is nothing more or less than a diverse group of people working together to nurture and sustain this knowledge-creating system, through improving theory and method, through enhancing people's capabilities, and through producing practical results.

From Organizing around Structures to Organizing around Purpose and Principles

We were very fortunate to have Dee Hock as a guide when we sought to determine the organization of the Learning Center. Hock helped found Visa International over 30 years ago and helped make it the unique business venture that it is.

Hock refers to Visa as a "chaordic" organization (from the words "chaos" and "order"). The core principle of the chaordic organization is that all formal structures, processes, and procedures should be secondary to the organization's purpose and principles. That is, the fundamental sources of authority and power lie in a body of central ideas, not in a group of people in positions of power. Only when purpose and principle are primary is it possible for structure, process, and procedure to evolve continually and readily.

Instead of trying to create an organization, we thus tried to create what Hock calls "conditions that allow organization to emerge." With that, our focus shifted from organizing around structures to organizing around ideas.

The core principle and purpose we formulated reflect the three central activities we consider essential in a learning community:

- We are a global learning community dedicated to building knowledge about fundamental institutional change through integrating research, capacity building, and practice.

■ Our purpose is to discover, integrate, and implement the-
   ories and practices for the interdependent development of
   people and their institutions.

Governance for Self-Organizing:
Tripartite Equity and Subsidiarity

Having reached consensus on purpose and principles as indicated
above, the Learning Center team went on to reach consensus on the
next two stages in Hock's process for developing chaordic organizations: concept and structure. (The entire process involves iterat-
ing between six stages or "lenses on an emerging reality": purpose,
principles, concept, structure, people, practices.) Each step of the
consensus-building process included not only the approximately 25
members of the team but also iterations with the respective organizations or communities they represented (e.g., MIT, many individual researchers and consultants involved in Learning Center
projects, and the 20 or so individual member companies).

Eventually, five goals emerged to express the basic concept of
the type of organization the team felt was needed to put the above
purpose into practice:

1. To found the Society for Organizational Learning (SoL)
    as a membership organization that involves corporate
    members, research members, and consultant members as
    a differentiated network of colleagues, not as employees.
2. To build a system of self-governance throughout the SoL
    Community based on the principles of tripartite equity.
    SoL would be governed by a council elected by its mem-
    bers, with equal representation of all three subcommuni-
    ties in the council. The council's powers would be only
    those which could not reasonably be discharged by the
    members acting on their own, in keeping with the principle
    of subsidiarity (localness). These powers, along with the

SoL's other basic governance processes, would be spelled out explicitly in its constitution, which itself could be modified, according to certain processes, by its members.

3. To create an enabling and interweaving organization (the SoL organization) that would provide a range of coordinating and community-building services aimed at enabling members to be aware of and continually develop the quality of their relationships with one another.

4. To be financially self-sufficient (membership fees from all members) and act as research venture capitalist by way of allocating seed funds to innovative research ideas and then helping those projects grow to attract more substantial funds; by articulating an overall research agenda; and by linking researchers, practitioners, and consultants for tripartite knowledge-creating ventures.

5. To link to a global network of similar learning communities at the local, national, and multinational levels as "fractals" within a global community (perhaps connected formally through SoL International, whose establishment would be explored).

This new body of tripartite self-governance enables the evolving learning community to develop and grow more locally and more globally at the same time.

Toward Collaborative Core Practices of a Learning Community

Boston, April 3, 1997: All 19 initial corporate members of SoL (former corporate members of the MIT Learning Consortium), almost all 40 initial research members (from MIT, Harvard, University of Michigan, Yale University, and others) and most of the 60 initial individual consulting members came to the first SoL meeting, in order to officially found the society. As a matter of fact, the room was packed with twice as many people as initial members, the others being observers on behalf of other organizations interested in joining SoL or interested in establishing their own, similar consortia in other parts of the world. After generating inputs for the future research agenda and after electing the first council, then the real work began: developing collaborative core practices that interweave and engage the whole community.

With regard to developing collaborative core practices, the first seven years of the Learning Center worked to establish basic practices, at the individual and small group level, of systems thinking, dialogue, and reflection on mental models and deep aspirations. The following issues currently guide our focus of attention, establishing core practices at the community level:

1. How to organize knowledge creation in a way that allows all members of the community to engage as researcher.
2. How to organize capacity building in a way that allows all members of the community to engage as coaches and teachers (of their peers).
3. How to organize governance in a way that allows all members of the community to participate and express their own voices.

Each of the goals focuses on how to interweave and cross-fertilize the core activities across the whole community. With regard to organizing knowledge creation in a way that enables everybody to engage as a researcher, the problem is that research and universities often work in ways that are disconnected from practice and practitioners. One potential way to leverage the knowledge of practitioners and consultants involves engaging all members of the community in the process of developing a research agenda. This work is just now beginning, led by the newly formed research committee of the elected council. Another example may be to have senior faculty members teach basic research skills to consultants and practitioners, who then work together in community-wide field research activities.

With regard to organizing capacity building that enables everybody to engage as coaches and teachers (of their peers), the problem is that capacity building is often disconnected from practice and research, such as in much traditional university education and corporate training. One potential way to leverage the knowledge of practitioners and researchers for collaborative capacity building may involve establishing annual peer learning review processes in which all members reflect in small groups on their own evolving theory of practice.

With regard to organizing governance that enables everybody to participate, the problem is that governance is often disconnected from firsthand experiences of the respective individuals. One potential way to leverage the tacit knowledge of experience for community-wide self-governance may be community dialogues, such as those occurring during the practitioner conferences or semi-annual meetings and a planned electronic strategy forum for ongoing dialogue among the council and the whole community.

In all three cases the challenge will be met by continually encouraging new ideas and self-governing practices from the entire SoL membership and helping people to realize that the members are the organization. Nothing short of this can possibly begin to overcome the deep fragmentation of research, capacity building, practice, and governance that currently exists in contemporary industrial societies.

Conclusion: Learning Communities as Triadic Differentiated Networks?

With that we return to the questions that underlie the story presented above. In answer to the question "How do you organize learning communities?" we are finding some evidence that learning communities seem to evolve best when organized as a triadic network in which

- a community-wide consensus on purpose and principles provides a clear and distinctive common ground for collaborative knowledge creation;
- a tripartite system of self-governance implements inclusiveness, localness, and efficiency as guiding principles for decision making;
- and a set of collaborative core practices interweaves and cross-fertilizes research, capacity building, and practice within and between individuals, institutions, and communities.

Rather than creating a rigid organization, these represent necessary conditions that allow an organization's emergence—that is, a philosophy of organizing that does not destroy the spirit of the community we are seeking to organize.

As for the question "How can leaders cope with problems that are high in all three types of complexity—dynamic, behavioral, and generative complexity?" we are finding some evidence that perhaps this leadership challenge can only be met when conceived as a challenge for collective as opposed to individual leadership. In the case presented above, leadership emerged through engaging diverse participants in the creation of a triadic network based on shared purpose and principles, self-governance, and a set of interweaving, collaborative core activities.

Only through such differentiated networks of common purpose can we begin to reweave what has become critically fragmented in contemporary organizations and society: practice, research, and capacity building. Only through reweaving these three elementary building blocks will there be the requisite organizational complexity for system-wide knowledge creation in an era of growing dynamic, behavioral, and generative complexity.

References

Ackhoff, R. L. 1974. *Redesigning the Corporate Future: A Systems Approach to Societal Problems.* New York: John Wiley & Sons.

Argyris, C., and D. A. Schön. 1996. *Organizational Learning.* Vol. 2: *Theory, Method, and Practice.* Reading, Mass.: Addison-Wesley.

Forrester, J. W. 1971. Counterintuitive Nature of Social Systems. *Technology Review,* January.

————. 1969. *Urban Dynamics.* Cambridge, Mass.: MIT Press.

Hippel, E. von. 1986. Leading Users: A Source of Novel Product Concepts. *Management Science* 32, no. 7 (July): 791–805.

Nohria, N., and S. Goshal. 1997. *The Differentiated Network: Organizing Multinational Corporations for Value Creation.* San Francisco, Calif.: Jossey-Bass.

Roth, G. 1996. AutoCo Case, Learning History at the MIT Center for Organizational Learning, Sloan School of Management, Cambridge, Mass.

Roth, G., and P. Senge. 1995. From Theory to Practice: Research Territory, Processes and Structure at the MIT Center for Organizational Learning. Working paper, Organizational Learning Center, MIT Sloan School of Management, Cambridge, Mass.

Scharmer, C. O. 1996. *Reflexive Modernisierung des Kapitalismus als Revolution von innen: Auf der Suche nach Infrastrukturen einer lernenden Gesellschaft—dialogische Neugründung von Wissenschaft, Wirtschaft und Politik.* Stuttgart: Schäffer Poeschel Verlag.

————. 1997. Was ist Personal Mastery? 21 Thesen. Zwischen Selbstführung und Persönlichkeitsentfaltung. In R. Benedikter (ed.), *Wirtschaft und Kultur in Gespräch: Zukunftsperspektiven der Wirtschaftskultur,* 112–123. Bozen: Verlag Alpha und Beta.

Schein, E. 1995. Learning Consortia: How to Create Parallel Learning Systems for Organizational Sets. Working paper no. 10.007, Center for Organizational Learning, MIT Sloan School of Management, Cambridge, Mass.

Senge, P. 1997. Leading Learning Organizations: The Bold, the Powerful, and the Invisible. In *The Leader of the Future: New Visions, Strategies, and Practices for the Next Era,* edited by Frances Hesselbein, Marshall Goldsmith, Richard Beckhard, 41–57. San Francisco, Calif.: Jossey-Bass.

————. 1996. Infrastructure for a Learning Organization. *Journal of Innovative Management* 2, no. 2 (winter): 4–18.

————. 1996. Towards an Ecology of Leadership: An Emerging Systems Theory of Leadership and Profound Organizational Change. Working paper in progress. Cambridge, Mass.: Center for Organizational Learning, MIT Sloan School of Management.

————. 1996. The Ecology of Leadership: A Guide to Organizational Learning and Executive Development. *Leader to Leader,* no. 2 (fall), 18–23.

————. 1993. Transforming the Practice of Management. *Human Resources Development Quarterly* 4, no. 1 (spring): 5–31.

————. 1990. *The Fifth Discipline: The Art and Practice of the Learning Organization.* New York: Doubleday/Currency.

Senge, P., and C. O. Scharmer. 1996. Infrastrukturen des Lernens: Über den Aufbau eines Konsortiums lernender Unternehmen am MIT. *Zeitschrift für Führung und Organisation,* no. 1, 32–36.

Freedom and Organization

8

The Virtues of Corporate "Disorder"

John Kao

Our customary business frameworks revolve around the virtue of order. The industrial revolution, from which we still derive much of our managerial and operational inheritance, is itself inherently based on a business model that derives value from order. Cardinal elements of this business approach include economies of scale, the design and implementation of long production runs, reduction of errors and conversely the enhancement of quality, the necessity of control, and the primacy of efficiency. The culture of the industrial revolution is mirrored in a set of sought-after and well-rewarded psychological skills, including the ability to apply rational standards to business problems, and to handle complexity through attention to detail. And this business approach also implies a particular managerial mindset. The general manager is seen as a decision-maker, one whose key responsibilities involve bringing order to chaos, reducing ambiguity, creating closure; in short, effective decision-making.

But what if this traditional approach is dysfunctional or at least only partially relevant to the contemporary business environment?

What if the truly relevant business model involves generating value from an ability to embrace uncertainty, to respond to wild cards and the unpredicted, and to find innovative ways of turning the ability to sense what is interesting or "cool" into an organizational capability? What if the key issues for corporate leaders are enhancing the ability to find novel phenomena, to increase intellectual diversity, to foster the efforts of creative talent, and to manage the creative resources of the organization? What if the key psychological skills are the ability to sense something new through intuition, and to harness the passion of people to inspiring but unpredictable goals and outcomes? What if the manager who successfully drives this business model has the job of being an agent of disorder, of bringing a potentially valuable form of chaos from an order that at its worst leads to bureaucratic rigidity? What if this role involves increasing ambiguity, giving up control and maintaining openness to possibilities? What if, in short, the job description involves deferring decisions in the interest of discovery, of finding a virtue in disorder?

This set of assertions will most likely attract two broad forms of responses. Some will get it, find it intuitively obvious or at least agree with it somewhere in their gut. Others, simply, will not. These two responses also define an interesting diagnostic for those who see, or do not see, the emergence of a new way of doing business. Leaving aside for the moment the issue about whether the concept itself is valid, there are those who "get" and others who do not "get" what we might call the new economy.

What do we mean by a new economy? It is a much talked-about and much to-be-talked-about topic. If one boils it down, simply put, this is an economy in which competitiveness is defined by speed, originality, intelligence, and agility. It is an economy in which the key assets are ideas, the talent that creates them, and the systems that bring them to fruition. They are those in which the winners, by setting standards, experience the potential for what Stanford's Brian Arthur has called increasing returns. They are those which most importantly require a new managerial mindset.

In what follows, I intend to explore the "virtues of disorder" with specific reference to the notion of organizational creativity. Creativity in business is inherently disorderly; it is subversive to the established order. It is the process of bringing something new into being, something that challenges the status quo, that contains elements of what the economist Joseph Schumpeter called "creative destruction." And competitiveness in the new economy is integrally connected with mastery of the art and discipline of business creativity.

If we are to develop new products and services, we need to harness our creative resources. Equally, creativity involves the ever present possibility of developing new processes, new ways of doing things. Perhaps most importantly, it involves new ways of perceiving. For example, who is an entrepreneur but a person who is able to perceive opportunities that others do no? Creativity is inherent in the process of seeing differently, or reperceiving, which in turn leads to strategic perspective. How we see things is fundamental to the kind of strategic insights we can develop. It was Pierre Wack, the head of group planning at Royal Dutch Shell a number of years ago, who introduced us to the notion of strategy as "the gentle art of reperceiving."

As such, strategy is not just about extrapolation; it's about fundamental reinvention and discovery. It's an inherently creative process. And without the bright flames of creativity, and without an equally creative process for developing strategy, the result will be nothing more than a dull and ultimately limited reprocessing of what is already known.

Such a refreshing point of view on strategy is an imperative because of the increasing uncertainty in the environment of most businesses, a change in the rate of change if you will, an increase in the white space, in industry turbulence. So, whatever the language you choose to use, whether you want to "find the white space," or "compete for the future," or "organize your business ecology," or "define your strategic intent," or any of the other new imperatives of next-generation strategy, creativity is at the heart of that process. And to master creativity is to understand and realize value from the virtues of disorder.

The Context That Requires Creativity

There is a popular notion of creativity as being something like brainstorming, lateral thinking, or ideation. Today, however, creativity must go beyond mere idea generation: the light bulb that goes on over the head of a talented person. It must become an ongoing process, not just momentary and isolated epiphanies. Creativity is a process that has a grammar. It is also a process that's linked to the way knowledge is managed, because it is inherently defined by quantum leaps in understanding that lead to the realization of value.

As I have surveyed the topic of creativity in business as both an academician and practitioner, I have been impressed by the fact that the practice of creativity translates into organizational capabilities in many organizations. In some, these capabilities are so deep-seated and hard to copy that they translate into a competitive advantage. One of the more unlikely data points on my journey has been the Coca-Cola Company. Mr. Douglas Ivester, the company's president, speaks of his emphasis on the discipline of creativity. At his company, creativity is not seen as an epiphany "du jour." It is not valued as a transient campaign or management development exercise. Rather it is seen as a discipline practiced 365 days a year, that is reflected in the way people interact with one another, and at all meetings as a definition of the desired style of collaboration.

Creativity is not just a way of distinguishing successful companies. It will increasingly be about successful countries as well. Singapore, now number 5 in GDP per capita worldwide, was far down the value chain in terms of economic development 30 years ago. What did the Singaporeans do? What are they doing today? They invest explicitly in innovation capability.

A $700 million innovation development scheme in Singapore gives grants for innovation infrastructure. A billion dollars of new money has just been advertised for innovations in school curricula, including training in creativity skills for children at the primary and secondary school level. Knowledge management, knowledge capabilities, technology, and creativity skills are all being blended together in a powerful set of national capabilities for the generation of wealth. This phenomenon of creativity as part of international competitiveness is also captured in the landmark science fiction book *Neuromancer* by William Gibson, who originally coined the term "cyberspace." As a text for strategic insight, it is quite unusual. It portrays a future world in which wars are fought, not over territory or tangible assets, but over the brains of talented people. We may be there already except we call it "executive search," and they don't use guns, at least not yet.

We are always looking for ways of doing things that go beyond simply doing things better. We're increasingly concerned about survival and renewal. Leading organizations are increasingly dealing with broad issues:

- How can we survive?
- How can we reinvent ourselves?
- How can we come to know which things are truly valuable?

The willingness to ask precisely these kinds of questions is a necessary precursor to the effective organizational practice of creativity.

Information technology is also pushing us toward an era of renewed interest in creativity. IT increasingly becomes, in the words of Albert Bressand of Paris-based think tank Prométhée, not IT but RT, the relationship technologies that connect us to each other and to provocative sources of knowledge. Technology takes us in the direction of new possibilities for collaboration, for linking the conversations that occur among people, and for linking people with new bodies of knowledge. It enables links between companies and experts, customers, affiliates and friends. These relationships can lead to a continuing stream of new insights.

The possibilities of technology also present us with a great challenge as we learn to travel back and forth between the physical, tangible world of most of our business processes as we understand them, and the intangible and virtual spaces that we will be working in as technology continues to open these doors. The tools we have now, such as group-ware and e-mail, are a fraction of what we will adopt as technology expands and opens up vast new possibilities for collaboration and, in turn, for the kind of creative capability that leads to strategic insight.

It is one thing to think that creativity is fundamentally and strategically important for your business. It's another to have a system in place for managing creativity, a system that people understand, that works effectively, and that regularly leads to the realization of significant value for the company. In most companies, there's a huge aspiration to narrow the gap between wanting to be and actually being creative. The question of a creativity methodology will occupy our attention for some time to come, until we develop a set of seasoned, tested tools for the practice of creativity.

Creating the Idea Factory

Part of my quest has been to find how such a system of creativity can be installed in organizations. What characterizes the systems that seem to confer competitive advantage? That's a trick question, because all organizations have such systems. People develop ideas; ideas pop out, they're talked about, they're developed, they're killed, they're filtered, they're screened. Sometimes they are funded, advanced, developed into formal corporate initiatives, and then shipped.

For most organizations, however, these systems are unconscious and unrecognized, and they don't work very well. So the question becomes how to make that intangible idea factory explicit. The challenge is to develop the realization that a creativity system isn't just the physical artifacts of people and infrastructure in an organization. It's also the intangibles of ideas and conversations about ideas. It's the realization of insights, the development of knowledge, and the connections between the inside and outside of the organization that produce a point of view and lead to creative products, services, processes, and perceptions of opportunity.

Learning Creativity and Improvisation through Jazz

In determining how creativity occurs in organizations, I have found a very useful metaphor in the world of music. There are two basic ways to play music. One way is to go to the music store and buy sheet music—which is rather like dehydrated music. Sheet music tells you exactly what notes to play, how loud to play them, how fast to play them, and so on. Anyone with a basic level of skill can sit down and play those notes. Mozart was very creative when he wrote his music, but he didn't want you to be creative when you play it. We use sheet music so we can play the pieces the way Mozart intended. Musicians who play from the sheet music can play one of two ways: correctly or incorrectly.

The other way of making music is jamming, a word that comes from jazz. The notion of jamming highlights the importance of improvisation. Improvised music has no sheet music to dictate how it should be performed. Instead, in jamming, there is a set of understandings that guide the execution of the music, and there is no distinction between rehearsal and performance. The talent of jazz musicians is that they pick up their instruments and immediately play new notes that sound good. Then they pick up their paychecks and go home. They just do it. For them it's a discipline, a job. If we can understand the art and discipline of jazz improvisation, I think we can learn a great deal about how to practice that art in the business world. Improvisation is probably one of the two or three cardinal skills for businesses to learn in the future, and the process of improvisation must underlie how organizations formulate strategy going forward. Jamming is about establishing a context for disorder. It's about the balancing act that must always occur between form and freedom, discipline and art. It is where form and the new meet on a continuous basis, where discovery occurs continuously.

In the traditional setting of large institutions, competitive advantage is conferred by scale and by ownership of resources. In this environment, sheet music is important as a means of coordinating activity. Planning in these organizations is about insights that originate in the command module and then are disseminated throughout the organization. The infamous vinyl binders from the planning department that Jack Welch did away with at GE were nothing more or less than corporate sheet music. The functionality of sheet music is obvious, but so are its limitations in a world where you have to be fast, smart, extremely agile, and, above all, very creative if you are to be competitive.

If we use jazz as a metaphor for creativity, we can identify the processes that have to be harnessed in the service of strategic insight. The person who can jam is someone who knows how to create new notes continuously in a way that will satisfy a number of tests: It has to sound good, and the listener has to want to stay and listen. If it's too alien to our ears, it won't sound good, and if it's too familiar, it will sound like elevator music. It has to balance a number of paradoxical elements. Improvisation has a grammar, just as creativity has a grammar. If you could hear a jazz musician play four renditions of the same tune, you would find them to be completely different. You would hear new notes that sound like a vibrant interpretation of the underlying structure, but each rendition would take us where we hadn't been before.

There are three signature skills of improvisation that are as relevant in business as they are in music. They are: clearing the mind, clearing the place, and clearing the beliefs. The entire methodology is all-encompassing, but these three skills are key.

Clearing the corporate mind becomes the first big agenda item. When jazz musicians get up on stage, they're not there to play notes they already know. They're there to start from the beginner's mindset. They're there to play something new—to move away from what is known into what is unknown.

This is very difficult for most organizations, because they tend to deal with what they already know. They reward people for being proud owners of expertise. They attempt to reproduce new insights in the image of the insights they already have. This thinking permeates the organization. But perhaps it is through the abrasion between different perspectives that the organization could come up with something genuinely new.

It's like a problem in the philosophical discipline of epistemology, the philosophy of knowledge. How do companies come to know things that they fundamentally don't know about, but which would be valuable to them if they did? Some companies have developed methods for clearing the mind. Some systems are extremely complex, while others are relatively straightforward.

For example, Meiji Seika, a buttoned-up Japanese confectionery company, created one extraordinary job description. One of the company's employees moved from Tokyo to Brussels; his job description was to eat dinner in restaurants and visit grocery stores.

His nickname was "the tastebuds." This was not a frivolous investment. Meiji was after the off-the-radar-screen knowledge that might
have no obvious value today but could be important in the future.
As a corporate leader, consider the following questions:

- How do you bring the outside, the environment, in?
- How do you take the inside out, in the sense of exposing
  your insiders to fresh contextual and market-related phenomena?
- How do you facilitate different kinds of conversations
  within the organization from those that support the day-
  to-day?
- Who is your chief knowledge officer? Your chief awareness officer? Your chief creativity officer?
- How do you systematically sense the environment?
- How do you represent, disseminate, and learn from new
  knowledge?
- How do you create a culture that systematically overturns
  its preconceptions?

The second signature skill is clearing the place. Jazz musicians,
when they want to develop something new, go to an isolated, protected environment to make it happen. Charlie Parker was the first
person who said, "I'm going to the woodshed," and it literally was
a woodshed behind his house. He played the saxophone for a year
until he came up with a new kind of music called "be-bop." He
didn't want any advice or criticism. He wanted to be alone. It's
about finding a protected environment that is free from judgment,
that enables different conversations, that may involve offsites, but
more importantly suggests a range of experiments in the integration
of environments, technology, and process.

It's not just an issue of designing the physical place, but also a
matter of designing the virtual spaces in which collaboration can take

place. Above all, it's a matter of creating an environment by suspending judgments until enough ideas have been put on the table that a new direction takes shape. Creating an environment where people feel brave enough to step forward and present their best idea is a management truism, but it's very difficult to practice in actuality.

Oticon, a company in Denmark and a prime example of how to manage creativity as a strategic capability, actually hired an architectural firm to widen the staircases in the building. They wanted to ruthlessly eliminate anything that would get in the way of people lingering and talking together as a spur to idea creation. They wanted their company to feel like a gigantic watercooler.

Considering how to clear the place involves a number of questions:

- How do you clear the place?
- Where is your company woodshed?
- Where is the place in your organization that allows people to think differently?
- Where is the environment that is like a Hollywood sound stage with a flashing red sign that says it's a hot set with hot things happening?
- Where is the environment that enables you to take a leap and generate something new?

Finally, we come to clearing the beliefs. A colleague of mine is fond of saying, "Creativity is like Santa Claus. If you don't believe in Santa Claus, he is not going to come down the chimney on Christmas Eve." An astute manager must try to increase the tangibility of creativity by fashioning a meaningful brand identity for creativity. He or she must build a culture, a system of meanings that translate into everything from compensation to the design of work flow in order to create believability and tactility for a set of attributes that are completely intangible.

Olympic Gold medalist Edwin Moses wore golden shoes when he ran. That was his brand identity for his aspiration to achievement. Managing the beliefs of the organization requires crafting a brand identity for creativity so that it becomes part of the mentality and the expectations of everyone in the organization. These days, the leaders of just about every company will claim to support risk-taking and the spirit of innovation. But this talk is meaningless unless it has practical value, and unless it truly relates to what people believe in and how their expectations are managed.

Relevant questions include:

- How does your culture lever your organization's creative aspirations in very specific terms?
- How does it translate into systems, structure, rewards, and the way jobs are defined?
- How do you make creativity tangible and practicable so that people will know that it's important?

The Implications of Creativity in Organizations

The three broad principles of improvisation explain how to enhance creative capabilities in the organization. They also portray successful creativity management as a balancing act between the twin poles of form and disorder. They can translate into hundreds of specific methods and tools that organizations can use. The next generation of organizational process around creativity will require a very different integration of technology, processes, facilitation, and structure to make that happen. In a sense, it's like moving from a mainframe model to a PC model. In the mainframe model, the decision is made in the command module. Then someone has to go to the computer room and have cards typed up and run through a computer in order to answer a vexing strategic question. In a PC environment, the process becomes one of rapid iteration, testing out hypotheses, low-cost experimentation, design exercises. It's not about specialists, it's about creating and flattening communities of discourse—it's about bringing in unusual points of view.

Corporate processes must be informed by a new managerial mindset. The new economy requires new metaphors for managers. They may be about what Louis Rossetto at *Wired Magazine* calls his job description—chief instigator. Or what Lou Platt at Hewlett-Packard says his job is—to encourage conversations. Or about management being an irritant and creating challenges that have a dramatic flair and resonance. For example, Jan Timmer started off Project Centurion at Philips Electronics by handing out a newspaper dated a number of years in the future with the headline, "Philips goes bankrupt." That newspaper started some very interesting conversations, which led to a great deal of strategic insight. Timmer's role was that of a producer, one who facilitates creative conversation, not that of the traditional manager.

Managing in the new economy is increasingly about finding great people, linking them with ideas and resources, and enabling them to produce something remarkable that leads to value. It involves creating an environment that supports creative work, and provisioning the efforts of creative talent. It may be that Steven Spielberg and not Alfred Sloane will become a leading example of the new managerial mindset needed to compete effectively in the new economy.

In summary, the art and discipline of the business of creativity is fundamental to corporate strategy. It's about being able to perceive with ever-greater detail and resolution what might be unforeseen and outside one's understanding. Today's heresy will most likely become tomorrow's orthodoxy, and we need methodologies to help us think creatively about that possibility.

To accomplish this we need to define different ways of working. It's about finding new ways of connecting people. It's about an intentionally designed work environment where conversations can lead to the desired level of strategic insight. It's about embracing the virtues of disorder, managing in terms of a new mindset, being open to the possibility of new business models. What is the right way to manage creativity in the interests of heightened strategic insight? Look at the sheet music in your organization, and then feel free to throw it away, in full appreciation of the virtues of disorder.

9

Endless Innovation
The Charles Schwab Strategy
An Interview with Daniel O. Leemon
Erik Calonius

When *Forbes* magazine designated Charles Schwab & Company "Company of the Year" in January 2001 the honor was for more than a single bright idea. Charles Schwab, a bespectacled Stanford University graduate, founded the company in 1971 and made it the most prominent discount brokerage house in the United States. But that was just the beginning of a string of innovations—ranging from the first "supermarket" of mutual funds to the groundbreaking e.Schwab online trading system. In between, the company has launched all kinds of product improvements—from a string of small, street-corner offices to such high-tech programs as Sell Analyzer (an online tool that evaluates the cost basis of securities in a portfolio and recommends which to sell for tax losses).

Daniel O. Leemon began his association with Charles Schwab & Company in the early 1990s. At the time he was a consultant with The Boston Consulting Group in San Francisco, where he was a vice president, and a lead member of the firm's financial services and consumer goods practices. Leemon joined Schwab in 1995 and is now executive vice president and chief strategy officer for the firm.

It was during the 1990s, with Leemon's help, that Schwab took its greatest strides forward. In 1993 came its Mutual Funds One-Source, providing one-stop shopping for investors; in 1996 came Internet trading through e.Schwab; and now, Schwab's "new model of full-service investing."

You wouldn't necessarily expect a financial services firm to be particularly innovative. Yet when you review the history of Charles Schwab, "innovation" and "innovator" are words that frequently pop up.

That's true. We started in the wake of a wave of deregulation in the brokerage industry. We're a firm that began in reaction to almost everything that had been before. And here we are, 25 years later, still thinking of ourselves as an upstart firm.

Schwab has had periods of disruptive innovation—the really big innovations, such as Mutual Funds OneSource and e.Schwab. And then there is a continuing record of incremental innovation. How do you focus on disruptive and incremental innovation, and how do you foster both of them?

I'll give you a top-down/bottom-up answer. The top-down stuff is driven by a very cohesive team at the top. We all know that innovation is important. We all know it's what our boss will rate us on at the end of the year. And we are all very big shareholders in the company. So some of the traditional impediments you get to innovation—I have my parochial interests, or I don't want to rock the boat, or why should I—go away when you know it's something your boss and the team look at. The executive committee, the executive vice presidents, even down to the top couple of hundred people in the company—the senior vice presidents—agree on that.

Each business head is constantly looking at his business saying, "My God, I've got a 20 percent growth bogey and I've got to keep increasing my fundamental business margin." Almost by definition, innovation leads you to those kinds of dramatic leaps. You can't afford an incrementalist's business plan.

Beyond that, innovation is just a natural part of our management process. A lot of ideas hit the table at the business-unit and corporate level. A lot of ideas come from our co-CEOs, Charles Schwab and David Pottruck. And then the rest of us try very hard to think those ideas through. If we were the customer, would we think that that is a good idea? And if so, then how in the world would we start getting it implemented? One of the key things is that this company focuses relentlessly on the customer. I know everyone says that, but this company really does it.

From a bottom-up point of view, most people here have a greater chance at making incremental changes than huge, disruptive ones. But since innovation is one of our core values, and by emphasizing it and by making sure that everyone is a stockholder, we create a great amount of incentive for people to come up with different ways of doing things. And we have an innovation process that rewards and recognizes people quarterly who come up with innovative ideas. In every way we can, and on every level, we are always trying to anticipate the needs of the customer.

That's an interesting point. A few years ago I interviewed Jeff Hawkins, who invented the Palm Pilot. We were standing in his garage, where he made the first prototype out of a piece of wood. He was telling me that he would carry that little slab of wood around in his shirt pocket, trying to imagine what it could be used for. That's certainly anticipating the needs of the consumer.

That's right. We've learned that you actually have to think *ahead* of the customer. Customers rarely articulate innovations. They may say, "I would really like a beer that makes me drunk but doesn't give me a hangover." Well, that's chemically impossible. But you can listen to what the customer says he or she is unhappy about, and then, if you know enough about the basic plumbing of your industry, you can put yourself in the place of the customer and ask, "How can we solve that problem? How can we make something really great?"

Tell me about the mechanics of that process. Do you get started with customer surveys? Do you contemplate the problem in a think tank?

We do everything. We love focus groups. We are probably overly addicted to focus groups, because they are usually quick and relatively cheap. We also do a lot of concept testing. What about this? What would you expect us to do here? What *wouldn't* you expect us to do? We used to think that our present customers were the only customers we had. But now we spend a lot of time on our noncustomers. We focus hard on what their dissatisfactions are. We ask them, "What are you unhappy about? What do you worry about?" What we usually find is that no one in our industry is hitting the bull's-eye. For example, the big brokerage firms want you to trade stocks and the big private banking firms want to manage your money. But the opportunity is in targeting the middle—and you find that by listening to the customer.

Innovation at Schwab has two steps. First, we listen to dissatisfactions so that we can anticipate what customers could possibly want, and try to articulate that idea in a great deal of detail. Second, we wonder how we can do this economically. It's like a game some people play when they go to a Chinese restaurant. When you get your fortune, you put the words "in bed" at the end of the fortune.

I've never played it, but it sounds like a great game!

It goes, "You will have much success and notoriety . . . in bed." Or "You will find great business opportunities . . . in bed." Well, the game around Schwab is "for free." Almost any time Chuck or Dave says, "You know what we ought to do? We ought to do x, y, or z," the end of the sentence has to be "for free." We'll do that for free. So the second part of the innovation process is how close to "for free" we can get. We work very hard to make the cost structure work, to do something very, very efficiently.

So you find a customer complaint and then slap "for free" on the end. How do you decide when to move forward with such innovations, and how do you implement them?

The running joke at Schwab is that at Schwab a pilot means the beginning of a rollout. The reason is that speed to market in our business is so important that we really have a "tweak as you go" mentality. Our experience with online trading is a great example. It's a no-brainer to have customers tell you that if you would just keep doing what you're doing now—but do it cheaper—that would be great. So it was in the middle of 1995 that the senior management team went offsite and came back and said, "We've got to get serious about online trading." It wasn't so much because there was competition at the time. Rather, our people looked at what having a screen and a keyboard and a data feed could do for people. They said, "You know what? It's not just different, it's better. And it does all the things we've been hearing customers for years say they want to do. It gives them control over what information they seek. It gives them second-by-second access to the market. It gives them the ability to track multiple stocks."

We decided that we had to get very serious about online investing. We then realized that the people who were already doing online trading were doing it very cheaply. So we decided to introduce e.Schwab, which was also cheap. It was exactly the same online trading, incidentally, that we were offering at Schwab in general, but with a different price point on it and a different name on the diskette. Part of the reason we did that is that if low pricing didn't turn out to drive a lot of volume, and if online trading didn't turn out to make the cost structure very productive, we would be a footnote in history today. We would have been out of business. So e.Schwab was constructed to put a speed bump between our mainstream business and this new business.

Did it succeed?

In fact, when we introduced e.Schwab in Florida in late 1995, it was a disaster. We advertised: nobody came. Many companies would have said, "OK, the market has spoken. And actually, we didn't want to do this in the first place." But we looked at it and said, "Something doesn't seem right. This doesn't make sense." Now, we had test marketed in Florida because it was the cheapest place you can buy an isolated edition of the *Wall Street Journal*. But when we looked at the demographics of Florida, we began to see why it had flopped. You have elderly people and people for whom English is not a first language. So in the end, we rolled it out in Texas and California, where, of course, it took off. The moral of this story is: don't give up on innovation while you are still sitting around saying, "But I want this. I like this! How come nobody else is buying it?"

Are you saying then that intuition plays a role in the innovation process?

Absolutely. I don't think I've ever seen an innovative idea that started with analysis. But there is a wonderful symbiotic relationship between intuition and analysis. The decision to do e.Schwab, for example, was not highly analytical. But there was a tremendous amount of analysis done under various cannibalization scenarios to make sure that the e.Schwab business was not going to unbalance the rest of the company. Then there were further analytics to prove to us that bringing the $29.95 price into the rest of our customer base would be good for us. So it was a mix of analysis and intuition. In late 1997 it was co-CEO Dave Pottruck who was saying that we needed to lower the price of e.Schwab across the company, that intuitively this is right, that we've just gotta do it. And it was the management team beneath him that looked at the analytics and said, "Yes, we *can* do this, and we know how to manage it."

Do you have an "intuition A-team" that makes these big moves?

Frequently it's Dave or Chuck. Chuck is conspicuously good at thinking up good ideas. He will start talking about something he would like to do and if you just go back and see him two or three times and ask a bunch of questions, it begins to take shape in your mind. For instance, Chuck would like to see us get more heavily into the checking account business. So Chuck would come into the room and say, "We ought to buy a bank." Now, some people listening to a billionaire like Chuck would say, "Yes sir, I'll go out and buy a bank." But we say to Chuck, "What are you trying to do? What are we trying to accomplish?"

If you take buying a bank literally, you get into all kinds of regulatory and capital ratio questions. But when you ask him questions and get underneath it, he's really saying two things. First of all, that all of our big clients have an account at these banks, and then that they are not getting good service from them. We ought to do a checking account that is better for our customers than the one they've got. It should pay higher interest. It should have lower fees. And, by the way, if we do it right, that would give us a nice piece of competitive insulation and probably a nice profit source. Notice the order of that: it does end with the economics. But it starts with what is good for the customers.

We have in fact issued a product called Schwab Access that we will be promoting a lot. We aren't a bank, it's not a checking account, but you can write an unlimited number of drafts on it. It comes with a debit card. We created a money market fund that is a government fund, with a very high rate of interest. We charge enough expenses against this fund to pay for all the checking and everything else, but it still gives you much higher interest than a bank.

Of course, between the beginning and the end of this innovation story there's a huge amount of work on what we do with the systems: Where will we promote this? How many customers have to pick it up for our investment to make sense? What does the average balance have to be?

In designing a company that runs on innovation, isn't there a danger that the ideas will dry up and the company will run aground? Doesn't that make strategy-by-innovation a risky bet?

It is, and that's why the analysts always ask us, "How long can you keep doing this?" But my boss has an interesting saying: "You can always get back your money, but you can't ever get back your time." What he means by that is that if you get ahead, you should be able to stay ahead. While your competitors are figuring out what you did and how to copy it, you're already on to the next thing.

We have little danger of running out of room for innovation. We don't have 100 percent market share, after all—we have about 5 percent. And we're already looking at the next thing. We're working hard right now, for instance, on our international business. Right now, our U.S. business is growing at 25 percent a year; our investment manager business is growing at 30 percent a year. Right now the overseas markets are not terribly exciting. But some day the U.S. markets will flatten out. I was just talking with Dave Pottruck this morning and he was saying that the challenge of being good management is building your next business while you're on the steepest part of the S-curve in your current business. Wait till the S-curve flattens out and it's too late. Someone else has probably already built it.

But many products reach the end of fruitful innovation. They can't be improved much. They become commodities. Do you see some point where you've satisfied the demand, where you've delivered everything that anyone could possibly want?

I think it depends on how narrowly you define financial services. We are lucky in that we are in the part of financial services that tends to make the biggest difference in people's lives in the long term, and they therefore have the biggest emotional attachment to it. It is these emotions that keep our products from becoming low margin and commoditized. In this respect, we are luckier than people in the credit card and mortgage business. But our mission statement used to say that we wanted to be the most useful and ethical provider of brokerage services in America. Now it is to be the most useful and ethical provider of financial services in the world. And I can imagine that one day we will say that we want to be the most useful and ethical provider of life-assisting services in the world. In other words, if 30 years from now everybody knows how to save for a comfortable retirement and there is no magic in the financial theorists to figure it out any longer, there will still be other services that people will need at the time of retirement that we ought to be able to help them with. In the long run, in the very long run, our competition is Disney, Microsoft, Wal-Mart—companies that have a high mind share and make people's lives better and more convenient.

So are you saying that Schwab is really a group of innovative people who can apply their energy to almost anything?

I'm not sure I would give us that much credit. But I do think that we have a very strong culture and very strong values. About 75 percent of our hiring process is based on values, compatibility, energy level, and what the individuals want to do with their careers. Someone who comes in here who is complacent or thinks we are stupid because we don't charge our customers more money—well, we

don't like them and we won't hire them. We have structured ourselves to emphasize the values we want. There is much more employee ownership here than in a typical company our size. There is
a much higher financial upside than in other companies our size.
That's what gets our people on track here. And there's excitement.
You walk the halls here and everybody will speak the vision and
speak the values with real excitement. They all feel they are part of
something. It's like the story of the guy who walks up to the janitor
in the hospital and says, "What do you do here?" And he replies,
"We save lives." That's the kind of company we want here. That's
what you get from Schwab. In a press interview a few years ago an
interviewer asked Chuck, "What keeps you up at night?" And
Chuck replied, "All the Americans who retired yesterday without
enough money to live comfortably."

*You've recently been rolling out a new model for full-service in-
vesting that has been called the reinvention of full-service brokerage. Are you hatching another disruptive innovation here?*

I think so. It's not as easy to describe as the others because it isn't
a product. But to provide open platform advice while keeping the
customer in control and without any conflict of interest is radically
new. Nobody in our business does that. No customer will sit down
with you and say, "That's what I want!" But if you describe it to
them, they will say, "Wow, can you do that?"

And now, all you have to do is figure it out.

Yeah. And we're working on that one right now.

10

Molecular Designer
An Interview with Roger Y. Tsien

Steven Adler

It is quiet in Dr. Roger Tsien's La Jolla laboratory on the bright and breezy January day that we meet. His graduate students and postdocs at the University of California, San Diego, work quietly; the atmosphere is relaxed but purposeful. Tsien's unprepossessing inner sanctum is cheerfully cluttered and furnished in a style that can best be described as *université moderne*. The small whiteboard on one wall is covered with chemical and biological equations and formulas. Roger Tsien works at the confluence of several scientific streams—chemistry, molecular biology, neurophysiology—and has conducted a dynamic investigation of the way cells communicate. Tsien's unique, interdisciplinary approach to cellular research, which eschews rigid departmentalization and actively encourages cross-disciplinary fertilization, has resulted in groundbreaking discoveries with a broad range of applications in both theoretical and practical biochemistry. His passion for his work is immediate, and it is laced with self-effacing, gentle humor.

You have a joint academic appointment at UCSD, in the main cam-

pus's Department of Chemistry and Biochemistry as well as the School of Medicine's Department of Pharmacology. Do you consider yourself a chemist or a pharmacologist?

That's hard to say. Immigration forms or tax forms give you space for just one word to describe what you do. I usually put "biologist," since I don't want to confuse bureaucrats. I came out of a biological background, and that's still the driving force. If I could use two words, and they didn't have to be a standard combination, it would be "biomolecular engineer." The core of what we do is designing and engineering biological molecules in interesting ways.

I believe you trained initially as a chemist. What drew you to pursue other disciplines?

I tried a lot of things in college. There was a brief stage where I thought I'd be a chemist, but chemistry courses at Harvard burned that out of me. You're forced to take them, you hate them, and you move on to something else. I dabbled in oceanography, neurobiology, astrophysics, a bunch of things. By the time I got to graduate school at Cambridge, I figured the most exciting problem was to study the brain. In some ways the existing methods people had to study the brain were both too blunt and too cruel. The main method then, and to a considerable extent now, is to cut a hole in the skull of an anesthetized animal, drop an electrode down, and record what you get in the brain. It's very much like ice fishing. You cut a hole in the ice, you drop a line blindly, and you see what you catch. As a grad student, if I caught six hundred neurons and analyzed them, I'd do a taxonomy of those "fish" as my thesis, and I didn't like the idea.

There's a great analogy from Donald Kennedy, who was the president of Stanford and a neurobiologist. He said to imagine a bunch of Martians trying to analyze and understand the game of baseball from way up in their spaceship. One approach would be to cut a hole in the top of the Astrodome and drop a microphone all the way down to a fan in the stands and record what the fan is saying. The Martians hear "Kill the ump!" or "Hot dog here!" You can imagine how hard it is to understand baseball from what one person says. Another way is to take a global pattern and analyze it. The Martians note, "Gee, it's usually about two o'clock on Saturday, and there's a big crowd, and by five o'clock they leave." They keep analyzing the population flow around the stadium or the general noise level at certain times of the day, and they try to understand what baseball is. This corresponds to the two traditional ways of exploring the brain. There is single-unit recording, where you try to record from one neuron; and EEGs, where you record the mass activity of millions of neurons, but you don't know what any of them does.

That was my dilemma. I felt that we needed a way to see neurons flashing lights, almost like in the old sci-fi movies, where the fronts of computers always had flashing lights. It made you feel as if it were thinking *really* hard. If we could see the neurons flash lights as they talked to each other, we could see them converse. So the question becomes, How do you make neurons change colors or flash lights when they are changing their biochemical or electrical activity? Most of the things we have made in the subsequent three decades are dyes or proteins that will change color or brightness in response to some biochemical signal. It enabled me to indulge my liking for pretty colors—my taste in art is more for Matisse than for Braque. This work allows me to feel that I'm being useful to this long-term goal of understanding the brain. I most likely won't reach that goal myself, but maybe I'll make a few of the tools that somebody else will then use. Maybe we'll also help with some clinical applications and assist people in finding drugs along the way.

On one of your many Web sites I came across the statement that the overall goal of your lab is to understand how living cells and neu-

ronal networks process information. Does that accurately convey what you do?

We are trying to understand how cells and neurons process information. We do so by building molecules, both little molecules in the domain of organic chemistry and big molecules in the domain of molecular biology. In another Web site you might have found the simile that these molecules are like spies that we train and then parachute into unknown territory, and they report back to us what they find. They're supposed to find out how that territory works.

Much of your current work involves the development of proteins that act as dyes to aid in understanding a variety of cellular interactions. Can you describe the evolution of your involvement in this groundbreaking exploration?

Much of what we work with is called GFP, green fluorescent protein, which is developed from jellyfish. It made a bit of news in the last day or so when there was all this publicity about a transgenic monkey. That first gene put into the animal was for a variety of GFP with a crucial mutation originally discovered by us.

Was the work with GFPs of your devising?

Partially, but there was a huge amount of ground covered before we became involved. We did not discover the GFP first, but our contribution was to make the changes in it that made it the most useful for other people. I know that you work in the theater, so I'll try to put it in theatrical terms. We're not the playwright of GFP. We're the stage director of several particular productions that happen to be popular.

What drew you, then, to direct this play? Why did you decide to work with GFP?

I think it was 1992, right after the cloning of the gene had first been reported, that I became involved. To continue the theatrical analogy, it was when the play was written but had never been performed. There was an even earlier stage, at which the novel had been written but it wasn't yet a play, and somebody had to write the play. That was the cloning of the gene by Douglas Prasher, who published it in 1992, and he is actually one of the unsung heroes of this area. He did it when nobody thought it was interesting. He worked practically alone for about five or six years. He faced funding crises toward the end of his work, and just before his research grant ran out, with a last gasp he pulled out the full-length gene. However, he had no more resources to go back and do more work with it. He decided that he didn't want to continue with the research. When I read his paper and phoned him up to talk about this treasure trove, I was astonished when he said, "Take it. I'll give you samples. Just promise to put my name on the paper if it ever works," which we did.

Why do jellyfish produce such a viable marker?

The ability of some jellyfish to glow in the dark has been known since Roman times. The particular protein we work on comes from Puget Sound jellyfish. Nobody really knows why they glow when they do—it happens when you disturb the water, and it happens at certain times of the year, but we don't really know why they want to glow. It's obviously a fascinating phenomenon. The first biochemistry on it was done in the early 1960s or so, when a scientist named Shimomura discovered that the jellyfish had two proteins in it as part of its glowing system. The primary protein glows blue, but the animal glows green because it has the second protein, the GFP, which changes the color.

Normally, proteins don't have this ability to glow, at least not in any visible wavelength. So the critical question then became, "How does it do this?" Most people thought the answer would be relatively trivial. There are proteins that glow, but never from the proteins themselves. They always pick up a dye or a pigment from their environment—that pigment is what is really glowing—and the protein may provide a nice shell around it. That's the astonishing thing about this jellyfish protein. It didn't need anything else, it knew how to do surgery on its own guts, sort of hara-kiri. It makes its own dye out of its own intestines, so to speak, and that's why everyone likes it now. You just tell the cells to make the protein—any skilled molecular biologist can issue the orders—and right there, by itself, it turns itself fluorescent, without needing to be fed anything else.

What are some current applications of GFP in science and medicine? Why was it used in this transgenic monkey, for example?

Any time you want to mark a cell or mark a protein, you make GFP express in that cell, or tag it to a protein. You fuse it in such a way that wherever the protein goes the fluorescence goes too. You can *see* it while it's alive; you don't have to break open the animal or the cell. Most individual cells, and some entire small organisms or embryos of larger organisms, are transparent enough that one can view their innards with a microscope while the cell is alive. Macroscopic opaque critters are more difficult, so one either has to do some surgery—admittedly opening the animal, but at least not destroying the individual tissues—or use pulsed infrared beams, which penetrate much farther into tissue than visible light, or switch to some nonoptical forms of imaging like MRI. With GFP you can see where that protein goes because it has this fluorescent tail on it.

I'll give you an example that's more visible to the lay public. Land mines are a big problem around the world—they've been left around in the soil and it's expensive and dangerous to remove them. You can now raise special strains of bacteria that can turn on some genes when they sense TNT in their environment. The gene you choose to turn on is GFP, so the bacteria will glow if they are growing in the presence of TNT. A little TNT leaks out of land mines, since they're cheaply made and are not hermetically sealed. In the neighboring soil there will be a little trace of TNT, and the hope is that you can come along with a helicopter and spray the bacteria all over the field. They'll replicate, and later another helicopter scans a laser beam to see the glowing patches where the land mines are, without people having to set foot and risk their own necks. That's the coolness of the potential.

A bit earlier, when discussing your work with GFP, you mentioned that Douglas Prasher, who first cloned it, was really the playwright and you were the director. If you allow me to torture the analogy a bit further, you apparently staged a spectacularly vivid production. On what projects, though, have you been the playwright, the creator?

One critical area is in small molecules you build from scratch. This started while I was a graduate student. Here we have invented quite a few molecules from nearly first principles. By contrast, the field of protein design is not far enough advanced for any of us to design a protein from absolute scratch. We always have to go to nature and ask how to do it. Evolution figured out how to make these marvelous proteins, and we exploit them.

The San Diego area is now one of the nation's leading biotech centers, and you have become involved with research in the corporate sector. Can you talk a bit about some of your ventures in this arena?

I'm the scientific cofounder of a couple of companies. The first is Aurora Biosciences. The company name is meant to suggest lots of colors and the dawn, but to be honest we also chose the name because the venture capitalists like to start with the letter A. Presentations to stock analysts usually go in boringly alphabetical order, and you want to get your material presented while they're all still fresh!

Aurora uses fluorescent technologies to develop cells that help the pharmaceutical industry identify drugs for potential uses. It helps them test and screen millions of compounds very rapidly.

Senomyx is the other firm. You'll probably now ask how it ended up starting with a letter at the other end of the alphabet. It was going to be Ambryx—as in ambrosia—until the lawyers discovered that another company already had a similar name. Senomyx uses the recent discovery of the actual protein molecules in the nose and tongue that mediate smell and taste to try to find novel things that will either make new odorants—or block them—or make new taste sensations. For example, kids don't know how to swallow capsules. If you have a bad-tasting medicine they have to take it in syrup, and the drug companies have to slather it with sugar to make it go down. But it still tastes "yecchh," and they don't want to take it. If we could actually block the taste of bitterness instead of trying to overload and mask the taste, they would take the medicine, and that would sell to the drug companies. We could make deodorants that, instead of just trying to pile a new fragrance on top, could actually block the original bad smell. We're applying modern molecular biology and drug screening to the old problems of perfumery or cooking.

Curiosity seems to be a critical ground zero for scientific research. Did you always indulge your scientific curiosity? Did you play with chemistry sets when you were a kid?

I did play with chemistry sets, but found it rather pedestrian, since the makers were too concerned with safety! I found a book in the school library in junior high that had much cooler experiments with much more dangerous substances. That's what made me think, when I was in high school, that I could be interested in chemistry. Funnily enough, it was burned out of me at Harvard and reinstated in the "other" Cambridge. It was not so much because of the institutions, though. The difference was that when you take chemistry as an undergraduate, you are being lectured *at,* you have to memorize stuff for exams, which I did and immediately forgot it. When I got to Cambridge, I realized that chemistry could be a tool to find a distinct way of studying the brain that wasn't being used by other people. So I had a goal in mind, and suddenly all those reactions that I couldn't remember as an undergraduate, I remembered now. It is totally different when you learn it for yourself, when you know why you're learning it.

At Cambridge, was the teaching of creativity and innovation intrinsic to the education process? Did a mentor lead you to think in an innovative fashion, or was it innate?

There was no overt statement: "We're going to teach you creativity." Of all places, Cambridge has been around more than six hundred years. They would laugh at that stuff as a bunch of jumped-up educational theory. You don't teach it, you do it by example. Of course, the British system is very keen on one-on-one instruction, much more so than the Americans.

I eventually got on to a wonderful teacher who had no students left, and he mentored me personally for nine months before he left. He didn't have to teach me creativity, in the sense that I already had far too much of it. I had too many wild ideas, but he gave me the ability to actually execute some of them by helping me begin to synthesize the molecules I was designing.

In synthetic chemistry, creative designs are of little use unless you can execute them and test them in reality. The analogy would be if a budding architect had to do his own construction or a songwriter had to perform her own work, rather than work with a separate builder or singer. No one had ever given me that degree of tutoring in chemistry before. It was vital training to have done some of it myself and was the other reason, together with having a biological purpose, that I decided that chemistry wasn't so bad after all.

I wish I had the time now to do the same kind of tutoring, but American labs are not organized like that. With one professor and one student you'd never produce results at the expected rate. You have to have ten to twenty postdocs and students, raise the money, and write recommendations. As I've gotten grayer and more bogged down in committees and supervision, my personal role has shrunk back toward the conceptual design aspects, leaving the hard experimental work to my students and postdocs. There isn't the time to give them what my chemistry mentor at Cambridge, Ian Baxter, gave me.

Does the idea of innovation have particular resonance for you as a scientist?

In a way, yes. I'm conscious that the type of science I've done emphasizes the sort of innovation that's like Edison's style of inventing. To that extent I work in a more applied fashion than my colleagues, by developing molecules or techniques that we can use in a concrete way. In biology, "technique" is a bit of a dirty word; you can put someone down by describing him as working on techniques. On a higher plane is pure biology, how nature works, for example, how it made us with one head and two arms and two legs. Academics probably value pure over applied science for two good reasons: as a defense mechanism against the rest of society constantly demanding practical (if possible, profitable) applications, and because if you discover something fundamental about nature, it is eternally true and credited to you; whereas if you develop a technique or engineering innovation, it often becomes obsolete and forgotten in a few years. Where this attitude hurts is when a student or postdoc who may be very good says, "I don't want to join your lab because you guys work on techniques." What they often want to work on is frequently much more mundane. It won't get them very far, but it's what they're *told* is the better thing to do, which is to ask in a very pure, abstract way about how existing biology works, not about how we can change it. Of course, when you want to invent drugs or cure disease, you then need the same sort of activist approach to reengineering biology as we take in our efforts.

To that extent we are *more consciously* innovating, because we are always wanting to make some new means to answer the question rather than to just answer it by using existing techniques. For a long time this bothered me a great deal. I was eventually a bit comforted by—and here's another analogy you might like—the fact that Woody Allen had his phase where he tried to be Ingmar Bergman. I guess he had the impression that these deep, artistic Swedish movies about the meaning of life and death are somehow higher cinematic art than just plain fun things that make people laugh. But in the end Allen had to realize what he is good at. He's not Ingmar Bergman, he can't try to *make* himself Bergman, and he might as well stick to the more mundane, "lower" art. If this business of making practical inventions is considered low science, that's OK. I would like to have as much involvement as I can in solving the pure biological questions, too, but I can't kid myself anymore that that's where I'm going to make my biggest impact.

We often talk of varying degrees of innovation, from incremental stages to the breathtaking breakthrough. Can you identify one singular contribution you made that achieved breakthrough status?

Well, probably right now the most frequently used technique out there involves GFP, but I also have to admit that our role was the least fundamental. We just modified something that someone else had discovered and yet someone else had cloned.

The important contribution, I feel—the place that we *really* built from almost ground zero—is in the field of calcium. Sometimes, the way you can judge things is to ask, "If the inventor had been run over by a bus the day before the invention was made, would it still have been possible?" The answer with the GFP is yes. With a lot of the calcium dyes, though, if I hadn't come up with the idea, I'm not sure anyone would be working on them or using them now. Maybe someone would have invented the same molecules, but would anyone else have written the exact same play as another playwright? Not *exactly*. Would anyone have written on the same general themes? Maybe more so. Obviously, when you're the playwright you have a far greater fundamental role.

Why do you consider your earlier work with calcium a breakthrough innovation?

When cells in the brain fire, or signal, there are some things they always do. Voltage spikes in the neuron create calcium pulses, which turn on lots of complicated biochemistry, some of which results in encouraging or discouraging voltage spikes in adjacent neurons, where the process repeats itself. If we want a generic way of seeing when neurons fire, you can measure either the voltage spike or the calcium pulse that the firing produced. I wanted to see neurons flash, and I had struggled with voltage dyes in order to do so.

So I began to experiment with making calcium dyes. At that time, the most fashionable calcium dye in biology was originally built by some Eastern European atomic energy commission to measure uranium and plutonium. It also would measure calcium, although not very well.

I was working on my thesis—and it too wasn't working well enough—and I heard about this Eastern European dye, and I realized, "Hey, that wasn't found by any *rational* means." I thought, "If you're *really* looking for a calcium dye, you could do better." Fortunately, I wasn't working under close supervision. I wouldn't have been allowed to pursue this in an American lab with proper supervision. I had already worked on three failing projects, and with only a year more before I had to turn in my thesis, I started working on another project. But nobody was watching me. I came up with a design and thought I'd give it a couple of weeks, no more, and if it didn't work I would go back to my other failing projects. And though it didn't make a dye, it fortunately proved that the principle of the design would work. People still use this building block as the core that binds calcium very specifically in a biological context. It was one of the better ideas in my life.

How do you find new ideas? Can you articulate a process by which you identify new directions or new applications you want to explore?

Maybe this question is like asking playwrights where they get their ideas for new plays. A certain amount of my inspiration comes from hearing talks or reading papers. You find that people have a need—and they often don't know it themselves—and suddenly you say, "Gee, if we had a molecule that would do *this,* it would really change things." GFP started that way. Sometimes you can't judge the impact it will have. Thomas J. Watson of IBM thought, after the first big computer had been built, that the worldwide market might be five computers, or something similar. People had no idea how pervasive computers would become. On a much more humble scale, that's what this biology is about, at least when it's successful.

Determining where to go next comes, in part, from trying to fill needs. Often we realize that there's a little bit of a need, and I think, "Gee, it would be cool and, yes, I happen to know of something that I could slot in here." There is a huge number of needs, and you don't want to start in until you know there's a hint of a lead. To that extent we're a bit like drunks under the street lamp. We go where we *think* there's a little bit of a glimmering of light. Actually, there are thousands of keys all over the place, and you might as well go for ones that are under the street lamp, under some sort of flickering candle, at least.

You don't work as a solo creator, though. You're dependent to a great extent upon the creativity of the people who work in your lab. How do you encourage innovation in your staff?

I don't know that I do a good enough job. I encourage students to devise topics for their theses that are plausible. I know they'll work really hard if they're working on their own ideas, which may not happen if I impose a topic on them. We have group meetings, which can be painful for some people, because we cover an enormous territory. Someone may talk about organic chemistry and the struggle to build a certain kind of molecule, and then a minute later someone else gets up to talk about problems in handling brain slices. The organic chemists often don't understand what the hell the biologists are talking about with brain slices, and the biologists find the chemistry totally baffling.

I keep hoping that the cross-fertilization will work. I keep encouraging them as much as possible to try both ends of the spectrum, as a theater director should try writing a play once in a while. You must decide it's doable, it's worth learning a little of the other language, and if you do, there are tremendous benefits from the cross-fertilization. But you can't force people.

How do you develop methodologies to manage your labs so that the work is concerted and pointed in a certain direction, toward a goal?

It's not very concerted. It's actually very diverse. Most people who come to my lab want to have their own project and not be part of a team or cogs in a wheel. Most other labs have one or two main goals and everyone performs a piece of it. The people who come to me are the ones who want to get away from that. I allow more diversity because I received it myself at Cambridge. I was left to swing on my own rope. My PhD supervisor at Cambridge said that if he had trained one good scientist in his life, that was enough—he would have felt as if he had reproduced himself in the scientific world. So

I try to give people a little bit of that freedom. To be honest, though, most of them are not quite as crazy and rip-roaring and ready to march off in their own direction. They need a little more guidance than I did back then.

So we attract these crazy people who want to do their own thing among a group of like-minded colleagues. They may make a contribution to a group effort, but mostly they want to innovate on their own.

How do you focus such a flurry of activity that can lead in so many different directions?

I've never taken any management courses. I've seen little bits of management training in these biotech companies. I shudder at the thought of trying to apply some of those systematic principles to my own lab. They teach that you should set a whole bunch of defined goals and a defined time line, and if you don't meet it, you should have the courage to cut it off decisively and move on.

In the business world you may have to be cold-blooded and set those goals. We don't do that in my lab. It's more free-flowing. That's why I can still cherish the notion that eighteen years after a project didn't work, I am still going to *make* it work somehow one of these days. The only justification that I can offer is that we've been lucky a number of times. We have produced, with relatively modest resources and by a process that the business schools would totally abhor, the relatively wild innovation that then allowed bigger enterprises to be systematic.

Have you developed your own barometer for determining success and failure?

There's a story about Einstein at a cocktail party. He saw a man who pulled out a little notepad just after a conversation and started scribbling in it. Einstein asked this man, "What are you writing?"

The man answered, "I just heard a good idea, and I wanted to write it down before I forget it." And Einstein said, "Oy vey! I've had only one or two good ideas in my lifetime, so few that I don't need to write them down." He had pretty high standards.

I do cherish some ideas that I think are more clever than a lot of the things that have become successful but haven't worked yet, and I can't quite give them up. I keep hoping that one day I'll find the right combination of people in the lab with the right interests, or I'll find some new development that will remove some of the technical problems, and we'll solve it. On the other hand, when I do come out with these ideas, some of the people who have been in the lab for a while will roll their eyes and say, "Oh, not *that* one again."

Do you publicize or market your developments differently from other scientists?

No, I don't think it's any different. We publish papers and give talks at meetings. I don't think I do anything that is unusual.

So to what alchemy do you attribute your success?

We happen to have made some things that were very useful to other people. When we started using the chemistry approach in biology, it was almost unheard-of. There was an almost total lack of communication between chemists and biologists, although that wall has broken down to a large extent now, in a small part because of us. I never tried to set up institutes. I just tried to solve some scientific problems. Now this sort of cross-pollination and collaboration has become much more fashionable, and some of our uniqueness is going away. We've created some metatechnologies and have engendered a huge amount of competition for ourselves. And we're starting to find ourselves scooped on what I hope are some of the more minor things. So I'm trying to pull the focus of our work back to things that I hope have not become as commonplace yet.

Do you have a guiding ethos that helps you define your work and your process?

It would be nice to say I did. Instead, I would have to say that we basically try to put one foot in front of the other, and try to do it in a good way. I don't have some overall master plan. Woody Allen has said that 80 percent of life is just showing up, and I agree. A lot of it is just hacking away and doing your best. I'm not a shining example to anybody in that regard.

When people look back at your work, what do you hope they will feel was your major impact?

If they can say that I created some of the tools that helped people understand how cells work and how the brain works, I think that would be a significant accomplishment. It would also be very pleasing if some of the structures we created would be appreciated as intrinsically interesting examples of molecular sculpture or architecture. Is that too pretentious, to imagine that designed molecules could have esthetic merit, distinguishable from commercial utility? I don't suppose this "art form" will ever interest mass audiences, unlike photography, movies, and video, which are more accessible art forms also born relatively recently from technical innovations. Even among the professionals, chemists often find it hard to judge biological significance, just as chemical elegance is often lost on biologists. That's the downside of working in a thinly populated interdisciplinary area. The upside is the abundance of opportunities relative to the number of competitors, I should add. But a lot of smart young people are entering this area, so I hope and expect that this field will expand and flourish.

11

With Us There Are No Titles
An Interview with Michael Hilti
Michael Gatermann

The head of the company arrives in shirtsleeves. Like all other employees, he has a name tag clipped to his breast pocket.

In Michael Hilti's empire there are hardly any privileges anymore: "We have no executives' club, don't lend company cars, have abolished titles," says the 51-year-old president of Hilti AG, the largest concern in Liechtenstein. This family business dominates the small Alpine monarchy. Its bright-red trucks are familiar in the landscape, and when the employees at headquarters in the small town of Schaan, three kilometers from the capital of Vaduz, go home for the day, there's rush hour in the whole country. "It's good to work here," says Hilti, "and life is good, too."

Its own worldwide sales representatives sell their customers locking devices for almost 2.5 million marks a year. And with such technically simple products as drills, padlocks, screws, and dowels the Liechtensteiners bring in a profit of about 10 percent.

Through all the economic ups and downs, the business's lock on success has held. Why? For Michael Hilti the key ingredient is creativity: "Creative colleagues lower costs, invent new products and marketing strategies, they like working, and they produce quality."

So he makes an effort to "create an environment in which people feel comfortable and let their creativity unfold."

That sounds great, but how do you do it?

The key words are "openness" and "accessibility." Everyone is challenged to think and discuss along with the others. In our facilities next to the belts there are clipboards everywhere, and the workers note what improvements could be made. There are no masters anymore; the workers' groups elect a coach once a year.

So there's nothing left for management to do.

On the contrary, demands on them have been intensified. Whoever wants to lead mature workers must show competence at all times. And the managers have to be catalysts for change.

Do you really have a team that consists only of high achievers?

Of course not. But while we concentrated solely on the development of the top people previously, for some time now we've concerned ourselves increasingly with the next generation of managers, who are lagging behind in achievement.

How does that work?

Every six months the superiors have to report with their action program for their team members, and they are evaluated according to their success in this area.

It sounds like an island of the blessed, where the weak are protected and encouraged . . .

Naturally there are limits. We see ourselves as a high-achieving team, and those who can't play in this league should step down. And there are also positions there in the concern. But we've learned something: it pays if you concern yourself especially with the weaker members of a team and encourage them, rather than concentrating on the top.

What does it bring you?

We raise the quality of our management. Picture the Gaussian normal distribution curve of talent in a concern—few bad people, many average to good ones, and few top ones: through our encouragement we push the whole distribution curve to the right in the direction of better achievement.

If employees are encouraged to constantly question things and criticize, their superiors have to have superhuman tolerance and patience. In every suggestion for change there is an implicit criticism of the organization and its leadership.

That's exactly how it shouldn't be understood. Here there is no expectation that those in leadership positions have a monopoly on good ideas. On the contrary, we judge them also on the basis of how much creativity they foster in their people and incorporate into the business.

You work in a conservative business. How do you prevent creative kooks from blowing the whole thing to bits and ruining your business?

We set limits and ordain that certain things must be accepted. These things are called "accept its"; for example, the definition of our line of work, lock technology. The "accept its" are outnumbered by the "form its," the questions, problems, and ideas that must be generated by our fellow employees.

How do you maintain the desire to innovate? After all, there's little promise of promotion, since you've abolished hierarchies.

That's right. We don't want any titles. What we offer is a rotation system. That takes our managers around the world and through all areas of the business. That's how we provide variety, which keeps interest up. For example, our former director of personnel in Germany was previously marketing manager in Japan and is now director of finance.

Is he competent?

He's learned those things. We love these career paths that don't follow a straight line. The advantage is that these people know the business. And they see to it that don't bring in any worn-out structures and ways of thinking.

Will your next generation want to go out in the world at all?

Yes, certainly, because here no one advances who does not have multicultural experience. And we tell the young people that quite openly.

And if he still doesn't want to travel?

He knows the consequences: he won't have a career here with us.

With flat hierarchies careers aren't spectacular. How do you encourage achievement in your people?

With interesting jobs. We offer targeted lateral moves—leaving one area in order to grow from new challenges. For example, our director of physical plant is moving into personnel right now.

But most people don't work for fun. They work for money, status, prestige.

And there's money here, too. All positions are evaluated according to the duties. The salary is based on that. And I know that there are a lot of people who are crazy about titles. But we're absolutely firm on that point: with us there are no titles.

But you have money. How does it work with money?

We're generous. We have a share system according to which the employees participate in the success of their departments. We do expect them to think in entrepreneurial ways.

That seems to be the trend for the 1990s. But it's not plausible. Those who think entrepreneurially will become entrepreneurs themselves and won't settle for being an employee.

But here with us there are totally different possibilities. If you start a small business today, you're to be pitied.

How so?

You have to do everything yourself, whatever comes down the pike. Here you're part of a network, and there are specialists for all problems. Our entrepreneurs have totally different market chances from the single combatant. And that simply makes it fun.

How do you find your young entrepreneurs? Does your personnel office have a goldfish pond, so to speak, in which the greatest talents of the business are virtually collected and evaluated?

We don't have such a thing. Of course there is evaluation of the next managerial generation's potential. But above all they have to prove themselves in the field. We don't think much of staff divisions, certainly not for the next generation. They simply have assignments, and we see how they hold their own. We don't need any assessment center, we don't have a lot of extra training. The business determines the course of action. We only want people in leadership who really know the business.

And how do you keep your top managers enthusiastic?

Exactly that: through their jobs. It no longer suffices to develop a core proficiency. We have to be excellent in all areas. So we're always trying to determine where we can learn something. We study the logistics, distribution, and production of successful firms in totally different industries.

But those are assignments in old-fashioned staff divisions.

And because of that we act immediately. At the beginning of 1993 we reorganized the distribution. Instead of regional responsibilities we've organized it by groups of customers and branches. So just in Germany 70,000 customers got a new company representative—an enormous undertaking.

Was it worthwhile?

Yes, but naturally not alone. We constantly keep moving. At the same time we dissolved the central R&D department and production management and coordinated the business areas. Then there was the reengineering process and the "Time Factor" program. Now we've set down out our strategy for the next ten years and formulated new goals.

That sounds a bit breathless.

On the contrary. That's exactly the trick—you have to keep the business in motion.

12

Pioneering Spirit versus Regulation Mania

Ron Sommer

The future can best be predicted by inventing it." This slogan can be found at Xerox's Palo Alto Research Center, the almost legendary powerhouse of ideas in California. A kind of categorical imperative for the creative: If you do not want to be taken by surprise by what you do not know, then create it the way you would best like it yourself!

Creativity has been the crucial "production factor" throughout the history of business. It first of all takes a good idea, turns it into a monumental idea, and launches a gradual process of development culminating in a great leap forward. Creativity has taken on great importance and is always mentioned in any advertisement recruiting managerial staff, along with equally heavily criticized dynamism.

If one asks an advertising manager how he arrives at his brilliant creations of copy and pictures, he gives the rather corny reply: "99 percent transpiration and one percent inspiration." Or put another way: there is no creative flash of inspiration; developing products is laborious and methodical work.

And yet, is human creativity the only door through which new ideas come into the world? How does a society living with and feeding off new ideas keep this door permanently open? How does it create a climate and environment in which the capacity to think creatively is constantly encouraged?

Even psychologists have difficulty describing this nucleus. In research into creativity they remain rather vague and, at times, ambiguous. They describe the creative brain as being independent and open-minded, intellectually flexible and unconventional in thought, with a high capacity for tolerating frustration. Intelligence is necessary to allow creativity to flourish, but certainly not every intelligent person is also creative, for even the very gifted fail to cope when faced with new sets of problems.

"I can tell straightaway whether the company I am walking through is innovative or not," says the economist Prof. Dietger Hahn (Giessen). When asked what signals he would look for, he spontaneously replies: "The staff are good-humored and often laugh, and they move quickly rather than slowly and ponderously." So the most relaxed atmosphere possible at work is a peripheral, perhaps even important, secondary factor for creative thought. The talents of a creative person begin with inner questioning, with the stimulant of a supposedly insoluble problem. He works on it and tosses it around, examines it from an intellectual perspective, dissects it, distances himself from it again so that he can approach it from a new, different angle, circles it, questions it: the intensity of the problem is rooted in its questionableness.

Circling and circumscribing the problem in this way results in a string of ideas and associations which are intended to merge seamlessly into a single strand. Psychologists, for example, study creativity by posing such simple questions as what can one do with a tin can? Or from our own field: which language and images can one transmit by telephone? Or, what annoys people using the telephone most of all? Or conversely, what do they like most about the telephone? Do they find holding the receiver tiresome? In which position do they enjoy phoning, in which position do they not? Would they like to see whom they are talking to? How does conversational and communicational behavior change when the call number is displayed? What will neuronal calls be like, and so on.

However, fluidity of ideas must be combined with high levels of motivation and the willingness to work hard to find a solution for the idea to reach a critical stage and be ignited. In so doing, it is important to accept uncertain and questionable intermediate steps, risk reaching impasses and taking the wrong road—including the respective investment.

This tolerance of ambiguity goes hand in hand with flexibility and originality which are in turn closely linked to the somewhat vague term "imagination." For example, the well-known Rorschach test classifies a solution as being original if it appears just once in a hundred test solutions. Innovations in today's products or services certainly demand higher quotients.

The triad of identification, analysis and hypothesizing is then followed—hopefully—by the magic word "Eureka" which marks the final stage of incubation and illumination. Creativity has a sisterly bond with curiosity which gives the initial impetus. It acts as the starter, whereas creativity acts as the engine in producing an original solution to a problem. So being curious alone does not help because then the starter turns without the engine starting. The outcome is that the problem is not solved.

The decisive motivating force behind present-day global competition is the speed with which ideas are converted into products. Inventing the product is followed by sizing up the market. This talent to spot and gauge the marketability of a new solution to a problem is the icing on creativity's cake. It represents an unexpected barrier for many original thinkers.

Unlike his competitors, Alexander Graham Bell, who is credited with inventing the telephone (even though he did not), was blessed with a brilliant ability to gauge the market and its possibilities. Biographies put forward an original explanation for this. Bell taught the deaf and dumb—his wife was also a deaf mute—and was keenly aware of the value of human speech. His constant struggle in a room devoid of speech had perhaps rendered him particularly susceptible to the idea of transmitting speech to a remote location via a wire. Maybe Bell's circumstances gave him the gift of what today's computer researchers called "expanding the senses."

Perhaps experts will disagree with me on this but I believe that there is a human characteristic without which innovation does not survive in the long run: laziness or—expressed somewhat more nobly—the tendency to rationalize. Because people were too lazy to press tomatoes, they invented ketchup. Because they were too lazy to walk, they invented bicycles and the car. And because speaking is easier than writing, they invented the telephone.

There is no shortage of original questions. Why does a car not run on water (in which, after all, the energy of hydrogen lies latent)? How can one arrange it so that bacteria not only produce and accompany waste but also consume it? Why does one not grow square trees so as to reduce offcuts (as is currently being attempted)? Where do the cancer and AIDS genes lie in the DNA chain? Is it worth crossing a tomato with a potato to create the tompotato?

In the media-oriented future, too, there will be no shortage of questions of varying originality, many of which will be widely available. To mention but one field, in Houston, Texas, it is already possible in the field of telemedicine to watch on screen prominent heart surgeons at work. And microinvasive procedures during which the gall bladder is removed via an opening the size of a penny in the abdominal wall are simply not possible without the aid of state-of-the-art data transmission.

Creativity and innovation require a microclimate which is fertile and encourages the flow of ideas. This applies to any group in a factory, the business as a whole and, first and foremost, the society in whose environment the products and services of the future are supposed to be created. It is in this area that the main deficiencies can be seen, for there is no shortage of creative people in Germany either—despite the serious or supposed difficulties arising from its location.

Establishing this social microclimate in which marketable ideas break new ground and take root is probably the main problem faced by the highly regulated industrialized nations. In Germany people's lives are regulated by 4,874 laws, 85,000 individual provisions, thousands of decrees and court judgments, and also a good 50,000 standards. Experts estimate the cost to companies of this vast body of legislation at around 60 billion Deutschmarks a year.

However, the self-strangulation of the economy and the society which is robbing it of the means to innovate is a much greater obstacle than these costs. Creativity is surrounded by provisions, regulations and prohibitions. The bureaucracy which is wont to regulate cucumbers' radius of curvature and the pitch of living-room staircases, which causes large-scale investments to be blocked because the site is presumed to contain a path for toads, is the real enemy of future market opportunities.

Wags would claim that the legendary Bill Gates, who began by tinkering in a garage, would never have had a chance in Germany. Using a garage as a permanent base to do business is strictly forbidden by numerous laws and ordinances. To give creativity and innovation a free rein, management must work to ensure an open environment encouraging discussion. But a company is not a planet orbiting society by itself—it is a part of that society. Using carefully devised psychological methods it is often possible to create an innovative atmosphere within a company. On the other hand, making a society more forward-looking is a much more complicated process.

This is where Germany runs into problems. While its political classes—led by the Federal President and the Federal Chancellor—constantly issue reminders of a "new culture of independence," people's inner state is not conducive to risk-taking. The German blueprint for life involves a fulfilling and, where possible, life-long position in a trade. Soap-box oratory denounces mobility and flexibility, and hard graft and playing it safe are the order of the day at work.

Of course, societies which are rigid and have grown tired of reform have been presented with two strict taskmasters: technical change (symbolized by the computer) and globalization. Both create the pressure of competition and teach society with its plural interests about mobility. Germany is currently undergoing this reform process, compelled from within and supported from without. It revolves around the key phrases tax reform and reviewing all social security systems, and also the efforts to create a "lean state."

These rationalization processes are progressing at an extremely laborious pace because each stage of the reform is tied in with giving up the usual living standards. As surveys show, the majority of the population is poorly informed regarding the direction and aim of these reform processes. Pollsters even talk of disorientation.

If society and the economy are sucked into the undertow of structural change, people have difficulty grasping the logic behind this movement and keeping up with the pace required. It is part of human nature to see the difficult path ahead. Only a few will set their sights on the horizon. It is the job of the élite to lend their support to achieving this.

This is not about the distorted image of a computer-controlled and inhuman "brave new world" but rather the visions of a society worth living in, in which new ideas are devised and realized, not to work against people but rather to work for them. At this point the grafter asks "Why?" but the creative person asks "Why not?"

People must be informed about the vast range of opportunities afforded by the communications-based society of tomorrow—which has already begun—not just as users but primarily as free individuals. Many are dominated by uncertainty and fear. But any experience gained during times of change has shown that fear dissipates the more familiar one becomes with the innovation.

The same applies to teleworking and telemedicine, intelligent traffic-routing systems and networked data systems. Germany currently has only about 30,000 teleworkers. For the year 2000 the EU envisages a potential figure of 800,000 teleworkers in Germany who could work at home without ever encountering the rush hour. Just recently Deutsche Telekom launched an initiative in conjunction with the Federal Ministry of Education, Science, Research and Technology, focusing on teleworking within the medium-sized business sector. "Let the data flow rather than the people."

Combined with a little enthusiasm for adventure, the pioneering spirit has not yet reached its limit. Here I am not (just) talking about the smart running shoe or the infallible toaster but about virtual worlds which help us to understand the real world. The cosmos of neuronal networks and the possibilities of artificial intelligence are still waiting to be discovered.

Anyone finding all this too complicated because his environment seems to be ruled by a maze of uncontrollable parameters can fall back on new forms of simplification. Fuzzy logic is a pointer in this direction. It dispenses with (perfectly possible) precision and consciously keeps things fuzzy. That way, they become easier to use because what matters mainly to users is not precision right across the board but rather simple situations; the user-friendly recorder, the economical washing machine, the smooth elevator or the sharp video image.

Consciously indistinct fuzzy logic uses fuzzy modules to stay more faithful to reality. This approach disproves the thesis that technical systems are constantly becoming more complicated. They should not constantly get on our nerves, but they prove that any progress made can also be accompanied by a new form of simplification.

The communications-related opportunities offered by the new electronic media do not lead to the distorted image of "Big Brother." Rather they give life to those democratic values which threaten to be stifled in bureaucracies: equality, freedom of information and freedom of choice, equal opportunities. In this respect the chip is the best lobbyist for freedom. It is the natural opponent of tutelage and authoritarianism.

Putting these thoughts into practice in corporate cultures is a difficult undertaking. Proof that it is slowly taking effect is provided by the fact that technophobia is no longer a source of complaint but that all schools are required to be connected up to the network. People have long appreciated the fact that they stand to benefit from the transfer of vast quantities of data and that it makes their lives easier. The fact that switching to computers is extending processing times for official procedures is part and parcel of the transition process and, in the main, it is only the public services which have been affected.

New ideas come into the world if their inventors are granted freedom of thought and anything liable to inhibit their creativity is removed. In this respect, the economy is much broader than society. But, in the final analysis, the longest journey for both begins with the first step.

13

More Disorder in the Enterprise
Berthold Leibinger

More often than not, creative innovation in business processes occurs in response to external pressures, such as economic downswings. This essay provides a case study of one business's solutions. The successful reordering of the business gave it a competitive edge during recession and made for a more efficient and more creative workforce during prosperous times as well.

In 1991 the machine tool industry employed 100,000 workers in Germany. The sales in that year were 17 billion DM, of which 55 percent was from exports. The biggest competitors were—and are—the Japanese and the Americans. From mid-1990 until the end of 1994, income from orders sank continually; on the average, there was a decline of 50 percent. Almost 40 percent of the employees lost their jobs, mostly skilled specialists and technicians. Numerous companies had to declare bankruptcy; many merged out of necessity.

At TRUMPF GmbH & Co., a major company in the manufacturing of machine tools, income and sales sank. They fell less than the industry average, but the drop was pronounced enough that two years in the red couldn't be avoided. A radical change of course was necessary—and was accomplished. Already in 1995 the highest sales before the crisis had been topped. In the meantime, sales increased on average 16 percent a year. The company is profitable.

Almost all German companies report that in the global marketplace they're about 20 to 30 percent more expensive than their competition. Only occasionally more, but almost never less.

When one tries to explain this increased cost with benchmarking against the best competitors in the world market, we frequently find that one-third of the increased cost can be attributed to the product, one-third to the organization of the business, and one-third to institutional requirements.

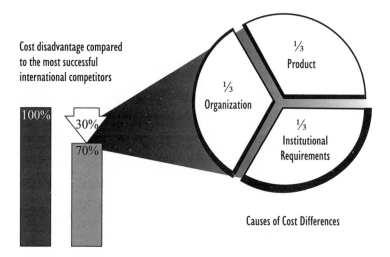

Figure 1. Innovation is relevant for all a company's activities. Source: VDW

Let us begin with the product. We often hear that German machinery is overloaded with technology and offers more than the customer needs or is willing to pay for. This was also the case at the beginning of the 1990 for TRUMPF's products, or at least for a significant portion of them. It was the result of a decades-long endeavor to react almost reflexively to every competitor's challenge in the world market by adding more technology. The lofty goal of the German R&D engineers was: faster, more precise, and more multifaceted.

The challenge to make a machine cheaper but with the same quality seemed like a cultural revolution. This was, above all, because in Germany the art of simplification is not considered to be creative. But it is possible and often truly necessary.

For a vigorous change of course a number of measures are necessary. The most important are:

- For a new product the business must produce target specifications along with product development in accordance with market demands.
- The desirable market price one determines for this product should not be exceeded.
- The actual development must be ushered through by a company-wide project group that participates in production, purchasing, operations, and control. Several attempts are necessary if the desired cost is not reached after the first run-through.
- The R&D effort must primarily focus on the most important sources of income—the core products.

As a result we can determine that not only the required cost reduction is possible but also that staff time is reduced through product simplification.

The structure of our companies in many ways resembles the monarchical past of our country. The pyramid begins on the top with the tried-and-true figure of the president or CEO. Goals, directions, and decisions are passed down from the top through clearly defined divisions. This takes up a lot of time, and mistakes in transmission are significant. The pyramid is also clearly divided vertically in terms of the various areas of responsibility.

In today's competitive world, success is a matter of being quick. A company must be flexible in response to changes in the market, the entity that determines everything. So a first step is to divide up the big pyramid into several smaller ones, each of which in turn contains all the essential functions of company. These small divisions correspond to the various departments or areas of the company.

The next step is to divide these pyramids into divisions that communicate with each other but are themselves responsible. The head of the business gives the divisions only the general goals and set procedures.

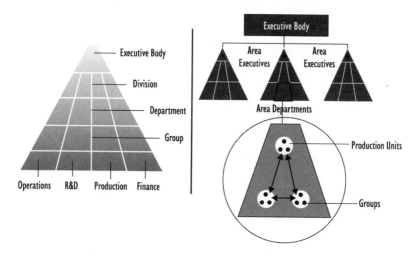

Figure 2. The ability to react after the structural reorganization of a company, depicted on the right.

We call these autonomous divisions production units; each is responsible for a product or important group of components. They consist of 50 to 100 individuals. All essential machinery that is needed for the particular product is part of the production unit. The disposition of materials and the responsibility for deadlines and quality are the purview of the production unit. The central storage of parts is not necessary, because processes have been shortened and parts move directly from the machinery into assembly. Communication is simplified. Mistakes are discovered on the spot and dealt with. Within the production units self-organized groups are responsible for the work as much as possible.

Through this reorganization, productivity—that is, sales per employee in production—sharply increased by more than 20 percent. Production time and expenditures were both reduced by around 50 percent. As important as the simplification of the structure is the increased motivation of the employees resulting from the responsibility granted them. They work not only more intensely and reliably, but also with pleasure. Stated in another way, because working is fun, productivity is greater.

There is usually the least room for change in the area of collective wage agreements. At least that's the case with companies that belong to an employer's association. However, changes in that area are most crucial, because the contractual arrangement is totally divorced from reality. We especially need creative solutions here.

Frank exchange with numbers and facts is important in conversations with company heads and unions; it is the first prerequisite to credibility. In our experience, it is easier on the operational level to convince others that both sides have many common interests.

One of the most important requirements is to adapt the amount produced to demand. In machine manufacturing there have been distinct cycles in the last decades. The deviations in demand appear consistently. In the past, the dips in demand were made up for during the periods of high demand. And in the peak periods workers were on overtime.

Recently, however, such periods of high demand have been no longer attainable in many areas of machine manufacturing. The global market has become so transparent that demand can always be quickly satisfied from somewhere. The difference in quality between products from Europe, Japan, or the United States is no longer so great that customers rely on one vendor. Therefore it is necessary to find new ways to adapt to business cycles. As figure 3 shows, a cycle encompasses several years. The length of time needed to balance out overtime and work reduction must run more than a year, as opposed to the unions' concept.

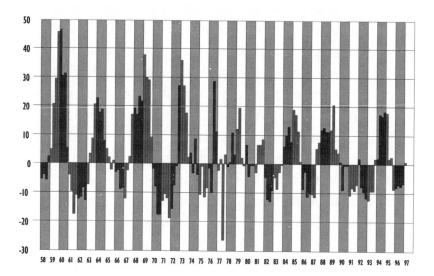

Figure 3. Receipt of orders in machine manufacturing;
real deviations in percent by quarter. Source: VDMA

Working with the 35-hour week, we agreed to 200 hours of overtime (and the same amount of reduced worktime) to correspond to the ups and downs of demand. The worktime that deviates from the 35-hour week—it can vary from 30 to 40 hours—is tallied up in a debit/credit time account for each worker. Of course, the account is evened out if a worker leaves.

Further, we agreed on increased time spent at the company for all employees. This refers especially to continuing education and training, which is not counted in the 35-hour workweek. The company head and the workers' committees also negotiated a reduction in sick time, which was necessary to adjust it to global norms.

The concessions the employees made are dependent on the promises management made. We are thus obliged:

- to build a new laser factory in Germany, although it would have been more advantageous for us to build it in France or Switzerland;
- until the year 2000 not to make any terminations for business reasons;
- within the same time period not only to hire all trainees but also to create 50 to 100 additional jobs.

Of course one can see in these promises—which we consider rather broad—that element of disorder that we're considering in this essay. But we've been talking about imagination, and here we're only dealing with practical, unspectacular steps to get out of a slump. Creative, unexpected solutions—perhaps revolutionary ones—were surely expected, but pedestrian ones offered. Where's the disorder in that?

There's no doubt: we need new ideas, impulses, changes, the much-vaunted creative destruction of established patterns. But at the same time we need to respect the existing order and obligations. In a complex world with thousands of dependencies and in a sea of information, perhaps revolutions just aren't possible any more. It's less a question of sudden changes than of changes in direction.

Imagination has to be directed toward the feasible. Visions are fine for those who have time on their hands. Everyone's asking for free time nowadays, but creativity and order aren't contradictory notions. We see this in the example of art, where one might expect that complete independence and self-determination are required.

Johann Sebastian Bach contracted with the city of Leipzig to put on a cantata every Sunday. It didn't have to be one of his own, but this pressure occasioned Bach to compose 300 cantatas during his time in Leipzig, and 200 of those cantatas survive. And what glorious cantatas! Friedrich Schiller, in his efforts to finance a theater in Weimar, made an agreement that obliged him to write a tragedy a year and hand over the receipts to pay off the debt. He kept his promise.

Free time is crucial in an enterprise. One has to be able to converse about the ways and means. But the direction and goal have to be spelled out. It's an element of the art of management to encourage, even demand, creativity, but to restrict it to clear goals. For this, taking delight in action and enthusiasm are as necessary as disciplined thought.

At the outset we postulated that it was necessary to combine ideas with the will to carry them out. To accomplish this, perhaps our industries don't need *dis*order, but rather *re*ordering.

14

Developing and Marketing an Innovative Idea
Chasing the Goal of Commercial Success

Heinrich v. Pierer

Well over a hundred years ago, Werner von Siemens said that "making your fortune with inventions is a very laborious business at which only a few have succeeded and which has been the ruin of many talented people!"[1] He knew what he was talking about. For by the time he made that remark he already had a whole series of very different inventions to his credit, from guncotton to a gold electroplating process. He had also largely perfected Wheatstone's pointer telegraph, developed a new method of insulating electric cables using gutta percha, designed water meters, and electric fire-alarm systems and much more.

Today, when anyone speaks of inventions or innovations, the topic still seems to be shrouded in mystery. One thinks of the great inventors of the Renaissance and the Industrial Revolution, such as Leonardo da Vinci or James Watt. To this day inventions and innovations are considered to be the work of geniuses, tinkerers or eccentrics. If we take the more recent past, the focus of attention seems to be on garage-based upstarts or self-made men.

But there is more to innovation than that. It is an all-encompassing concept that includes spectacular successes, but also everyday routine in labs and development centers, includes brilliant flashes of inspiration, but also arduous work on small but significant details, major scientific or technological discoveries, but also the refinement of processes and methods, starting with the research process itself and ending with financing and marketing.

How do such innovations come about, how can we promote them, and, above all, how can we get them accepted? If society, the state and the economy are to meet the challenge of the future, peoples' attitudes to change will be crucial. An unwillingness to accept it will of course impede it. But if change is understood as an opportunity to take new bearings, and if new behaviors, methods and strategies are developed and adapted to altered circumstances, the climate for change will be substantially more favorable. In other words, what we have to do is use innovations to get ahead. That is why it is important to consider the many different aspects of the complex process that gives rise to the new.

The Context in Which Innovations Take Place

"Not facts, but opinions about facts determine communal life," observed the Greek philosopher Epictetus in the first century after Christ. As far as innovations are concerned, this means the basic attitude of a society to innovations and individual initiative is not a negligible factor.

The *Gründerjahre* in Germany, from 1870 to 1873, the German economic miracle following World War II, and, more recently, America's success in creating so many new jobs, were and are all based on objective circumstances such as new technologies, improved business conditions, economic booms, etc. But subjective circumstances, too, such as states of mind and future expectations, play an important role as well.

If innovations are to arise and gain acceptance on a broad scale, there has to be an underlying attitude in society characterized by an entrepreneurial spirit, curiosity, and the determination to do something for oneself and thus improve one's own lot. What can be achieved in such a climate is proved by the unprecedented rise of Asian countries. The enormous dynamism of these societies is not just based on the creation by the government of conditions favorable to business, but above all on the fact that the people there are highly motivated, ambitious and determined to achieve better conditions for themselves and their descendants. "He who does not think about the future today will spend tomorrow ruing the present," says a Chinese proverb that is typical of the forward-looking attitudes, enthusiasm and desire to build that prevail in that part of the world.

But there is no need to look as far as Asia. In the USA, too, an atmosphere prevails that is quite different from that in Europe. It is no accident that when one hears of miraculous rags-to-riches careers one instinctively thinks of America, not of Germany. Only eight percent of German students want to start their own business, while over fifty percent want to join the civil service. By contrast, in the USA it goes without saying that the best students want to join dynamic high-tech companies or go into business for themselves. Readiness to take risks and entrepreneurial initiative enjoy little social recognition in Germany, where successful young businessmen are often viewed with condescension, or are envied for the fruits of their success. Founders of companies that have gone bankrupt, on the other hand, are privately and publicly stigmatized as failures and frequently boycotted by capital investors. Things are quite different in the USA. Founders of companies are held in the highest esteem. Innovators and successful businessmen are the pride of their country and of their fellow citizens. And when one of them who has risked a lot takes a fall, he still counts as a "great guy" who unquestionably deserves a second chance. It is a completely different entrepreneurial culture.

But there is something else, too, that determines the climate surrounding innovations: the general attitude to technology. In 1825, when the railway line from Liverpool to Manchester was about to be built, it was feared that the noise of the locomotive would keep cows from grazing and hens from laying eggs, that the "poisonous smoke" would cause birds to drop out of the sky, and flying sparks would set fire to houses beside the track, causing them to burn to the ground. It was complained that horses would become superfluous and that producers of oats and hay would lose their livelihood as a result. Above all, many were convinced that the steam engines would explode and tear the passengers to shreds. None of these things happened. Instead, the railway brought an enormous gain in mobility and affluence.

Technology itself is only an instrument and thus has no moral bias. It would certainly be wrong to have blind faith in technology. At the end of this century, which has witnessed so much suffering and horror, including perfectly engineered genocide and tragic catastrophes, to do so would be naïve and irresponsible. But those who only stress the risks and potential abuses stand in the way of solutions to such pressing global problems as feeding and supporting the world's ever-growing population or preserving our natural environment. Such solutions are needed urgently. But they can only succeed if technology and research are welcome and enjoy public support. Although surveys show that attitudes to technology in Germany have improved recently, a third of the population still persists in the view that new technologies entail more risks than opportunities.

Naturally these are only general statements. Technologies we use in the home or in everyday life—things like cars, refrigerators and telephones, which offer us immediate tangible benefits—meet with widespread acceptance, where-as other technologies often face considerable skepticism. Examples include large-scale installations such as refineries or power plants, activities seemingly unrelated to everyday life, such as basic physics research or neutron-based research in the field of solid-state and materials science, and cases in which it is felt that there is a more obvious alternative, such as the concrete choice between genetically engineered foodstuffs and those cultivated using biodynamic methods.

Why use nuclear power, when wind, water and sunlight are "more natural" sources of energy? Why use genetically altered tomatoes, when naturally cultivated tomatoes grow in your own garden? Arguments like this are often heard from people who are especially sensitive to issues of global relevance, such as environmental protection. But when faced with the question of using new technologies, they choose to ignore the global aspects. They often overlook the fact that the world's energy requirements cannot be met without the use of nuclear power, that only a green revolution will make it possible to feed the world's growing population, and that modern medicines and hardy, abundant crops can only be obtained in sufficient quantities with the aid of genetic engineering. Instead, they paint an idyllic but unrealistic picture.

What is needed is a broad horizon and the courage to change or, as Robert Musil once put it, an attitude which doubts that the current state of the world is sacrosanct, "not out of skepticism, but in the sense of the climber who knows that the firmly planted foot is always the lower of the two."

Knowledge and Observation as Starting Points for Innovation

"Inventions are seldom successful if they are not based on sound technical knowledge and if they are not intended to fill an existing and acutely felt gap. Ninety-nine inventions out of a hundred are based on inadequate understanding, and the supposed gift of inventiveness is based on conceit."[2]

The basis of every innovation—whether in technology or in marketing—is knowledge. Only someone who understands the intricacies and causes of a process or the workings of a product can improve it. Only someone with an eye for what is lacking—whether in a product range, production process, or a product's functionality—is able to think of ways of closing the gap. Knowledge is the raw material of innovation.

A far-reaching structural transition towards a knowledge society is under way. Today, according to OECD estimates, one in every three or four gainfully employed persons works with new, knowledge-intensive technologies. Traditional manufacturing jobs are increasingly being replaced by new occupations in software, engineering, service, and consulting. This trend is also perceptible at Siemens. Over 50 percent of our value added now stems from knowledge-intensive services. But that is only the average for all our operating groups taken together. In areas in which product cycles are particularly short, such as in information technology or telecommunications, the share of knowledge-intensive value added is considerably higher.

Knowledge-intensive products and services promise growth. Since the mid-1980s, for example, sales of computer software have risen by 12 percent annually, a rate of growth far in excess of that of hardware. The ratio of hardware to software on the world information-technology market was 51 to 49 percent in 1989; in 1997, it was 41 to 59 percent.

Today, a new chemical formula is discovered every minute, a new physical relation every three minutes, and a new medical finding every five minutes. More information is printed every day than in the entire period between the invention of printing and World War I.

When Werner von Siemens founded his first company 150 years ago, the largest technical libraries possessed fewer than 100,000 volumes. Today, the world's largest library, the Library of Congress in

Washington, D.C., has four million volumes of scientific and technological works.

As our knowledge expands, two key factors come to the fore: first, our capacity to find our way through this mass of material, to identify and define problems, and to absorb knowledge in a focused manner; second, the technical means needed to obtain access to all this knowledge quickly, precisely and in a manageable form. Today's employees are responsible for managing knowledge themselves. They have to both acquire and apply knowledge in parallel throughout their working lives. So we have to move away from the established sequence of *first* taking a degree to acquire knowledge, *then* finding a career in which to apply it. Instead, we need to establish a culture of lifelong learning.

Given these altered circumstances, the requirements that training has to meet have also changed. There can no longer be any question of completely absorbing all the knowledge in a given area of specialization. Rather, the focus must be on acquiring a basic store of knowledge that facilitates the assimilation of the relevant parts of a specialized field at a later stage. Of course, David Ricardo's foreign trade theory, thermodynamics, and constitutional law must continue to be taught to those studying for degrees in economics, physics, and law respectively. But the degree courses and training syllabuses must be systematically stripped of ballast and geared more to real life. Other skills are also important, such as the ability to keep one's bearings, to assess criteria, to manage time, and to work and communicate effectively as a member of a team entrusted with complex projects.

In addition to personal skills, technical and organizational factors play an important role in the acquisition of knowledge. According to recent estimates, the Internet, that loose combination of 120,000 computer networks, has nearly 100,000,000 users, and the number continues to increase by leaps and bounds.

Soon the degree of networking will be just as much a measure of a country's development as literacy or the number of telephones. And at present there are marked differences even between industrialized countries. Last year 23 out of every 1,000 inhabitants in the USA had access to the Internet, while in Germany the figure was just six. And with regard to investment in information technology, the industrialized countries of Europe are clearly lagging. In the USA in 1995, $724 was invested per inhabitant on information technology, whereas the European per capita average was just $350.

The Europeans will have to see to it that they do not fall further behind. The new forms of communication and exchange in a knowledge society also give rise to new market opportunities and openings for innovation. The ability to organize knowledge, to provide high-speed access to large quantities of it, and to select and prepare it, is becoming increasingly important, both in-house and as a service offered to third parties. Of course, knowledge management is also of strategic significance. Only those who master it successfully will be able to stay on the ball as far as technology and business ventures are concerned.

People with Ideas and Stamina

"Not many individuals are cut out to be inventors, for few have the necessary courage of their convictions or the requisite stamina."[3]

This assessment by Werner von Siemens is still valid today. A study by the Schloss Garath academy came to similar conclusions. Having the courage of one's convictions, stamina and single-mindedness of purpose are among the most important characteristics of successful inventors. The influence of what is old and established is persistent, so a considerable expenditure of energy is needed to think up something new, get a new idea off the ground, and make it work.

In 1866 Werner von Siemens discovered the electrodynamic

principle. In retrospect, this was the breakthrough that gave rise to electrical engineering. But initially it was just the beginning of a long series of experiments resulting in improvements to details and further developments. Although two years later Siemens was able to demonstrate the use of dynamos to generate electricity to operate arc lamps, fifteen years would pass before the first regular power plant would go into operation. In 1881, in the little town of Godalming in southern England, Siemens Brothers built the world's first public power station. It was followed in 1884 by the first German "block plant," on Berlin's Friedrichstrasse.

Long intervals between an idea and its appearance on the market as a product are not unusual. Chester F. Carlson needed six years just to find a company that was interested in the copying process he had invented. It then took another twelve years of intensive development work and high entrepreneurial risks to turn the idea into a marketable product—the first dry photocopying machine, the Xerox 914. A team of developers at Motorola invested fifteen years of research and development work before the idea of wireless telephony gave birth to the first marketable mobile phone in 1983. And Dave Duke and other specialists at the U.S. company Corning Glass Works took over a decade to improve and develop fiber optic cables before they finally achieved market success in the mid-1980s in cooperation with Siemens.

Besides patience and stamina, however, success also requires versatility, an ability to take criticism, a readiness to make course adjustments, and critical detachment from one's own ideas. It also helps to be able to work on a team in which individual members with a wide range of different interests, broad experience, and different ways of thinking and working interact harmoniously. It has been proven that a motley mix of characters in teams makes for successful innovation. At any rate, our experience confirms that teams with members from different backgrounds generally achieve the best results.

While awarding our annual Siemens prizes for inventors I had the opportunity to get to know some of our innovators personally and was struck by their wide range of interests. There are not only enthusiastic skiers and mountain climbers among them, but also keen theater- and concert-goers and dedicated musicians. In addition to these hobbies they generally have a wide range of other interests covering cultural, historical and philosophical topics that extend far beyond the limits of their area of specialization. If asked when their new ideas come to them, most innovators reply that it is generally not in the office or the lab, but in their leisure hours when they are pursuing their hobbies.

Although essential to the process, creativity, spontaneity, and intuition make it hard to plan innovations. For it is individuals—complex personalities—who spot the gaps, develop solutions and thus bring about the birth of the new. And to do this they need personal freedom and trust. It has to be assumed that employees will perform their work in a motivated manner, that they will use resources responsibly, and that they recognize and respect corporate objectives. This is the only way to create an atmosphere in which creativity and initiative can flourish.

But allowing scope for creativity does not mean abandoning all organizational constraints. Systematic analysis of problems and precise detection of weaknesses in technical equipment, in processes, or in organizational or social procedures remain fundamentally important. The key questions leading to the discovery of potential innovations are still: What is wrong? What is missing? Where are the gaps?

These are then followed by the actual search for a solution. The process of inching toward success naturally involves errors and setbacks as well. It must not be taboo to mention them. Instead we must put them down to experience and do all we can to learn as quickly and as thoroughly from them as possible. Frederick W. Smith, founder of the U.S. transportation company Federal Express, which constituted a remarkable market innovation, puts it this way: "Failure is an essential part of the process of renewal. You must be ready to talk about your failures, otherwise you will never score a major success."

The more systematically errors are registered and dealt with, the sooner the blind process of trial and error can be overcome. For this reason companies need a robust and resilient attitude toward error.

Sound theoretical knowledge, a broad base of experience, a systematic approach to work and a sound, healthy attitude toward errors are essential requisites if innovations are to flourish. The most important aspect, however, is to ensure that the process of innovation is directly related to market and customer needs. Only then can a climate arise in which creativity, cost-effectiveness and responsiveness to customers and markets come together.

Corporate Strategies and the Market

"It is absolutely fatal for an invention to be launched onto the market too early and too hastily. There will inevitably be some kind of setback that also destroys the healthy nucleus, which needs time and tranquillity to grow."[4]

Today, the problem Werner von Siemens describes here is more topical than ever in view of constantly shortening product cycles and the increasing rate of innovation. Just about all high-tech companies all over the world are working to reduce their time to market. Little time remains for maturing, and for "tranquillity" a good deal less. On the other hand, launching innovations onto the market prematurely carries the risk of disappointing customers with underdeveloped products, thus damaging the company's reputation and destroying the basis of long-term success. Nor must we underestimate the opposite danger of launching a technically perfected product onto a market that is not prepared for it. This danger is primarily associated with revolutionary innovations, for which customer interest and market behavior are hard to predict. Disappointments of this kind are one of the hazards of the innovation process, and as much should be done as possible to reduce the risk by means of careful market studies. Even so, they can never be entirely excluded. The sluggish acceptance of the video recorder and the compact disc, for example, shows what can happen when a market is not yet ready for an innovative product. In both cases the breakthrough to large sales volumes did not occur until years after their initial presentation.

At the same time, there are many examples of innovations that were launched onto the market at just the right time. This was the case with numerous Siemens products, including the pointer telegraph, the dynamo, the telephone and switching equipment, the first electric dentist's drills and X-ray machines, the electron microscope, the technique of drawing monocrystalline ultrapure silicon, neural networks, flexible, modular automation systems, state-of-the-art, super-efficient power-plant and environmental protection technology, and, finally, small but important components such as surface acoustic wave filters, chip cards and the logic chips used in telecommunications equipment.

In the final analysis the vital question for a company is, how can we guarantee that innovative products geared to customers' needs are launched onto the market at the right moment? There is no patent solution for this. According to the writer and essayist Arthur Koestler, "All great inventions, all great works, are the result of a liberation, the liberation from the routine of thinking and doing." The integration of these spontaneous and creative processes with an up-to-date corporate organization based on division of labor, and, above all, a feel for the needs of customers and the market, is the other precondition for successful innovations. For it is ultimately customers who pay for the innovative product, and it has to be of use to them. Innovation policy must steer a course between these two poles.

Siemens's innovation initiative operates simultaneously on different levels: With mobilization and communication measures, idea and innovation competitions and an increased tendency to assign responsibility for projects to the originators of the ideas, we not only encourage better use of new ideas, but also show that creativity, imagination and commitment are also recognized in practice and pay off. We promote and perpetuate the learning process in the company by educating employees in best practices and by heightening awareness of processes and customers. To this end we draw upon the experience of the company's—and the world's —best.

We encourage better use of the world's knowledge base by optimizing all methods of accessing it. We do this by cooperating with universities and independent institutes, by entering into global research alliances with industrial partners, by internationalizing our own research and development activities, and by perfecting our internal communication structures. Appropriate patent strategies are used to enhance the economic benefit of the ideas and solutions conceived at our company.

We constantly review our core competencies to see if new business can be developed from them. To this end we have set up "white space" projects, in which Siemens's operating groups cooperate to open up new business potential. We have taken a new initiative to further expand our software capacity, as software plays a key role in the creation of innovative products. We have strategic innovation projects in which we systematically scan customer and process requirements to identify new trends at an early stage and introduce appropriate innovations.

An effective innovative strategy must on the one hand promote *long-term* thinking, stimulate visions and create scope for the development of the kind of revolutionary innovations that will open up completely new markets. On the other hand it must register *short-* and *medium-term* trends, focus on today's customers and their requirements, and retain and expand existing market share by introducing incremental innovations.

At Siemens both approaches are reflected in an intense dialogue between the operating groups on the one hand and corporate research and development on the other. In our medium-term technology planning we compare the products planned by the operating groups with the findings and forecasts of our central R&D department concerning the evolution of core technologies. Our product planning is based on a system that extends over several generations, and on a method of defining core technologies whose future lines of development are sketched out in what are known as core-technology road maps.

The multigenerational product planning system requires operating groups to indicate what products they intend to rely on in five and in ten years' time. For example, the Automotive Systems Group aims at developing an engine-management system for an ultra-low emission engine. Such a system will reduce exhaust emissions by means of high-precision fuel injection, permanent monitoring by sensor of pressure cycles in the engine, and individual monitoring of the various cylinders. When proposed, it was to be ready for the market in five years.

The road maps are then used to determine if the company possesses the necessary core technologies to enable it to develop the envisaged product. In the case just described, for example, these would include piezoceramics, a special hydraulic system, sensors and thin-film technology. If the company has such core technologies at its disposal, development can start. If not, the question is whether to purchase the necessary technology or to enter into a cooperation agreement—or, in some cases, whether to get out in time.

We are dealing here with a two-way feedback process. On the one hand, *short* and *medium-term* product planning is balanced against the future scenarios of the core-technology road maps. This enables us to estimate the costs of going ahead with specific products. At the same time the opposite process also takes place, in that new technological developments are examined for the possibilities they offer, and a systematic search is conducted for products in which these possibilities could be exploited.

By contrast, *long-term* technology planning involves drafting detailed scenarios of society's future needs and problems that allow us to draw conclusions about which applications, business opportunities and technologies might be important. These are then compared with the extrapolations of the medium-term planners. Comparisons of the different perspectives offer pointers to key future technologies or areas of research, and help to shape current technology and innovation strategies.

These planning instruments are of assistance in the search for opportunities for innovation, but they are not enough on their own. Equally important input often comes from customers and suppliers. That is why it is important to involve both in the development process at an early stage—the customers so that account can be taken of their actual requirements during the development phase, and the suppliers so as to keep a substantial portion of costs under control from the outset. Cooperation with customers and suppliers who are technological innovators in their own fields is particularly fruitful.

But all these strategies and attempts to anticipate the future cannot alter the basic fact that innovations are never devoid of risk, especially when they concern ventures into technologically uncharted territory. Lines of research can turn out to be technological dead ends. Competitors may turn out to be faster in the race against time. The market and society may not be ready for a given innovation. In the worst case such innovations may even be nipped in the bud.

The road that inventors and companies travel, from an initial idea to commercial success, is not without risks, and it is essential that these be identified and managed as quickly as possible. Only in the rarest cases do innovations take off immediately. Strokes of genius are the exception, not the rule. "In rare cases, it can happen that a spontaneously conceived invention achieves immediate success, but this is more or less like winning the jackpot in the lottery."[5] And we know how slim the chances are. Developing innovations that pave the way ahead is hard, requiring not just creativity and knowledge, but also stamina in mastering the many individual steps involved. As Goethe put it, "knowledge alone is not enough, one must also apply it; wanting something is not enough, one also has to do it."

Notes

1.   Werner von Siemens in a letter to his brother Carl, September 30, 1855.

2.   Werner von Siemens in a letter to the state building contractor von Busse, December 16, 1890.

3.   Werner von Siemens in a letter to his wife, Matthilde, July 1857.

4.   Werner von Siemens in a letter to J. Stein, January 27, 1880.

5.   Werner von Siemens in a letter to the engineer Gilli, January 16, 1866.

the
Individual
and the
Environment

15

The Individual

Franz Emanuel Weinert

In principle it is an irresolvable dispute whether the person makes the circumstances or the circumstances make the person. Similarly open to question is the role of the individual as the creator or creation of culture, science, the economy, and technology. We are inclined to extol the individual as thinker and discerner, as agent and former; we presume that there is in him a mental strength for the creation of the new, we consider him to be the embodiment of great cultural achievements and those of civilization, but also as the cause of numerous social problems. Is this the case? Or to pose the question more precisely: To what extent is this the case?

The Genius as the Creator of the Significant New

Are geniuses nature's gift to society? This question, which is just as much a trusted thesis of materialist thought as of the idealistic or romantic intellectual framework, refers to the individual who is extraordinary and is equipped by nature with superhuman abilities as the real source of the new in the world, if one understands thereby not the many small new things which are constantly arising everywhere, but the great epochal developments in knowledge and cultural achievements.

No wonder therefore that both actual and supposed geniuses have aroused the imaginative speculation of their fellow humans since time immemorial, in so far as there was and is also at all times and in all societies a cult of genius—regardless of whether one expressly supports it, practices it hidden in seclusion, or vehemently criticizes it. A good example of this is modern research on genius which as often trivializes as heroizes its object. But what is the inspirational force in genius? Many old cultures shared the mythical belief that in the thoughts and works of seers and of artists both a divine and demonic force is manifested, a conception that still continues to have consequences into the present in the hypothesis that genius is related to madness.

It ranks among the intellectual achievements of the seventeenth century to have gone beyond the idea of genius as being magical with the idea of a genius as a person to whom outstanding intellectual or artistic potential is attributed, a potential which only very few people have. The expression "genius" was indeed furthermore applied in a very variable way in the time thereafter, but gradually three essential features of the genius became apparent. Firstly, he has innate gifts and talents which come to light early in life (as in child prodigies) and a strong inner developmental dynamic, the lack of which cannot be compensated for by averagely gifted people even by efforts at learning, however intensive. Secondly, this intellectual potential predisposes the genius to extraordinary cultural achievements, to the production of completely new ideas and works, which contradict the hitherto usual, customary and accepted ones and which are judged to be particularly significant and valuable by the world at the time and subsequently. Thirdly, the brilliant intellectual insights and artistic testaments are, as a rule, not the result of painstaking, step-by-step, hard, detailed work but rather the consequence of unconsciously effective forces which run through a characteristic sequence of stages of the creative act. The *preparatory phase* in which the conscious, painstaking work predominates and quite often remains unsuccessful; the *incubation stage* in which the task remains active below the threshold of consciousness and of its own accord leads to a convincing solution. In the *experience of illumination* the results of this unconscious creative process become subjectively evident—maybe as a sudden idea, or as the outline of a neat solution to the problem, or as a self-conscious insight or as an intuitive anticipatory act. Finally, in the *verification phase* there remains only the laborious presentation of evidence, elaboration and explanation of that which one believes with a high measure of self-certainty and self-confidence to know as an idea.

With the notorious uncertainty about what is really new, original and at the same time valuable, the difficulty of recognizing genuine talent in current actions and their results, and the widespread addiction to experiencing intuitive mental processes, it is no wonder that the world around us seems to be full of unrecognized, underestimated, chosen and self-nominated geniuses. Their number is far and away greater than the small group of geniuses who have been recognized without doubt from and in their works.

A recently published book edited by Oswald and Zegans, *Mozart—Freuden und Leiden des Genies* [Mozart—The Joys and Sorrows of a Genius] (1997), offers a good example of the facets of analyzing the work and life of a genius, and also the intellectual ups and downs of research into genius.

Creative People, Processes and Products

What distinguishes the genius from the highly gifted, the musical genius from the successful composer, the extraordinary from the ordinary mathematician? It is certainly not, or at least not in the first place, intelligence quotient as many strongly maintain, whereby an IQ over 145 counts as brilliant, over 130 as highly gifted and over 115 as very gifted. It is certainly also not (only) the public or specialist estimation of the worth of a learned person, artist, manager, or politician and his (life's) work, important as this factor is for the practical use of the concept of genius. It is also never the result of a lot of active and productive learning time, as many experts carrying out specialist research would have us believe—necessary and important as the acquisition of knowledge as regards its contents is even for geniuses, if they wish to create great works.

The question about the differences in talents between the poets, musicians, mathematicians, philosophers, natural scientists, engineers, politicians, and captains of industry who are geniuses and those who are not is often asked but never convincingly answered. This may be one of the reasons why both public and scientific interest has turned away from the rare genius to the many people who are creative. Added to this is the experience that the desirable changes in our scientific and technical world are brought about not only by the revolutionary ideas of a few but also and above all by the evolutionary contributions of the many.

Consistent with this, something began at the end of the nineteenth century which the German sociologist Niklas Luhmann with a certain amount of cynicism called the semantic path of the concept of creativity: "Creativity seems to be nothing other than democratically deformed genius. The trinity 'new, important, surprising' is still preserved, but its claims are being reduced. Whoever has talent and takes the trouble can make creativity out of it. One needs to have great staying power and, of course, a publicly funded post. With this transition to the small-scale no longer so rare and exclusive, the question about the recognition of creativity becomes all the more acute" (Luhmann, *Frankfurter Allgemeine Zeitung,* 10 June 1987).

Many prophets of the spirit of the times are, however, announcing that all human beings are creative to an equal extent, but that in the case of many people their potential for original thought and expression is not developed but is submerged or blocked or not sufficiently aroused, fostered or even permitted by the existing world of education and work. Of course it is not like this! If one measures the evaluation of creative products in a demanding way, if therefore one does not celebrate every small sandcastle, every abstract doodle or every modish extravagance as a manifestation of creative potential, then people become very clearly differentiated in their creative abilities for divergent thought, for identifying and solving difficult problems, for invention and discovery, and for the creation of works of art. According to the scientist J. P. Guilford, writing in 1950, these abilities include sensitivity towards the existence of problems, their particular nature and solubility in principle; fluency in the production of ideas, flexibility of thought, and the originality of the solutions to problems. In addition to a high general intelligence, prerequisites for all these are wealth of imaginative thought, the ability to draw analogies, and for metaphoric, associative, and playful thought, *as well as* the competence in analytical and constructive intellectual thought—hence a combination of cognitive predispositions that in popular psychology are mistakenly viewed as contradictory and mutually exclusive.

If one measures these cognitive prerequisites of creative achievement with the aid of reliable, valid psychometric testing processes, one experiences a great disappointment, however. More precisely, this multiplicity and diversity of intellectual characteristics does not permit one to make a forecast of school, professional, scientific, or artistic achievements which is satisfying in theory and workable in practice. There are two reasons for this.

The first is that creative achievements in life depend not only on the level of cognitive abilities of an individual, but also require an intelligently organized base of knowledge in order to become effective at solving problems which are demanding in content. Even for very gifted people and geniuses it takes many years as a rule to build up the necessary expertise through systematic learning, the acquisition of empirical knowledge and intensive practice. Contrary to many assumptions of everyday psychology and to scientific attempts at explanation, creative achievements are not dependent on creative abilities or a rich basis of knowledge alone, but come about, I am convinced, through the fostering of cognitive capabilities in the acquisition of knowledge as regards its content and through the practical use of this knowledge with the aid of advanced abilities of thought and structuring.

The second reason is that cognitive competence is a necessary but not a sufficient condition for creative achievements. Motivational factors also play an important role in the acquisition of these preconditions as well as in their use in demanding behavioral and problematic situations. These motivational factors include a strong curiosity and strong interest in learning, knowledge, and structure, often combined with behavioral tendencies which strike one as distinctly playful and explorative; a high level of demands as regards self-imposed targets and achievements, which are the object of personal aspiration; a certain measure of tolerance towards uncertainty, ambiguities, and contradictions during the solution of a task; a certain nonconformity in the personal formation of judgments and sufficient tenacity in the pursuit of one's own goals. Creative people are also often difficult partners in life and work, who need in equal measure a cooperative and a competitive social environment in order to fully develop their potential for achievement.

Individual and Cultural Creativity

The individual as cause and the cultural development as collective result—this thesis which promotes self-esteem is part of the basic assumptions of every idealistic understanding of the world. This idea is being questioned not just by Marxist thinkers but also increasingly by academics working in the social sciences and in cultural philosophy. Hence the American cognitive psychologist Jerome Bruner talks of "cultural creativity" and means by this the continued existence of intellectual and material tools, which every culture has created to compensate for the natural limitations of the individual. Even geniuses and highly gifted people use the cultural resources at their disposal as necessary preconditions for their creative work just as a matter of course. Furthermore, scientific discoveries, technical inventions and artistic creations are always embedded in a cultural context which at one and the same time defines the condition of the possibility and the boundary of feasibility for new discoveries. If one relates the development of a culture with a role which the individual can play in this, then the genius operates like a dwarf standing on the shoulders of a giant—to strain a well-known metaphor of Merton.

The analysis of the limitations of the individual in the creation of the new needs, however, to be taken a step further by including the immediate socio-cultural surroundings of the individual. New empirical studies confirm indeed what we all know from experience: the same people are more creative and productive in certain environments than in others. There are firms, institutes, laboratories and departments which obviously have the effect of stimulating their workers and fostering their creativity. Such places are characterized by a high level of demands, strong task-orientation, shared attentiveness towards new ideas, an open atmosphere for discussions, and a balanced relationship between individual competition and social common ground.

In Place of a Summary: Five Paradoxes on the Role of the Individual in the Discovery and Invention of the New in the World

The scientific state of knowledge at present permits no secure statement about the general laws according to which creative thought and action proceed. But perhaps the significant new is invented or discovered just because particularly individual constellations of conditions are in existence. The most worthwhile way of presenting a summary of the preceding look at the role of the individual for cultural progress therefore involves the formulation of a few obvious paradoxes.

Firstly, only the individual human being is capable on the basis of his intellectual equipment of discovering or inventing something significantly new, but he is able to do this only in the form of measured doses of discrepancy from the state of cultural development reached at any one time.

Secondly, geniuses and creative people stand out by their exceptional level of innate gifts, but they first have to acquire knowledge so that creative abilities become creative achievements.

Thirdly, cognitive competence is indeed a necessary precondition for creative achievements, but motivational factors play an equally important, often underestimated, role.

Fourthly, creative individuals need a creative environment in order to reach the highest intellectual, artistic, or practical achievements.

Fifthly, intelligence, imagination, and creativity are mental potentials which are distributed very differently amongst people, but intelligent knowledge is always needed for their individual development. Only the highly imaginative use of intelligent knowledge makes human thought creative.

Bibliography

Bruner, J. *Acts of Meaning.* Cambridge, MA: Harvard University Press, 1998.

Cox, C. M. *Genetic Studies of Genius: The Early Mental Traits of Three Hundred Geniuses* (Vol. 2). Stanford: Stanford Unverisity Press, 1926.

Ericsson, K. A. (ed.) *The Road to Excellence.* Mahwah, NJ: Erlbaum, 1996.

Feldman, D. H. Mozart als Wunderkind, Mozart als Artefact. In: P. Ostwald & L. S. Zegans (eds.), *Mozart—Freuden und Leiden des Genies.* Stuttgart: Kohlhammer, 1997.

Galton, F. *Hereditary Genius: An Inquiry into Its Causes and Consequences.* London: Macmillan, 1869.

Guilford, J. P. Creativity. *American Psychologist* 14, 1950, pp. 469–79.

Luhmann, N. V. Vom Zufall verwöhnt: Eine Rede über Kreativität. *Frankfurter Allgemeine Zeitung*, 132, 10 June 1987.

Murray, P. (ed.) *Genius: The History of an Idea.* Oxford, U.K.: Blackwell, 1989.

Ostwald, P. Genie, Wahnsinn und Gesundheit: Beispiele aus der Psychobiographie. In: P. Ostwald & L. S. Zegans (eds.), *Mozart—Freuden und Leiden des Genies.* Stuttgart: Kohlhammer, 1997.

Ostwald, P. & L. S. Zegans (eds.) *Mozart—Freuden und Leiden des Genies.* Stuttgart: Kohlhammer, 1997.

Simonton, D. K. Thematic fame, melodic originality, and musical zeitgeist: A biographical and transhistorical content analysis. *Journal of Personality and Social Psychology*, 38, 1980, pp. 972–83.

———. *Scientific Genius: A Psychology of Science.* Cambridge: Cambridge University Press, 1988.

———. Das schöpferische Genie in der Musik: Mozart und andere Komponisten. In: P. Ostwald & L. S. Zegans (eds.), *Mozart—Freuden und Leiden des Genies.* Stuttgart: Kohlhammer, 1997.

Wallace, G. *The Art of Thought.* New York: Harcourt Brace, 1926.

Weinert, F. E. Der aktuelle Stand der psychologischen Kreativitätsforschung und einige daraus ableitbare Schlußfolgerungen für die Lösung praktischer Probleme. In: K. U. Mayer (ed.), *Generationsdynamik in der Forschung*. Frankfurt/Main: Campus, 1992.

Weisberg, R. W. *Kreativität und Begabung*. Heidelberg: Spektrum der Wissenschaft, 1989.

16

In It for the Long Haul
An Interview with Harold Prince
Janet Coleman

Who could be better to comment on the relationship between artistic and commercial innovation than Hal Prince, Broadway director and producer? First as a producer in 1954, then as a producer-director in 1963, and then solely as a director from the late 70s on, Prince has enriched the musical theater—and rewarded his investors. This partial list of his shows tells the story: *The Pajama Game, West Side Story, Fiddler on the Roof, Fiorello, A Funny Thing Happened on the Way to the Forum, Cabaret, Company, Follies, Pacific Overtures, Sweeney Todd, Evita, Phantom of the Opera, Kiss of the Spiderwoman, Show Boat, Parade.*

When I look at the list of your shows, I'm struck by how many of them break new artistic ground and box office records. Can you identify anything about the way you think about the relationship between artistic innovation and commercial success that accounts for this?

I'm not much of a businessman. I think I have a reputation of being among the best producers that Broadway has ever had. If that's so, then it's because I wanted to be a director and I calculated that the only way that would happen would be if I could hire myself.

When you are a burgeoning artist, you face so much opposition, so many negative forces, so many people telling you, "You can't do it." More subconsciously than consciously I took the path that seemed clearest and easiest to me, which was to produce plays that George Abbott and Jerome Robbins directed, with an eye to one day hiring myself. For a period of six years I learned from two of the best. Abbott and Robbins are very dissimilar artists, but enormously successful and disciplined. I probably learned more of the work ethic from Abbott and more of the abstract choreographer's priorities and vision from Robbins.

I discerned that the first thing you had to do to be a good producer was possess enough artistic taste to know when to say no and when to say yes. If you deny an artist the money to support his vision, you have to know as an artist that he's throwing money away. I knew. I also knew where money would work. Sometimes it seemed as if I was being very indulgent, but I felt that the artist had a hook on something amazing and it was worth the extra ten thousand dollars to provide it. And other times I thought, "He's going to change his mind tomorrow. I will have blown ten thousand dollars and he'll say, 'Sorry, wrong muse.'" That would spend money rather more quickly than I could acquire it. So I knew when to say yes, and I knew more specifically when to say no and be responsible about it. I hated throwing money away. It is hard to find. And I provided enormous supportive enthusiasm.

Many industries have changed profoundly in the last decade, largely as a result of technological innovations. What has happened in the theater business?

Computerization has taken over the game. Tickets are sold that way. A vast audience is reached via the telephone—Ticketron and so forth. You used to buy tickets via the box office or via scalpers, as we used to call them—agents who sold tickets at a premium. Now you pay the premium, usually much less, and you do your buying over the phone with a credit card. What could be nicer? So the number of tickets sold has increased enormously. You can tell what your advance is instantly because it's in the computer. You can tell what tickets you've got available at night because it's in the computer.

Another innovation is the half-price TKTS booth on Forty-seventh Street, which sells unsold tickets on the day of the performance. People line up in the rain or in the frigid cold to get discounted tickets. It has enormous advantages and some disadvantages. *Phantom of the Opera* has never appeared at the ticket booth. If it did, it would unquestionably jeopardize our full-price ticket sales at the box office. But we are a phenomenon. It will be years from now when we finally do appear at the ticket booth. There are actually hundreds of thousands of people waiting for that day who have not yet seen the show or who have seen it and who want to see it again, but not at box office prices. When that happens it will have a deleterious effect on all the other shows at the ticket booth. The shows that most need TKTS to keep going cut their ticket prices in half, and so they have a much harder time meeting their break-even expenses every week. So you have the phenomenon of shows running on and on and on thanks to TKTS, which is lovely for theatergoers and theater owners, but not for producers or investors, because those shows never pay off.

An innovation that I have no respect for is this insanely competitive paid-for advertising game that everyone indulges in. Everyone advertises on television, pours hundreds of thousands of dollars a week into advertising a show that might have broken even at $200,000. They throw these sums at newspaper ads as well, but mostly television. Ironically, the newspapers—for example, the *New York Times*—have done very well as a result of competitive advertising. The *Times* generally has thumbs up and thumbs down on whether a show runs or not. It would argue this point with me, but it does. So fortunes are poured into the newspaper that gave you a bad review, running quotes from the newspapers that gave you good ones. It's a paradox.

When I was starting out in the theater, I didn't know much about advertising, and my priority as a producer was not to advertise before a show opened. Can you imagine doing that in the year 2001?

We used to have meetings in my office with the advertising agency and my staff. I would say, "Now we're not the show everybody is waiting to see. They don't even know what we're going to give them, so we're not going to spend any money on advertising. We're going to let the other guys do that. Then we're going to come in and upstage them with our production." That happened over and over again. But now times have changed.

The amount of money people spend on advertising today is so disproportionate to the money they spend on creating art, providing support to artists, it's obscene. Someone wisely said the other day that the only people who get rich in the theater today are the advertising agencies and the theater owners. The producers don't. Shows run on and on and on and don't pay back their investment. They look like hits to the uninitiated, but they are box office failures.

Why is that?

The theater owners keep you as long as they choose. They take the rent, the cream off the top, and when there's another show waiting to replace you, you're out on the street.

But there are moneymakers?

Yes. And they are worth talking about. Take a good look at *Phantom of the Opera*. *Phantom* has run fifteen and a half years in London. It is in its fourteenth year in New York. At one point it was playing seventeen productions simultaneously. Now, fifteen and a half years later, seven productions are running simultaneously. The average theater size is two thousand.

And here is a fact worth reckoning with: *Phantom* has grossed more money, and I'm sure netted more money, than any theatrical event in history—any film ever made. At this point its gross exceeds three and one half billion dollars.

Really?

It is this sort of success that encourages investment in the theater. There have only been four of these bonanzas in recent history: *Cats, Les Misérables, Miss Saigon,* and *Phantom. Cats* and *Miss Saigon* are gone. *Les Miz* is in its last years, and *Phantom* should last another four or five years. Bear in mind, all of this income comes from first-class companies—the original productions. Subsidiary rights kick in after the original closes.

The point is, if you look at the theater as a crapshoot, and people have forever, you're likely to wind up bankrupt. The theater is not a crapshoot.

It's an art form.

The reason I have staying power is that I never, ever thought, "Will it make money at the box office?"

I never thought, "Who's your audience?"

I've never analyzed demographics.

It neither interests me, nor am I persuaded that it works. Quite the contrary, I'm persuaded that it doesn't. You do what you do and some of your shows succeed artistically and fail economically, and

some succeed on both scores, and some fail totally. I've had my
share of failures.

*You just said that you don't begin where conventional marketing
wisdom says one should start—with a demographic picture of your
audience. Instead, you begin with an artistic idea and from that create a show. How do you stay true to your artistic vision?*

You just do. You pick the subject. I happen to love metaphors. I
love social problems. I love politics. I love to reflect on my own
frustrations with the times in which I live. I've been here a long
time. Times change. Politics change. Once I find an idea for a
project, I choose a composer, a librettist, a lyricist, a designer, and
a director (me). My artistic taste has betrayed me on occasion. I
cannot pay attention to that. I have to move on to the next project.

I'm very happy that I don't dwell on failure. I've had enough to
have stopped myself any number of times. In the 1980s, I did eight
shows in six years and they all flopped at the box office. I started to
read in the newspapers how it was all over for me, but I didn't take
it seriously. In forty-something years in the theater, six years is not
very long. *Evita* immediately preceded the six bad years. It ran so
long that while I was failing all over the place I still had a show running successfully for all but a year and a half of that period. Then
came *Phantom of the Opera.* Since *Phantom,* I've had some failures. I've also had some nice big hits. They just don't seem big
compared to *Phantom.* But *Kiss of the Spiderwoman* was successful, as was the rethink of *Showboat.*

George Abbott said to me way back in the beginning, "No matter
how secure you are about the show you're doing, always have another show ready for a meeting the day after opening night and have
them all coming into your office at ten A.M. First of all, it will get you
to bed earlier that night. If the reviews are good, fine, don't drink so
much, you've got an appointment at ten the next morning. If the re-

views are bad, you can't lick your wounds because you've got an appointment with another set of authors the next morning at ten." I've followed that most of my career except for the last few years.

Why the change?

The cost of doing things has escalated so much that we can't insist on working as often as we used to.

I think we are back to the relationship between art and commerce. Does doing fewer shows affect your ability to innovate?

Here's a paradox. When I was both a producer and a director, I not infrequently had three musicals running simultaneously on Broadway. To my three, David Merrick had five.

In 1959 there was a potential strike or lockout on Broadway. Merrick and I controlled the larger number of hit shows. We let the strike happen because we discerned that we wanted to be in the theater for the next 30 or 40 years. If we hadn't, costs would have started to escalate to a point where we could not enjoy our lives in the theater as we had previously. The strike lasted nine days. It took the momentum out of the shows we had running that year. I had a new success called *Fiorello,* which Abbott directed and which won a Pulitzer prize. After the nine-day strike, no question, it came back, but without the energy it had going into the strike.

Today, every time there is a labor negotiation, the producers cave in because they don't see it as a forty- or fifty-year journey. They see it for the moment: "Oh my God, I've got a hit, I may never have another one. Give them what they ask for."

And so today the costs of producing and maintaining—operating costs—are way out of proportion to the rise in the ticket prices.

For example, it cost $162,000 to do *Damn Yankees,* $169,000 to do the *Pajama Game.* Today each of those musicals would cost upwards of $8 million. So you see that you've cut way down on the number of productions you can finance. It's easy to find $169,000. It's much more difficult to find $8 million.

What does the perceived need for every show to be a big hit do to the art form?

It's hurt the art form terribly. But it alone hasn't hurt the art form. The shift in where money is has endangered the art form. We've lost patrons because old money has almost been erased from our society.

When I was a young man, there were all the famous old money names. And I knew them. They loved the theater and some were close friends. They're no longer in the game. You never read the names of all those famous rich families except for Rockefeller. You're sitting in Rockefeller Center and as of last week they no longer own it. So you see how much that's changed.

The theater used to have benefactors who produced shows. They were the equivalent of William Shakespeare's patrons. They were artistic. They were frustrated in expressing their enormous affection for the art form, because they could not write, direct, compose, or perform. But they could be in the company of the people who did. And they could legitimately put their imprint on what was in theaters. You could say, "I'm going to see a Gilbert Miller play. I'm going to see a Theater Guild play. I'm going to see Robert Whitehead's play." You could say, "I'm going to see" these productions, because they had a creative imprimatur. You could actually look at a play and say, "That's a Theater Guild play," and you'd be right.

Producers today are not primarily creative. They are often businessmen and women with access to a lot of money who want to make a lot of money. When I produced, I had a few large investors and many small ones: actors, stage managers, stagehands, dressers, ticket takers, my barber. They gave me $500 and enjoyed the ride. Interestingly enough, out of the first shows I did, a $500 investment made $2,500. Where else could a small investor do that? It's changed.

Today we have a cross-section of enthusiastic people who'd love to make a killing, who love being in the theater, but who try to dope it out the way a Wall Street investor at his computer would do.

It doesn't work that way.

How does it work? I'm going to guess that thinking long term has something to do with it. . . .

I'm living proof, along with my colleagues, that if you have longevity and keep your eye on the artistic prize, then you'll be OK. One caveat: you don't want to be way out there on the artistic limb. It's a wonderful place to be, but not when you're in a business where you need to raise money and return money.

We've talked about changes in the business and financial side of the theater industry. What changes have you seen in theater audiences?

The shifting of money has also shifted our audience. I think our theater audiences are people with newfound wealth who live in the suburbs. They are either less demanding or less perspicacious of the art form. They are very much contaminated by the sound bite on television, by the short attention span and lurid delivery of "entertainment." And they translate that into what they want to see in the theater, so it is louder, busier, more lurid, often more vulgar.

So how does that equate with *Phantom*? It is a visceral, emotional experience for the audience. It is not an intellectual experience. It was never meant to be. Predominantly, my shows have been somewhat intellectual experiences. *Phantom* goes against that totally. It's sung through. You needn't listen to the lyrics. You needn't even listen too hard to the text. What you need to do is sit back and let it happen to you like a kid. And that's what the audience does. Also, it appeals to an audience that doesn't speak our language, because our language is only secondary to the appreciation of *Phantom of the Opera*. It's a visual appreciation; it's a musical dynamic. It's let the music wash over you. It's let those costumes and that scenery and this basic plot—Beauty and the Beast—just happen. Having analyzed it in those terms, I am not disparaging it, I am simply explaining it.

I used to think that I was on firm ground with a project if I thought it was pretentious. I'd smile to myself and I'd say to my wife, "Oh boy, is this one pretentious." Then she'd say, "You're in good shape." That goes all the way back to *West Side Story*. I guess I can characterize many of the shows with which I'm identified as having a kind of self-importance. It wasn't conscious in the beginning, but it was there, and that was OK. Today it's not as OK.

Right now, the audience that is filling our theaters is diminishing our aspirations. The tail is wagging the dog. Being an optimist, I believe that at some point they will get more educated. They will start to see how repetitive and unworthy some of the stuff they accepted last year and the year before is, and how much they need something fresh. That's when you bring in *West Side Story,* which was remarkably accessible to everyone.

Which brings us back to artistic vision and sticking to it. Earlier you said that you don't take a conventional marketer's point of view toward an audience. From your description of how an audience experiences Phantom, I know that you think about what the audience feels when the curtain goes up. What else, imaginatively, goes on between you and an audience?

There seems to still be an appetite for new musicals. But the audience can't tell me what they are. I have to tell them. That's what nobody understands.

I've never given one moment's thought to whether or not an audience will want to see a show. People have run scared from a number of my shows. I picked up *West Side Story* with my partner when another producer dropped it. It seemed to me absolutely a wondrous project. And potentially popular.

What scared the other producer?

Look at *West Side Story* before the fact, not after the fact. It's a balletic musical about kids fighting on the streets of New York. The score is by Leonard Bernstein, who had just had a failure with *Candide* the year earlier; the lyrics are by a young man no one had ever heard of named Stephen Sondheim; and there are no well-known names in the cast, just a bunch of kids. Not only was it worth doing artistically, but it was a huge success from my investors' point of view, because, as well as it did on the stage, it did even better in film, and they shared in the success of both. Sondheim reminds me we had a hundred walkouts a night for a year and a half at *West Side Story*. People couldn't pigeonhole it.

When I directed *Cabaret,* let's face it, no one knew why the hell I was doing a Nazi musical.

Well, put it like that . . .

That's exactly how you put it: "I'm doing a musical. There'll be swastikas on stage. It's about the rise of the Third Reich and this little cute MC is going to change before your very eyes from an adorable entertainer into a Nazi."

Not infrequently people would find me in the lobby at the original *Cabaret* and say: "Why don't you sell Joel Grey dolls?" The question is staggering. I'd ask, "With or without swastikas?" "He's so cute, that Nazi." But of course that allure is exactly what we were trying to create. It's playing on Broadway right now in its third incarnation, and it's a gigantic success.

No one knew who Evita was. If you don't know who the vice president of the United States is, you surely don't know who Evita Peron is. But they know who she is now.

We've talked about escalating costs, concomitant difficulties raising money, and the shifting sources of financial backing. What about artists? Are they out there? Are there enough of them to create a vibrant theater community?

Our biggest problem isn't with our artists, but with our entrepreneurs, our producers. Playwrights are there. Composers are there. I know many of them. I just completed a show in Philadelphia: three one-act musicals, which are going to come to Broadway. They're all new composers, as are the choreographers, the book writers, and the lyricists. No one's heard of any of them. The only director anyone's heard of is me. The other two are new. The *New York Times* review was the best I've received from that paper in recent memory. But producers have yet to learn this lesson. They aren't nourishing their artistic juices and they lack courage. As long as that condition exists, the Broadway theater is in jeopardy.

When you say courage, do you mean the courage to stick to your artistic convictions?

Yes. Here's what I mean. Among the innovations that are epidemic in the theater is the workshop. You have a show written and then you have a workshop so the investors can hear it before they commit themselves to it. It pretends to be there to show you what to do to fix the material. It doesn't. Probably 80 percent of the musicals that fail on Broadway have had workshops, which didn't affect the subsequent production. I think that many producers would rather finance a workshop than produce a show. They can do a workshop for a couple of hundred thousand dollars, then they don't have to do the show. They can clearly see why it's in trouble or what its problems are, and that they can't solve them. So they do the workshop and then they walk away. And they didn't lose ten million dollars. They only lost a couple of hundred thousand dollars. It seems a little Alice in Wonderland, but it's true.

When the cost of productions was small, no one gave me advice about my scripts. I never let an investor read one—let alone see a "workshop." And I never chatted socially with them in the lobby about what was wrong with the show.

I was clear about the rules. I said, "I will make you money, but you have to be with me for the long haul. You will make. You will lose. You will lose. You will make. But what you make will outstrip what you lose." And once the rules were clear, substantial investors were willing to take a chance. I don't believe in the short haul.

What, if anything, do technological innovations contribute to an artist's ability to innovate?

During my lifetime they've talked about the potential of holography, the wonders of multimedia effects. Those techniques have rarely paid off.

The theater is an empty space that engages the audience's collaboration with the artist. You fill the empty space with just enough and then you say, "You fill in the blanks." But the audience contributes to this experience, something that films and television do not do. I think that will always be so.

Do we benefit from mechanization? Do the candles in *Phantom* come up out of the floor in a mechanized fashion? Absolutely. But in London they don't. In London they come up through the floor on Victorian machinery that goes back a hundred years. When we came to America, it was all mechanized, and I'd say, "It's too smooth. Let's rough it up a little."

We can be the beneficiaries of technology, but we must never lose sight of the fact that we are not at heart a technological art form, nor should we be. Any audience that asks for that is asking for what movie audiences are asking for.

As for movie producers, can't they see that one more body hurtling through a plate glass window in a movie isn't filling theaters any more? If I'm reading the newspapers correctly, they've had a terrible year. They haven't made great movies. Wouldn't it be wonderful if they went back to words and directors? Wouldn't it be wonderful if we did?

Look at reality television: *Survivor. The Mole.* Will that last? Of course not. Just hang in there. I guess I've been saying "Hang in there" a good portion of my life. "Hang in there. It will go away."

17

Composing with
High Technology
An Interview with Todd Winkler
Kent Lineback

You teach music at Brown University. You have a doctorate from Stanford. How would you describe who you are and what you do?

I consider myself a teacher, a composer, and a multimedia artist. I create interactive works of music and art where human action is the primary input to a responsive computer system. I've worked in several forms: interactive concert works for musicians, dance pieces using motion-sensing systems to generate music and images, and audio/video installations activated by user participation.

I started out my training as a composer in college and, before that, playing classical music and playing in bands. I've always been interested, even as a kid, in gadgets and technology. As soon as I got to college I took an electronic music class with Gordon Mumma, who got me involved in music technology. Gordon is one of the pioneers of electronic music. He started one of the first electronic music studios in Ann Arbor in the late '50s, and later worked with John Cage and Merce Cunningham. I've pretty much kept up with all the developments in electronic music from 1976, when I was a teenager, until now. Along the way I also studied classical music and traditional composition in undergraduate and graduate school.

What I've pursued my whole career is taking new technology —sometimes helping to create that technology, mostly in software— and then using it to realize a work of art.

Would you describe some of the work you've done?

The first phase of my work, starting maybe about 14 years ago, was focused on interactive concert music, a medium I continue to work in. I began writing pieces where a musician would play, and the computer would do some kind of analysis of the performance and then supply an accompaniment or act as a musical partner or alter the sounds in real time.

In these concert works I want the players themselves to feel like they are having a real musical dialogue with the computer. So what comes from the computer has to be somewhat unpredictable, but it can't be random. It has to make sense for what they are playing, and it has to have certain kinds of rules of engagement. Just like a good conversation, there has to be a kind of give-and-take.

For instance, I wrote a solo piece for an electronic drum set called *Stomping the Ground.* In that piece I have 16 pads, plastic pads—it looks kind of like a drum set—that actually don't make any sounds themselves, they're just a means of putting information into the computer. I could have the computer make sounds like a drum set when you hit the pads, which is what most people think the system is for, but actually those 16 pads, or locations, can be used to produce any kind of sound I want from the computer.

When the drummer plays on the pads, all the computer knows is which pad is being hit, when it's hit, and how hard it's hit. From that I am able to obtain a lot of expressive information that drummers are good at. Drummers practice over and over to get a kind of feel and sound. It's really their expertise with tempo and accents that makes them good drummers. I was able to capture this information, basically capture the drum riff, and then map that to the melodies. So actually the melodies are created by the rhythmic structure and accent patterns of an expert drummer, a human being who is playing on those pads.

Wait. "Melodies are created"? I'm confused about how those melodies are actually created. Where do they come from in that situation?

They come from algorithms, sets of rules that I've devised for generating melodies and put in the computer. The algorithm is a step-by-step procedure that describes a musical process. A round, for instance, is a well-known musical process. Based on what's coming in, the computer will pick the right notes, using the algorithms. So the drummer supplies the rhythm and tempo, and the computer creates the sounds and pitches for the melodies based on how the drummer plays.

Could you give an example of a very simple algorithm?

A very simple algorithm might say, "Here's a scale. Start on a particular note and play up the scale between two and eight notes and then turn around and play between two and eight notes in the other direction."

How is that related to what the drummer is doing?

It could be influenced by the accent pattern of the drum. For instance, I'll have the turnaround note be one of the louder notes the drummer plays.

A turnaround note?

A change in direction. Let's say the computer melody goes up a certain number of notes until it detects an accented drum beat. The drummer goes ya-da-POM and on that POM the computer melody starts going back down and waits for the next accented note from the drum and then starts going back up again. So you get a melody that's based on what the drummer just did. And the note selection could be a specific scale or specific intervals that I'm interested in. There are numerous methods I have to generate notes or chords or rhythms. This is just a very simple example. I am much more interested, these days, in creating or altering the actual sounds with the computer in response to a performance.

And randomization is what makes it sound never quite the same?

Exactly. I've set some parameters up in the melody generator to be improvisational or randomized, but other elements are always fixed. So as a result, in a given situation or a given set of inputs, the computer's responses always sound somewhat similar but are actually never the same twice. When I use randomization as a technique, I usually have constraints on the range of possible values. I might say, "Go up and down between eight and twelve notes." Or I might say, "Go up and down between two and four notes." One will make a choppy melody that always turns around on itself and the other will make longer, fluid lines.

When you write an algorithm, how do you do that? Where do you come up with an algorithm? Is writing a musical algorithm like writing music itself?

It might sound strange, but all composers have ways of coming up with notes and rhythms and ideas for putting them together, and many of those ideas can be coded into an algorithm. It's not always that logical, but sometimes you can get close.

One of my teachers was a guy named David Cope, and he developed this system, EMI (Experiments in Musical Intelligence), which is based on the parametric analysis of existing music and identifying various features of musical style. With EMI he has been able to create music that sounds like it was written by famous composers. He does it by feeding into a computer lots of Mozart, for instance, and then doing statistical averages on it and other kinds of analysis. He can generate new works in the style of Mozart based on the information and rules stored in his database. Apparently, his computer-generated Chopin or Bach has been good enough to fool some professional musicians. They can't tell the real versions from the fake.

Now that I have a better idea how interactive computer music works, I should let you return to your description of the work you do and how it's evolved.

As I worked on interactive music, I became more and more interested in using a movement-sensing system to allow people to create music by their movements. This might involve dancers, who are so well trained in controlling their movements, or it might be in the form of an interactive installation.

So I started looking into different kinds of visual systems that could analyze movement. I settled on one that I've been very happy with called the Very Nervous System. It was created by an artist named David Rokeby. His system uses a video camera as the input device to the computer. Rokeby's software detects changes in the video image, so I am able to detect the location and speed of someone moving in front of the sensing camera. I am able to impose a grid onto the video image, and the software reports changes in each grid space.

The Very Nervous System is similar in some ways to a MIDI (Musical Instrument Digital Interface) keyboard or to the electric drum set. Each of those systems simply tells the computer *where* something happened (a specific key or drum pad is struck, a person moves into a specific grid space) and *how quickly* (the velocity). And of course, a computer is good at timing, so it knows *when* something happens.

I've now spent about five years with the Very Nervous System, and I've completed three fairly large dance productions and several installations. My latest work adds dancer-controlled video projections and video processing, along with music and sound.

Some of the algorithms I used for responding to musicians translated well into the motion-sensing world, although I then got more specialized and started developing better and better musical responses specifically for movement, because the kinds of gestures dancers make are different from the kinds of musical gestures musicians make.

I've always been deeply interested in human-computer interaction. What is important to me is not just finding a way of generating music but also developing the way the computer responds to a human being. So I'm looking for different ways of analyzing human gestures and how they will correspond to the sound world.

In watching videotape of some of your motion-sensing work, I noticed instances when, say, the dancer's motion triggered a specific and distinct sound from the computer, and that motion always triggered that same sound. But in other instances the connection between the dancer's motion and the resulting sound was less obvious and more varied, richer.

I've developed some responses that are very obvious, sort of a one-to-one correspondence, and others are a little more mysterious as to how the movement is influencing the sound. I've created a big library of different ways to interpret and map gestures, everything from the very obvious to almost impossible to detect, and lots and lots of different kinds of musical responses. But the main work for me at the beginning was just thinking of all the kinds of ways the computer could respond musically to movement.

What's been the response of the people, the dancers? Did they like it?

They love it! All the dancers, when they start moving and making music, say, "Wow! I didn't know you could do this! I'm making the music." Dancers hook directly into being able to alter the sound. They feel it right away. They go with it.

So it's an infinite loop. The dancers hear it, and it changes how they dance. But how they dance changes the sound the computer produces, which changes how they dance. And so on and on.

Right. I've done a few workshop situations with dancers where I'll experiment with suddenly changing the sound. The computer will be making this big rumbling abstract sound, and all of a sudden I'll change it to bright bells and plucked sounds. And immediately the dancer's movement will change—especially a good dancer. And this also happens with untrained dancers. They will be doing the movement that they think will make that sound. I've seen this in my interactive installations. If I have a big percussive sound, people stamp their feet and move their arms up and down. But if all of a sudden I come in with some very delicate sparkly whooshing sounds that are more ethereal, people will pause and move slowly, sort of wave their arms around in the air, and their feet won't be stomping around so much.

I'm not sure I know exactly what you mean by "installation."

Interactive installations are works of art that are location-specific. Each is in a particular place, like a room in an art gallery. What makes it interactive is that it needs a human who's in the place, involved, to make it go, to make it work. In other words, just sitting there by itself, it isn't complete, it's simply a place, waiting for a person to participate in order to realize this work of art. People do not have to have any special training, as they do with my works with professional dancers and musicians. Everyone is invited to participate, and each person realizes a unique version of the work and is, in fact, part of the work. Each person who experiences the installation is a performer. They might even have some spectators acting as their audience. They are the dancers in the dance.

So someone goes into this location, this space, and does something. Maybe just moves around. Or someone picks up a picture and looks at it or opens a drawer, and then the room, the computer, reacts to that with sound of some kind or visual elements or something else.

That's right. An interactive installation doesn't have to have a computer involved, but more and more the computer enables these kinds of things to happen, because the computer is pretty good at translating human movement as an abstract series of numbers into something else. That "something else" doesn't have to be music. It can be an audio clip of someone talking or a video clip or even something physical like a door opening.

It's the physical world interfacing with the virtual world. I'm interested in both. How the physical can be enhanced and augmented by the virtual or by computer mediation.

I use two analogies to explain what I want in all of my interactive works. One is a good conversation, the way what each person says alters what the other says. The second is a jazz ensemble, especially a free jazz band, in which the way each player plays is affected by, and affects, the others. It's the same feeling of engagement as in conversation.

I'm not anywhere near there, but if I can get that with the musician, if I can have the dancers feel like they're participating in that way, and if I can have people in an interactive installation playing back video and sound and getting that kind of feeling, I think that will be fantastic. I think I'm getting there a little bit. But certainly I'm nowhere near the sophistication of real people in conversation or the jazz ensemble.

You use the computer in most of what you do. What is it you're basically up to in using a computer or technology to compose music?

I think of the computer as a tool. A very fancy, sophisticated tool. It allows me to do a certain kind of work I can't do without the computer.

You remain the composer?

Absolutely. My software is the composition. The computer is dumb as wood. It simply does what my software tells it to do. My software is the work. It represents all the potential outcomes. All the things it can produce are represented somehow in that code. There might be a million different melodies, and I've set it up to give it that potential. What happens in my interactive work is that that potential is only realized by human action. It doesn't happen on its own.

So if you say the computer is simply a dumb machine for realizing your musical ideas, then in effect it's you who are reacting to the dancer. Or, better, it's an interaction between your mode of thinking, as expressed in the software, and the dancer or the drum player or whatever.

Exactly. It's a mode of thinking that is open enough to generate many results. When I was in graduate school, I studied some of Beethoven's sketchbooks. They're Beethoven's outtakes, the stuff he threw away. I'm looking at this music and thinking, "Wow! This is great stuff!" The stuff that Beethoven threw away is fantastic. And I thought, "Wouldn't it be great if you could hear all the different versions that were running through Beethoven's mind?" People think this is sacrilegious. The Ninth Symphony, the Fifth Symphony, they're perfect in every way. How could anybody ever change anything or touch it? But he kept changing it constantly, and I would love to hear all of the versions that were running through his head.

So why not set my composition up in the beginning to have this range of possibilities? If I have a good idea, why not hear all of the variations? That's what I'm doing in my algorithms. I'm thinking, "Oh, it could go up or down, it could do this or that." Well, let's have it do all of it, let's allow the computer to be able to do all those things at some time, based on what comes up. So it's really an environment that has the potential for making lots of different kinds of things. I'm still keeping pretty good control over it, as an artist and as a composer. I don't want it to do just anything. I want it to produce music I want to hear and I'm interested in.

Yet sometimes, maybe often, you're surprised.

I am. Yeah, I am. And I like those surprises. I build into the software the ability for me to control almost in real time, as someone is playing or someone is dancing, how wide or small these random elements are. I can constrain various parameters to have a very narrow wiggle range, or I can make them very wide. And if I open up everything, if I open up all the parameters very wide, then I have no idea what it will produce.

Sometimes I'll walk into my studio, open up all the parameters very wide, and think to myself, "I wonder what's on today?" I just turn the computer on. Sometimes it's great. Most times it's horrible. But every now and then I'll go, "Wow!" And I'll jot down those parameter settings so that later on, or in a different piece, I'll plug in those settings again as a starting point for a new project.

Let's go back for a moment to Beethoven's sketchbooks. In the end Beethoven chose one of those variations he worked on. And what you do is not a choice of one thing.

True. I create the potential to generate endless variations. But it's different when I do a recording. I have to choose one version for a recording. A purist, whatever that is, might say that to do a realization of one of my interactive music pieces I should have somebody just play it once and put it on CD, and that would be the most honest way. That is to say, this is it from beginning to end, one realization of the work.

But in fact I have taste. I like things. I dislike things. So when I make an actual recording, I might do ten takes and then splice together my favorite parts to create an ideal version of the work. Part of my craft is knowing how to splice and process sound in the studio. So I use my skill and creativity to make a fixed version for CD, which is different from a live performance.

On the other hand, if I were to choose a fixed version for somebody to perform in concert, I would miss all the nice surprises. I would never hear all those nice things that happen spontaneously.

You've mentioned Beethoven and David Cope with his fake Mozart and fake Bach, and you studied classical composition. Where are you, or where is what you do, in the context of the history of music?

Music has always taken advantage of available technology. There's the electric guitar, which spawned rock and roll, there are new microphones, which allowed singers like Frank Sinatra to sound more intimate. And of course there's the piano, which evolved from the harpsichord when new building materials and construction techniques became available.

The last commonly used acoustic instrument invented was the saxophone, in the middle of the nineteenth century, and since then almost all the new instruments have been electrical. As soon as electricity was available, instruments started appearing. There was the telharmonium in 1906—which was, I think, the first electronic instrument that anybody knows about—the theremin in 1919, the vibraphone around 1925.

Then electric guitars, guitar pickups, in the 1930s. And, of course, as soon as solid state circuits were available, they made their way into musical instruments. As soon as the first Apple computer was available, people started writing music software for it. That started the whole MIDI revolution. And even CD recording was a big change—all music became digital.

So I see all of my work fitting in perfectly with how the history of music has gone, which is that new technology gives musicians and composers new ideas for making new kinds of music.

Well, for me—and I'm someone for whom music is important, especially classical music—that raises a very basic question. What is music?

A lot of people have different definitions of music, but my definition is usually "organized sound" or "sound organized over time." I think of music as a temporal art, so the time element is crucial.

What's the organization element? Is it that somehow the sounds are connected?

If you walked outside and recorded the sounds of birds singing, and you came in and played it, some people would say that's music. They would say any sounds are music. I would say, "Well, perhaps the birds are organizing it, but there wasn't a person who organized it"—though I suppose somebody had to turn the tape recorder on or off. But if you took that recording and spliced it a little bit or put different parts of it together, and they lasted a certain amount of time, I would say that's music.

That's pretty broad, but I usually think of it somehow as organized sound, even if the organization technique uses random procedures. John Cage used various random procedures to come up with certain features of his music, certain sets of parameters, but the way he did it was highly organized.

Then what is innovation in music? What is musical innovation?

Hmm.

Do you as a composer care about innovation? Do you get up in the morning and say, "I'm going to be innovative?"

Not really. I just follow the things that interest me the most. It usually turns out that the things that interest me the most are the new things. And that's what I want to go toward. Like a lot of other artists and academics, once I've figured something out, I'm not really that interested in going over and over it. Instead, I'm always thinking, "How can I incorporate this other, new thing into here?"

Usually I think of musical innovation as ideas, which may become techniques or instruments or whatever, but before anything happens you have an idea. I'd say the ideas that are the most influential are the most important ones. They're the ones that change the way future composers, or people in general, think about music.

Take John Cage, for example. He said, "Sounds are sentient beings. Any sound is music." Sound is music. Wow! How can that be? Noise is music. My refrigerator is music. But when you stop and really consider what he said, it completely changes the way you think about music. I don't think music would be the same today without a lot of John Cage's ideas. I don't know very many composers who sit around and listen to his music, but they would all say they were highly influenced by his ideas.

So the ideas that people have are what's infectious. They're the viral part of it. The idea invades people's minds and all of a sudden everybody starts thinking it and suddenly, Boom! Everything changes.

For instance, this movement-sensing technology. I didn't invent it. But just the idea that a dancer's movement can create music is a new idea. It bursts an old conceptual bubble, the idea that movement and music are two different things, or that the dancer moves to the music and not the other way around. It's like gravity. You drop something and it falls. If one day you dropped something and it floated, your whole world would change, and you'd have to think of everything differently. Movement-sensing is something like that but on a much smaller scale. You move and there's a sound. Wow! What do you do with that? The new dance piece I am working on, *Falling Up,* explores this whole subject of how technology changes what we believe by making the impossible possible. It's about flying.

I'm fascinated by the relationship between technology and art in your work. How do you view the innovations you create? Are they musical, technological?

I view myself as an artist, an experimenter, a researcher, and an inventor—not a gadget inventor, and not an innovator in the technology itself, other than writing software for a specific project. I'm waiting for other people to make the hardware available for me: a faster computer, a better hand-held camera, new sensing systems. Then I'll experiment with it and see if I get some new ideas for work that requires those new capabilities.

But in some ways, some piece of technology—for instance, something like the Very Nervous System—in and of itself shouldn't be impressive. If someone tells me that now the computer can know where people are and how fast they move around, my first response might be, "Wow!" Hopefully, though, everybody gets over that "wow!" response very quickly and moves to the "So what?" or the "Now show me what it can do" response. It's as if somebody invented the first piano and people said, "Wow! This is great. Lots of keys!" Then they would say, "OK, but now what can it do? Now play something. Play something beautiful or interesting or complex."

That's where I am, at that spot. Here are the new inventions, but there needs to be somebody who's artistic or smart or who thinks things through to show they can be used to realize some of the new ideas or to show some of the potential. We have had an amazing amount of technical progress in the last ten years, with very little memorable content to show for it.

All right. But now I'm curious. Given your interest in the human-computer interaction and your heavy use of technology, how do you actually work? How do you compose? What's the process for creating one of your pieces?

Well, I probably have a different process for each work. But the dance pieces may be good examples. I'll get together with the dancer, who's a choreographer also, and we'll improvise. I'll have my system running, and I have a whole library of sounds and responses and musical material that I can draw upon.

It's not that much different from jazz musicians who have a huge library of their own and other people's solos that they've memorized, sort of their whole experience. I probably have 200 different kinds of musical responses I can call up immediately, and each has about 40 different parameters I can change. So I can right away get to a certain kind of sound or response.

In the process of developing these dance pieces we might start with an idea and pursue it. Like the piece about flying. Or we may have no idea what we're going to do at all. In either case, we get together, I set things up, the dancer starts moving, we try this, we try that. It takes a long time, weeks and weeks and weeks, many sessions, 30 to 40 hours together or more. We're really just playing, like kids, we're brainstorming, we're experimenting. I like working that way. It's actually my favorite part of working. We haven't decided anything. We try out the craziest things. I've had people bring in toys. Somebody's gone on roller-skates. We're juggling balls. We're throwing stuff. We're trying to make music by flying toy airplanes around the room. We're projecting video onto the ceiling, walls, floor. Most of it doesn't work. Meanwhile I'm writing software like mad, and we have a video camera recording our sessions constantly. Each version of the software, with all of its settings, is cataloged to its corresponding place in the recorded video so that we can recreate any of the sessions.

Then the dancer and I will both sit down and watch all the videotapes. A lot of it, we'll say, "Well, that's boring." But we usually find striking moments or whole sections where images, movement, and sound all come together, and we mark those sections for further consideration. For instance, in one piece we had about twenty things that we loved, but only five or six of them ended up in the final piece because they didn't all make sense together as a single work.

When you start working on one of these, what's your goal? What's your purpose—not for the specific piece itself but overall—when you're doing a piece of art?

I'd say there are a few goals. One of them for me is that I always want to learn something new. There's some research aspect to every piece that I've done. I want to try out some new artistic ideas that I have based on this technology. I also might want to try a new software idea, because I'm writing software to make all this happen.

But that's not all I want to do. I also want to come out at the end with a work of art that stands on its own, that is intriguing and emotionally and intellectually engaging. I care most that the end product, the finished product, will be a complete and whole work of art and express something significant or inspire someone to have a significant experience. I think I've succeeded when somebody comes away with new ideas or has felt something deeply or learned something to the point that it has actually transformed him or her somehow.

So trying out things is a means to that end, not an end in itself?

Yes. I want to end up with artwork instead of something that just demonstrates how a technology works. I'm actually very aware of not simply making my artwork a demonstration. I'm aware of the danger of that and fight against it. Everyone is so easily impressed with technology just because it's new. They say, "Wow! isn't this great!" No. It has to say something or do something worthwhile.

When the Mac Plus first came out, people started writing these crazy documents with every word in a different font and some words were italicized and some bold and some underlined. But that didn't make the writing any better. It still said what it said. You could throw as much technology at it as you wanted—a better printer, a faster computer, better fonts—but in the end, there was some content there and it still had to mean something.

Then how do you decide what's junk and what's not, what's worthwhile and what's not?

A lot of artists and critics would argue that there are objective criteria for evaluating art, and I could list my objective criteria, which would be different from others' criteria. But what it all boils down to, for me, is that I have to produce something that I feel good about. I have to think that it's good. I hope I like it, too, but I keep it when I think that it's good.

I also would have to say—this is very personal for me—that exploration of new technology gets me going. It really engages me and I'm fascinated by it. It sort of fires me up, because it's fun and it gives me new ideas. There is an important aspect of play I described in the dance pieces. I also feel that I'm motivated by playing with new technology. I want to play with my toys, and in being interested in playing with my toys, I make artistic discoveries, which then gets me to do the artwork. I think I would do the artwork anyway, but I wouldn't be having nearly as much fun or be nearly as engaged if I were sitting at the piano with pencil and paper.

Doesn't this create a dilemma for you? There are more and more new whizbangs coming down the road all the time. How do you decide which ones are interesting to you?

I've seen a lot of my artist friends fall by the wayside by being attracted to every new thing that comes along. Everything that comes along requires a learning curve. No matter how good we are at whatever we do, and no matter how much similarity there is to previous things, it does take a while to get good at any new technology. For this reason, I choose my new technologies carefully.

I did my graduate work at Stanford, which had a fantastic center for computer music research. The program was well funded, and they were able to buy every new computer that looked interesting. Well, everything that came along was obviously much better than the previous thing. So every year or so, it was another new machine or whatever. But every new machine, of course, couldn't do anything by itself. Again, dumb as wood. So everybody would start painstakingly writing software for it. Then, one year later, another new machine, much faster, more processing speed, blah, blah, blah. So everybody would shift gears. Of course it had a different operating system, or you had to write in a new language. Six months later, another new machine, and on and on.

I have to say that many of the people there were engineers and computer scientists inventing the technology, so it was a very exciting time, and their goal was to keep pushing and improving the technology.

The thing is, composers needed much more time to learn and master these systems. They had trouble getting good at any of these things because they were changing too quickly. Suppose you play the flute for six months, and suddenly the guitar comes out. You can play more notes at once! So you switch to the guitar. Then out comes the tuba. Wow! Bigger, louder! Do that! Then three months later, the piano. Even more notes at once! The result is that although you may actually become a better musician for all this diversity of experience, you would never become good at any one instrument. You'd remain an amateur.

When I was in graduate school in 1989 and I was seeing this going on, I decided I would learn one thing and get good at it and stay with it for five years. I made a conscious decision to learn a certain kind of software and use it to pursue my interest in human-computer interaction. I said I would create a world for myself in that environment and stay with it. I was lucky that I picked a programming language, Max, that continues to evolve to this day.

One of my teachers once told me it took seven years to get good at anything. That made sense to me. For some reason people think technology should be easy. My students complain all the time. I show them something, and then the next week they expect to be the world's expert at it, and they're so frustrated that they actually have to spend time with it. This takes as long as anything else does to get good at.

Since you love working with new things, it must be a goal to do something new.

No, not to do something new just for the sake of newness. As I said, I want the end result to be some type of artwork that's really interesting, that has content that needs the technology to work. I actually try to talk my students out of using technology. I'll say something like, "You're writing an interactive piece. Well, can you put this on CD or tape?" If they say yes, I'll say, "Don't make it interactive then. Don't use any more technology than you have to. Don't use technology just because it's there."

Technology is difficult. It doesn't make your life easier. That's a myth. Technology makes it more difficult. Playing a video, a VHS, that's easy. Anybody can do that. Playing video off the computer, that's almost impossible, especially in real time in response to somebody moving. So if I have an idea and my idea could exist equally well in interactive form or on tape, tape's much better, much, much better. I would never choose the interactive form just because I could or because it's new. That would be a waste of my time, and the end result wouldn't be as good. I'm trying to find a reason to use the technology, a reason that's essential, that's required for the project and for the artistic idea. I do hope that the artistic idea is new, but if I had an artistic idea that wasn't new and that I thought was really good and compelling, I would go with it.

18

The Heart, the Head, and the Hand
Passion, Analysis, Production
Tao Ho

When Walter Gropius created the Bauhaus in Dessau in 1919, he identified what he perceived to be an emerging danger to the creative sovereignty of the architect. Unbridled technology would eventually alienate the human heart from the hand. He saw the sacred progression of the design process, which originated with impulses sprung from passion and emotion in the architect's heart and fluidity rendered by the architect's own hand, being irreversibly severed by the advent of mass produced building components. These components were designed independently, without any relation to the particular design problem at hand, and beyond the control of the architect.

Unlike painting and sculpture, architecture is not conceived of and produced by a single person. It is an art form that involves the participation of a team of specialized individuals who are overseen and guided by the architect. Gropius recognized that mass produced building components would undermine the architect's control over design,

235

and he proposed that industrial designers develop components in a way that would be in harmony with architectural design processes.

Today, the widespread misuse of the computer in design poses the most imminent danger to the human artistic process, and threatens to distance the architect further and further from the final product. If a design was originally conceived in the human heart, a computer filters out its passion, intuition, and emotion as it reduces its design to an objective quantity that it can "comprehend" and describe. It cannot distinguish a good design from a bad one.

In Gropius' time, it was not the computer, but mindless production—churning out pre-determined components without any thought to design —that threatened to isolate the architect from the details of buildings. This trend toward isolating the architect from the totality of the building continues when the architect often "loses control" from as early as the conceptual design stage. And since new generation computer draftsmen who lack any sort of design training are often the only ones who know the capabilities and limitations of the computer software, they wield a dangerously large amount of power over the ultimate design. While the architect has traditionally overseen the conceptual design and the detailed drawings as well as supervised on site, he or she usually lacks the skills and knowledge necessary to guide the work of the computer draftsman. Architects are, more than ever, faced with the urgent task of controlling the horizontal and vertical integration of such increasingly isolated roles.

Knowledge versus Wisdom

The way in which human creativity functions is determined by the left/right dichotomy of the structure of the brain. This will never change. Technological advancements will only provide us with ever-changing tools for making creativity manifest in the form of design, or in the worst case, computers will independently generate instant, fascinating illusions that deviously pose as artistic designs which were never conceived in the human mind.

With this foresight, it is important for us not to forget the creative potential within the "software" of the human brain. Jerzy Saltan, the protégé of the great twentieth-century architect Le Corbusier, referred to this function of the creative process when he described Le Corbusier's creative methodology. According to Saltan, all of the technical logistics and functional requirements of Le Corbusier's projects were systematically entered into the storage banks of his brain. These quantitative facts were then scrambled and recombined into an artistic form by means of inspiration, emotion, or intuition. This process is now scientifically understood as the dynamic interplay between the rational left side of the brain and the intuitive right side.

Compare the two diagrams shown on the following page. One represents the divided structure of the human brain, with a fibrous "net" called the Corpus Callosum linking the opposite left and right sides. The other is the ancient Chinese symbol of cosmic harmony. The yin and the yang are polar opposites, not unlike the left and right sides of the brain, in constant harmonic interaction with each other.

The left side of the brain is equivalent to the yang and embodies the "masculine" characteristics of logic, linear thinking, and cause and effect. The right side is equivalent to the yin and supports "feminine" characteristics of human nature such as intuition, holistic thinking, and free association.

The diagram of the left-right dichotomy of the hemispheres of the brain is well known. What is significant to the architect, however, is the process of communication between them—the process that resides in the Corpus Callosum, or "in the net" of the human brain. Without this fibrous communication network, an innovative work of architecture could never be created. Either it would be profoundly beautiful but unable to stand up, or it would be pathetically

plain but very structurally sound. It is the "net" which provides the necessary balance between function and beauty; or between rational knowledge and intuitive wisdom. A human being without a right side to the brain is a cyborg, and the person without a left side is a lunatic. Either way, without balance, you create a monster.

The "intelligence" of the computer is based on its ability to quantify the relationships between things based on their common characteristics. The "wisdom" of the creative mind, on the other hand, is based on its natural ability to contemplate a unifying relationship between entirely unrelated things; to envision inspired links between seemingly disparate phenomena. For example, only the human mind can contemplate the relationship between Chinese cooking and modern music, or illuminate the parallels between Ikebana (Japanese flower arrangement) and graphic design!

The analogy of the computer to the left side of the brain has often been remarked upon. We know the computer can only ever amount to half a human because it has no right hemisphere "brain" function. As the computer begins to take over the design process, architecture will exhibit fewer and fewer signs of authentic creativity and the beauty inspired by intuitive processes. A computerized robot is capable of playing Chopin's "Nocturne" by electronically scanning the score, but it will never sound like Rubinstein.

This is because the computer reads the score as a series of separate, distinct, minute dots of sound. Rubinstein, however, can simultaneously see between, and beyond the dots and transform them into a flowing line of musical feeling that transcends the individual notes into musical expressions. The computer cannot perform the functions of transformation and transcendence which are essential to rendering artistic materials as artistic substance. This will always be an ability unique to human creativity.

If the "net" which gives us balance, and the capacity to interpret and transform, is eroded, then only a tightrope spans the gulf between left and right. Keeping our balance on this tenuous crossing is now more difficult than ever, further challenging the process of artistic creativity.

The Importance of Forgetting

The human brain is carbon-based. Carbon has a weakness, in that things stored within it can get lost. This is commonly called forgetting. The computer brain is silicon-based. It is "superior" to the human model, because it retains everything in its original place forever.

Unlike computer brains, human brains change, develop, deteriorate and forget. This gives us the capacity to think subjectively, to change our opinions, and to forgive. It is the difference between a mechanical brain and a human mind. These are our flaws, and they make us human. They also determine whether our artistic creations will be spiritual, inspirational, and poignant. If we diminish our beautiful capacity to forget and to forgive, to err, and to gauge our surroundings with subjectivity, we render ourselves less human and our designs less personal.

Impact on Thinking

Computers have their own private language based on the simple function of zero (0) and one (1). Point five (.5) does not exist. The very simple and perfectly rational language of the computer allows it to perform mathematical functions with speed and accuracy that is "light years" beyond that of the human brain. This has led to the general perception that the silicon brain is superior to the carbon one. Thus the shortcomings of the human mind are made more evident by comparison. The efficiency of the computer brain mercilessly points out our faulty thinking.

To compensate, we struggle to understand the language of the computer and to pace our lives according to *its* schedule. Thus design becomes dictated by the limited probabilities allowed within its private language. Artificial intelligence now means that instead of computers becoming more human, we become more mechanistic! If we want to work efficiently using computer-generated design, we are forced to speak its rational language. Our human brains are fully capable of doing so, but as we surrender to left hemisphere brain functions, we surrender our natural balance and condition our design process more to its needs than our own.

The yin and yang, as the basis of traditional Chinese philosophy, is also a sort of binary system (see diagram on the right).

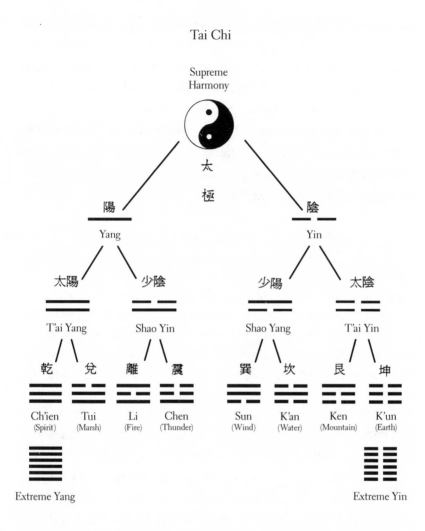

Tai Chi

Supreme
Harmony

太
極

陽
Yang

陰
Yin

太陽
T'ai Yang

少陰
Shao Yin

少陽
Shao Yang

太陰
T'ai Yin

乾
Ch'ien
(Spirit)

兌
Tui
(Marsh)

離
Li
(Fire)

震
Chen
(Thunder)

巽
Sun
(Wind)

坎
K'an
(Water)

艮
Ken
(Mountain)

坤
K'un
(Earth)

Extreme Yang

Extreme Yin

Different combinations of broken and unbroken lines of the two polar opposites yield a total of eight possible combinations. When the lines of both the yin and the yang are doubled, an "extreme" yin and yang are created. Then, different arrangements yield a total of 64 possible variations in between the two extremes. Each of these possibilities is a cosmic archetype that represents the variability and complexity of human situations. Whereas the binary logic of the computer recognizes only an "either-or," or "black and white" understanding of facts, the holistic wisdom of the yin-yang emphasizes the dynamic aspects of all phenomena and the on-going transformation of all things and situations. One might draw parallels to the concept of fuzzy logic. That is, to the undefined, unquantifiable "fuzziness" that exists in different degrees between polar extremes, the possibility of an open-ended "maybe" rather than a definite yes or no. This middle-ground is the sovereign realm of creativity, and it is outside the binary logic of the computer.

High-Tech Software and Low-Tech Hardware

For the architect, the line is alive, the plane has a soul, and the point has a pulse. Although the computer understands these as the fundamental building blocks of architectural form, it can register within them no qualitative distinction. To the computer all points, lines, and planes are created equal, without any subjective value attached to them.

It would be naïve to dream that we could put a halt to the frenzied pace of computer technology. If we still want to be master of our designs, then we also must master the computer. But this will not be achieved by a perpetual game of catching up with the speed of the computer and following its independent, fast-paced development. Instead, we should focus on developing the high-tech software of the human heart, head, and hand in parallel with the high-tech hardware of the computer. The 21st century poses enormous new and formidable challenges to sustainable existence. The foremost challenge of this century, especially for designers, architects, and engineers, is to make a crucial transition from the very high-energy oriented environments of the 20th century to more low-energy oriented ones. We have to learn how to modify our lifestyle and the "hardware" which supports it, not to reduce the quality of life, but

The Sixty-Four Hexagrams

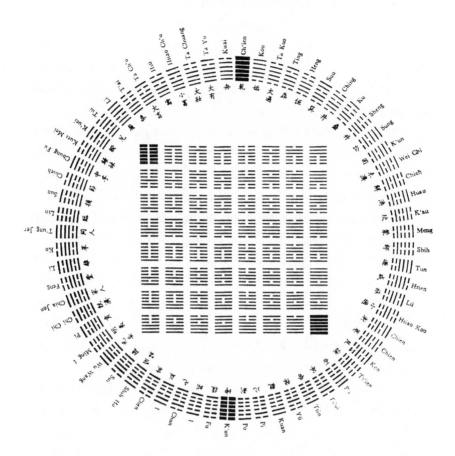

to sustain and even improve it through human advancements that simplify technology rather than complicate it.

The high-tech software of our own creative brains, as masters of the positive advantages of computer technology, should be developed and called upon to change the destructive course of the 20th century. Rather than allowing computer technology to dictate to us and lead us on a course where we lose control of our own destiny, we should "reinvent" the age-old process of creative thinking as the force which guides technology. We will then be able to come full circle, to live in harmony with nature, to return to a low-tech life pattern without sacrificing a high quality of comfort and aesthetics in architecture. The ecological and energy crisis that we inevitably must face will only be resolved through a holistic response that reunites Heaven, Earth, and Man as one entity, mastering technology for the sake of the future.

At the turn of the 20th century, long before the invention of the computer, or even the calculator, Einstein relied on the high-tech software of his own intuition to formulate his Theory of Relativity. There is no limit to what humanity can conceive of, and achieve, if we can liberate ourselves from the stifling constraints of computer intelligence. If Einstein had been relying on the "intelligence" of the computer, he might have mistrusted the high-tech software of his own mind and set aside the clarity and low-tech simplicity of his slide rule and chalk board (or he could have just as easily used an abacus and Chinese brush!). He did not require a computer to envision $E = mc^2$. Sustainable solutions to very real problems will only come about with a return to a faith in human intelligence.

Technology is inevitable, but let's not mistake it for God. If yin represents humanity at one extreme and yang technology at the other, then a strong and lasting balance can be achieved between them. It would be a mistake to continue to feed the "monster" while starving the creative potential of the human heart.

19

The Writer's Dubious Friends
John Barnie

In our culture the writer has many enemies masquerading as friends, who stand on the sidelines dealing out advice, courting the writer's attention, and feeding off his work for their own ends. Because writing is a lonely and isolating occupation it is easy to be seduced by the blandishments or diktats of these enemy-friends, but the writer needs above all to preserve his loneliness, that inner space where the creative act occurs which has no predetermined purpose.

William Faulkner summed up his life as a writer in his Nobel Prize acceptance speech in 1949. It had been, he said, "a life's work in the agony and sweat of the human spirit, not for glory and least of all for profit, but to create out of the materials of the human spirit something which did not exist before." I'd add to that, as a definition of what the writer is about, a line from Harry Martinson's *Aniara,* where the poems of a blind poetess are described as having their origin in "the human spirit's play with the soul of language."

This is not enough, however, for the false friends who want to

This essay is reprinted with permission from *Planet: The Welsh Internationalist* 144 (December 2000–January 2001).

use the writer and his art for their own purposes. A particularly destructive form of this is to be found among political ideologues of
the socialist and nationalist left who harangue writers to take a political stand in their work. It is exemplified in a quote from Lenin
used as the motto of the 1934 All-Russia Writers Conference: "The
writer is the engineer of the human spirit." Nearer home it is there
in Harri Webb's hectoring "Advice to a Young Poet" which, in full,
reads:

> Sing for Wales or shut your trap—
> All the rest's a load of crap.

Webb took his own advice. Beginning as a minor poet who produced two interesting volumes, he ended up as a bar-room ballad-
eer, the purveyor of beer-mug-thumping doggerel—because what
came to matter to him was the political message made simple and
popular.

Literary reputations are created, for a while, out of such rigidity
and over-simplification, the question of artistic achievement fudged
or avoided by critics who share the same political ideology as the
writer. Only in this way could the mediocre novels of Lewis Jones
be taken seriously in English departments at colleges in Wales. The
ideology, the working-class engagement in the fiction, have to be
seen as sufficient in themselves. But couldn't Faulkner's account of
his life as a writer also hold true for Jones? The answer is no—because Lewis Jones's main interest in the novel was its usefulness as
a vehicle for political purposes. He was not interested in creating
"out of the materials of the human spirit something which did not
exist before," but in using preexisting novelistic structures and conventions to clothe an idea and predispose his readers to a specific,
communist course of action. From the outset Jones wrote because
he had designs on the reader in a way that Faulkner did not.

English departments have proved increasingly attractive to
writers in the past fifty years, but they are dangerous places har-

bouring other kinds of false friends. Leaving aside the postmodernists who deny with a shrug that there are or can be such things as critical or aesthetic standards, who have proclaimed the "death" of the author, and have reduced the living poem or novel to something called the "text," the temptation for the writer is to see the university as a promising haven, a source of regular income in the form of a visiting professorship or residency. Often this will seem to involve little: a few lectures, readings, a creative writing class or two, with time freed up for writing. But this seductive package also holds the seeds of destructiveness for the writer, who is expected to perform, to discourse on "the creative process," to talk about and analyse his own work for student audiences. A writer, in his professional life, has to develop a finely tuned critical attention to what he writes, but he needs to do this from within, in a way that is intuitive rather than analytical; it is not necessarily even verbalized.

This isn't enough in an academic context, however. Faced with a postgraduate creative writing group consisting often of highly intelligent, articulate students, the pressure and temptation is to become an explainer of the creative process, the analyst of one's own writing from the outside, taking on the role of the professional critic or theoretician of aesthetics. For the writer this is almost always disastrous. With time, he creates a facsimile of himself as "writer," which he reproduces for public consumption; he becomes the adept who, in interviews and lectures, retells the same stories again and again, until they become what he is; and he is locked out from the private space within, his deeper creative identity. The writer as self-parodist, who can no longer write in an exciting way that even interests himself but produces endless simulacra of those past achievements for which he was first acclaimed, is a familiar figure today on the university circuits.

The fate of the writer as academic is akin to that of the writer as media star. If a writer has a London agent and a big-time publisher, he will be under pressure to perform, to get talked about in the press and on television, because being in the public eye helps sell books. The writer can see this too, looking around at his contemporaries, the ones who have "made it" and the ones who haven't. The temptation is to believe that it "doesn't matter," that he only has to do this for the duration of the book promotion, that signings across the country are fine, and chat show appearances—that any publicity is "good" publicity.

For those who depend on the productions of the writer in the publishing business this is true. But the media—including, in Britain, the broadsheet press—have only an ephemeral interest in literature. They are much more engrossed by literary gossip, the writer as sensationalist material. To cash in on this, the writer must be prepared to become the tool of the media professionals, to have his identity distorted, even created for him, in ways over which he has little control. This may sell books on a big scale if the cards fall right, but it creates out of the writer yet another engorged monster for public entertainment.

This is not a particular problem in English-speaking Wales, where poetry and most serious fiction are ignored by the media. Its destructive influence can be seen, however, in the press's obsession with the life of Dylan Thomas, almost half a century after his death. Tales of his chaotic, destructive existence are endlessly recycled by the Welsh papers, while the poetry, which is the only thing that gives his life any interest at all, is ignored. This media-projected "life" is like a rotting carcass chained to the poems.

In the technological, consumerist, profit-driven world we live in, we need great poetry and fiction more than ever, even when we don't know it; but it is the art we need, not the artist. Read the poetry and the novels, but leave the writer alone. Leave him out of the world of calculation and gossip. R. S. Thomas understood this better than most. He never held a creative writing fellowship and rarely lectured or discussed his poetry in public; his readings were minimalist and austere, keeping his audience at arm's length. In this way he reserved his privacy, the necessary creative space out of which the poems came.

There's a late poem by Robinson Jeffers that expresses it well, "Let Them Alone":

> If God has been good enough to give you a poet
> Then listen to him. But for God's sake let him alone until he is dead;
> no prizes, no ceremony,
> They kill the man. A poet is one who listens
> To nature and his own heart; and if the noise of the world grows up
> around him, and if he is tough enough,
> He can shake off his enemies but not his friends.
> That is what withered Wordsworth and muffled Tennyson, and would
> have killed Keats; that is what makes
> Hemingway play the fool and Faulkner forget his art.

Jeffers guarded that essential inner privacy with even greater tenacity than R. S. Thomas. He had a sign outside Tor House on the cliffs at Carmel. It read: NOT AT HOME.

20

Why Is It Easy to Be Creative?
An Interview with Gerd Binnig

Gunna Wendt-Rohrbach

What is creativity?

Creativity is a property of nature, although it was originally defined differently. The Brockhaus dictionary has a definition that only refers to humans. But it's clear that all of nature is highly creative. For example, it produced us humans, and that's certainly fantastic. We have not yet been in the position to achieve something of equal magnitude. What sort of mechanisms exist in nature that can produce such things? Do these powers have something in common with what we humans use to be creative? I have come to the conclusion that these two things are very closely related, that nature does indeed think—or something close to it—that it is in a way creative, and that humankind has too high an opinion of its own creativity. Human creativity is actually something very natural and simple.

Is human creativity an imitation of nature?

An imitation and a continuation. I don't think it is humanly possible to do anything else. For the creation of something new, there are good mechanisms, which nature has already discovered and implemented. They are simply the best mechanisms for evolution in a very general sense. People have rediscovered them for the evolution of intelligence.

What does it mean when you say creativity is the ability to evolve?

Everything we know originated at some point. It started billions of years ago. Life itself first formed out of a natural development, from an evolution. Making something new according to a specific mechanism is a creative act. We create new things with our brains, with our thought structures. These thought structures had to originate at some point, too. They have not always been here; they did not yet exist at the moment life formed in the world; they had to develop first, just like life or matter. We can assume that all these things have developed in accordance with similar criteria. I even think that the mechanisms through which they developed are virtually identical.

Can creativity be learned? Is it fostered in everyday life, or in science?

I firmly believe that creativity can be learned! Not that you can suddenly go from being an uncreative person to being a creative person by taking a one-week course. It's a very long process. Everything you should be able to do has to have been practiced for years, ideally since childhood. Infants and small children learn creatively. Maybe we got out of practice in school, at least in part, because there we have to absorb more things than these creative mechanisms can handle, since they were intended for dealing with things playfully. At this time, our creativity is put last, which is really sad. But later, when we are involved in a career—depending on what the career is—we must suddenly be creative. Certain career choices give you no choice but to be creative, and then perhaps you relearn it.

Isn't room to make mistakes a prerequisite for creativity?

Yes, creativity needs to have a protective space. If you are stuck in an everyday business in which your main objective is raw survival, then creativity is probably stifled. But business structures are designed in such a way that they provide protective spaces for some people. These people are expected to be particularly creative. There are creativity specialists who are granted this kind of protected space, which not everyone is allowed to enjoy.

Doesn't that mainly happen in artistic professions?

No, I don't see it that way. Certainly artistic professions lean in this direction. But even in art, there is a lot that is purely technical and superficial. The same is true of science. The percentage of science that is creative is about the same as the percentage for art—but artists claim theirs is higher, although I can't find that this is really so. Maybe it was originally different, but so much art is produced today that it is very difficult to always create something original. A lot of it is simply copied.

How does competition affect creativity?

Scientists are not always creative—they also perform everyday duties, and they compete with each other. This competition is not always directed toward productive results in the long term. It's often a matter of who will be the first to reach a specific result in the next few weeks. Of course, this stifles creativity, since any kind of creative development requires time. You need a long preparation time. You need this protective space in which everything can unfold. Certainly artists are granted that more than scientists. But even in universities, this kind of climate should prevail. Research is not a one-year business—it needs time. In the meantime, this attitude has been gaining acceptance.

Can you be creative alone, or is some type of dialogue necessary?

To answer that, I have to introduce the image of fractal Darwinism or fractal interactions. The term "fractal" is very important. It's relatively easy to explain. I see that the world is broken down into units. A picture is one unit. You can't buy a piece of a picture; you don't see just a section of the picture, you see the whole thing. And we, as humans, can see ourselves as units. We differentiate ourselves from the environment, we have a skin, and we also differentiate ourselves mentally. Two tigers approaching each another maintain a certain distance. All the units you see in the world interact with each other and mutually change one another. Evolution takes place, creative things happen. It's interesting that each unit is composed of subunits, and that this goes on ad infinitum. A human is composed of organs, the organs are made of cells, the cells from macromolecules, the macromolecules from smaller molecules, which are made from atoms, and the atoms are made from elementary particles. You do eventually reach an end, because we don't know how it continues. You have to have this picture in your head to be able to discuss creativity. All these units, regardless of whether they are large or small, are creative. Each of these elements is embedded in an environment, in a larger unit. If I think of myself as a creative person, I have to understand that I am embedded in a creative unit. The next-higher unit could be my research team. If this research team is uncreative, it will probably be very hard for me to be creative as an individual. We affect one another; we mutually stimulate each other. If someone were to repeatedly say to me: "Why don't you just quit trying to pursue these crazy ideas of yours?" then that would be a very uncreative situation. When every new idea is struck down—which is actually the case in some research teams—the individual can't be creative. Any unit that wants to be creative must be embedded in a greater unit that also wants to be creative, which must be embedded in a still-larger unit that wants to be creative.

Is this an unconscious process?

I believe all of this works more or less unconsciously, and that we have learned since we were very young to function like this. A child doesn't generally play by himself all alone—he has playmates, so he learns this kind of group creativity.

What reasons are there not to be creative?

There are bad reasons not to be creative, and there are good ones. Very often there are simple misunderstandings. You think that if you make a mistake, everyone will react violently to it. Why don't we give it a try? What happens if I allow myself to make mistakes? And I have to give myself this license in order to be creative! Over time, you develop a feeling for which areas you need to be cautious in and avoid mistakes as much as possible, and in which areas play, and with it the freedom to make mistakes, is downright necessary. I think simply not wanting to make mistakes, even on the playing field of society, is a bad reason for not being creative. If you make a mistake there, people cope with it. You must find out for yourself how many mistakes you can cope with psychologically. This in turn must be seen in terms of fractals. The group and larger group of which it is a part must also come to terms with it.

Is that what you call the ability to make a fool of oneself?

Yes, this ability to make a fool of yourself can be cultivated, and I find that you *should* cultivate it. It is an art you can learn through daily practice, whereby you observe what happens if you really disgrace yourself. This happens a whole lot less than you imagine in your fantasies. However, there are really good reasons not to be creative. Society consists of two elements: it develops, it evolves, it is receptive to what is new. But it also has a conservative element. We have to build on something. We need something tangible. This causes us to be disapproving of new things. You can feel this very strongly when you try to be creative. Nobody listens, or they censure you, and you have to be able to endure this. If you say, that's too much for me, then I would say that that is a good reason not to be creative. You have to decide for yourself how much you can put up with. To try to be something you aren't and let it destroy you is senseless.

Does being creative also mean making yourself vulnerable?

Yes, you have to develop an inner philosophy to be able to live with this vulnerability. You have to create a worldview for yourself in which this vulnerability is a component. You have to perceive that vulnerability is something positive.

What does intelligence have to do with creativity?

Creativity belongs to intelligence. It is a subfield of intelligence. Intelligence encompasses everything that has to do with our understanding, with our brain. Creativity is a part of this. The aspect of creativity is very noticeably excluded in intelligence tests. Spatial powers of imagination are tested, and how well you can associate certain things with one another. But there is a little more to creativity than that. It involves being able to develop something step by step. You must not only recognize a pattern, but be able to change it. Someone who is a market analyst must not limit himself to simply recognizing the situation. He must also be able to project the future. He must be able to imagine how development would continue, and he must try to make his own contribution to it. He must be an active part of changing these structures, otherwise he's only running along behind.

In your book, you name the creative stages of your life. They are all situations in which you decided to swim against the current. Does the creative moment lie in having made your own decision?

Isolation can be an important part of creativity. Isolation—that is, going your own way, differentiating yourself from other things. This has something to do with loneliness. When you take a creative path, it is usually a lonely path. You do things differently from others. No one goes with you. It is a lonely way, but it is the only way you can go. When I go with the masses, I might feel secure, but I am also miserable; I feel violated, because I am not going my own way. It is always a mixture, a trade-off, the old conflict: security or adventure. It is a balancing out between an individual road and one traveled by everybody else.

21

Ora et Labora
Seven Non-Benedictine Rules on Human Rights Regarding Idleness with an Introduction about Two Heroes of Vigilance

Jürgen Werner

Aristotle was an advocate of leisure as essential to the ability to think creatively; it is said that he also needed very little sleep. When he was tired, all he had to do was lie down and rest for a few moments. To prevent dozing too long, he usually held an iron ball in his hand, which would drop into a bowl as soon as he reached an unconscious state and his body tension relaxed. The clatter would wake him. The amount of time it took for the object to fall was just enough to refresh the philosopher.

Even if fictional, this story is plausible and fits very well in a series of anecdotes compiled by Diogenes Laertius, the collector of legends and biographies of Greek philosophers. Laertius documented the life of Aristotle, whom the intellectual heavyweights of the West portray as a man who could not afford a long-term state of "insensitivity" because of the magnitude of his duties. In his writings on the soul and on sleep, Aristotle asserted that being awake represented the resolution and release of the power of sensitivity; in contrast, sleep blocks and paralyzes the talent of perception.

Whoever sleeps turns his back on the world. In the meantime, if the world doesn't stab him in the back, he shouldn't be surprised that he experiences nothing. From time immemorial, sleep has been a metaphor for a lack of curiosity, even lifelessness. People like Aristotle who have made enormous discoveries in the history of intellect and who have had a significant effect on political self-understanding, the exploration of nature, or the development of all core areas of culture, ethics, and aesthetics—such people became the subject of stories that portray them as proponents of vigilance. When entire generations of decisive thought can be attributed to a single person, we have to be able to find special characteristics in the life of this person as proof of a fruitful breeding ground in which these ideas could bloom and flourish. We want to uncover the mystery of their thoughts, discover the laws of innovation; and as an example of "intense vigilance" we find nothing more than the existence of "microsleep." That which is new appears whenever people afford themselves the luxury of constantly being on guard. This is the simple point of the story of the tireless philosopher.

Vigilance has long been a characteristic of leaders. Those who had to catch a few winks could trust others to watch in their place. Leadership meant seeing things earlier than others and, even more importantly, being able to interpret what had been seen. The only thing missing was someone with vision sharp enough to interpret the world in a way that made it accessible to everyone as long as one took into account certain lines of thought. There was no question that this leader would have to be capable of telling others what he saw in a way that others could hear his message and understand what they had heard. It is this quality that made Aristotle famous for more than a millennium. He was the founder of a tradition of absent-minded certainty. It was no longer necessary to look at nature to know what it had to do with the world; it was enough to read about it in books, and later—after Christ—in the book of books. Anyone who understood the eternal laws could no longer be surprised.

Nothing is as tiring as always having to look at the same thing. A world that is presented as the established order because it has been thoroughly examined once and for all doesn't merit any extra attention. The need to ignore all factors relating to uncertainty and to force life's unpredictabilities into some sort of much-needed structure, whether in regard to the dictates of common sense or laws of divine creation as they were postulated by the Roman Catholic Church, moderated the latent horrors of the world. From this point on, what were regarded as irritating phenomena could always be explained, from a volcanic eruption to a cloudburst. We were only free from worry if there was nothing new under the sun. However, the beauty of this well-ordered cosmos was neither something against which we again had to close our eyes, because we could not bear what it showed, nor was it something which required our eyes to be opened wide in amazement because we could not take it all in. Rather, the world as an eternal creation from which one does not flee was not fascinating; it was a place of well-tended boredom.

Then someone decided leisure was valuable, which gave rise to idleness, at least among those who could afford it. Included in this group were the monks of the Middle Ages. Many of them suffered from having too much time on their hands. The quiet contemplation of the eternal order of the world and its unchanging ruler ended all too often in the sudden appearance of apparently incurable sadness. This paralyzing condition, for which there is no obvious cause, is called *acedia,* a particular type of melancholy, the experience of emptiness in a universe created by the Divine. It was considered a fatal sacrilege and undermined the foundations of monastic existence. While there is no fear when nothing new is anticipated, the abyss of nothingness becomes a tempting prospect. The leisure still celebrated by Plato and Aristotle as an attitude of the free citizens of the *polis* regarding the circumstances of their lives, and which they acclaimed as a prerequisite for the happiness of being creative in the knowledge of the essential, had become habitual, and was therefore dangerous. "Idleness is an enemy of the soul; therefore, the Brothers should alternate between physical labor and religious activities," thus states the first sentence of chapter 48 of the Rules of St. Benedict of Nursia. This particular passage of the monk's orders became famous with the formula "ora et labora." Accordingly, the rhythm of life requires us to vary our activities now and then.

To speak of Aristotle and St. Benedict of Nursia is to remember the two individuals who characterized the nature and the relationship of work and leisure perhaps more than anyone else in the social and intellectual history of Europe. As influential theorists, they symbolize the boundaries within which practical and purposeful actions are evaluated between such emotions as happiness or sadness, and intellectual motivations, such as curiosity or boredom. It all comes down to recognizing a basic form of behavior—for Aristotle, the interruption of whatever is usual, and for St. Benedict, whatever is habitual—that allows adequate space for leisure, thereby providing space for creative rest. But of course, the reception of the anecdote about "microsleep" makes the difference between the two very clear. Whereas Aristotle created a caesura that once and for all put those contemporaries capable of reflection—the philosophers —in a position to passionately devote themselves to the problems of the world, St. Benedict proclaimed a regular beat in the tempo of life's progress. Only this rhythm can transform idleness into leisure, which had been the original objective. Aristotle set tension in the contents and required uniformity in the circumstances, so that he consequently regarded the central question as "Which activities should fill up leisure time?" In contrast, Benedict required an alternation of external conditions in order not to endanger the eagerness for the one fundamental pursuit of monastic life—the contemplation of divine truth—and to increase concentration. The rule turned out to be an ordering of time that advanced vigilance.

What do these notes on two general presentations of the European tradition of leisure have to do with the question of how new things are introduced in the world? The answer is clear: vigilance is a way of looking at the world that isn't necessarily present just because one doesn't sleep. This view is nowhere more relevant than in periods of accelerated change. In accord with this line of thought, the dramatic present-day restructuring in the economy and society doesn't require "fully rested" contemporaries—as particularly attentive people were referred to until recently—as much as it does "wide-awake" partisans in the competition for social, political, intellectual, and economic survival. The metaphor of "being awake" steers the attention back to the essential: the ability to allow oneself to be interrupted. Hence, the evocation of Aristotle and Benedict in this context is governed by one intent: the talent for leisure should be conceived as an extremely hard encroachment into the normal activity of life and particularly work that is linked to a demanding task. Those who see leisure as a precondition for the discovery of something new are at first startled—because in the face of any creative activity we have to be disturbed in our well-ordered world of habits. Nothing impedes innovation as persistently and thoughtlessly as those efforts, so often pursued in the name of effectiveness, to remain as free from irritants as possible.

The following theses aim precisely at presenting the art of letting oneself be interrupted effectively as the necessary precondition that makes innovation possible. They are modern variations on the Benedictine formula of "ora et labora," which connects every form of concentration to this successful alternation and which presents a quiet but critical reaction to the Platonic and Aristotelian view that only those of us who are relatively free of everyday obligations can explore the great questions creatively. We may perhaps read them

as a corrective annotation to the social and political maxim according to which the programmatic lack of idleness is cultivated to the
degree that the right to freedom is a legal right. The cynicism of the
words from the "collective recreation park" would perhaps be more
on target if it were mirrored less in the immense unemployment
figures than in the countless overinflated options that help people to
kill time and that constitute the response of a society that doesn't
know what to do with itself.

Interruptions are disturbing. But do they not also destroy intense vigilance when they intrude? *First rule: That which is new
appears in the world when tensions provoke it. Creativity is consistently the result of a provocation of the habitual, the result of a successful disturbance. As a formula for the extent and amount of
work, the Benedictine "ora et labora" also defines the limits of leisure. Not every interruption serves to relieve daily activity or confront idleness with content.*

No word contains more indefiniteness, more freedom from obligation, than the small copula "and." Things that don't necessarily
have anything to do with each other are connected to each other in
a relationship by these three letters, without anything having to be
said about what kind of relationship it is. There is justification for
doubting whether prayer and work are related to each other, even
though long after the formulation of the central Benedictine theme
Thomas Carlyle pronounced their connection to be an identity: "To
work is to pray," he said (cited in Pieper), thereby imbuing product-
oriented pursuits with a connotation that was unflattering to any
businessman engaged in them. Indeed, the "and" leads to such ex-
aggerations, just as it leaves undecided whether leisure and goal-
oriented activity in this motto are anything more than two extremes
forced together. As an intermediate element, "and" only signals that
there is obviously something that limits work, and conversely protects the time for quiet contemplation, ideas, and creative rest from

extravagances. It translates equally as promise and obligation: a rest is prescribed for every goal-directed activity; every thought that goes beyond the status quo must be measured against the realities we imaginatively seek to expand. He who is oriented to "ora et labora" is free of the compulsion to overwork, since fixed periods of interruption are prescribed, and at the same, he has a standard by which to measure the reality factor of his discoveries or inventions.

When he captured the rule in writing, Benedict wanted to add a this-worldly note to his monks' prayers directed toward heaven. He therefore developed a litmus text for measuring the quality of thoughts that are not directed to what is, but rather strive toward what should or could be. Content was less of a determinant of value, of innovation. The forced rhythm intended to disturb work or interrupt meditation was much more decisive, because the constant, almost methodical, forced irritation increases the strength of our endeavors at least to maintain achievements from one field to another, even if it isn't enriched by the tension and the distance from its origin. Regular interruption is a guarantee of being able to achieve on a high level.

The conquest of uselessness is one of the greatest dangers to the creative person, because wastefulness is always a part of creativity. We must play in order to bump into something new; we must vary, try out, and change. The nonspecific, self-satisfying exploration of ideas must not be restricted at the outset. Aimless wandering with no specified goals is a part of change, discovery, and invention. Activities that appear to be completely pointless when judged by innovations that have actually been achieved—like running, showering, eating, driving a car, dawdling, or sleeping—in retrospect turn out to be catalysts for the creative process. However, it is important that we not lose ourselves on these detours. The Benedictine "ora et labora" as the guiding rule for rhythmic interruption of any course of action in life can help prevent this. Unlike the Aristotelian demand to define the content of leisure according to qualitative criteria, "ora et labora" leaves the issue of what should fill up leisure time wide open, aside from its unique perspective of monastic meditation. But it regulates daily life very precisely, and coerces compliance with the two needs—rummaging and wandering, and strictness—through the planning structure alone. We must always return from periods of inquiry along the detours back to the mainstream, and inversely, those who cling too tightly to methodical guidelines must be coerced to stray.

Benedict's rule is an attempt to strengthen the will to moderation without aspiring to mediocrity. His prescripts for a balanced way of life do not reckon with a well-balanced personality. This makes them a provocative motivational principle to guide the innovation process, because nothing is more foreign to the creative person than harmony among the psychological, intellectual, or social contradictions that characterize him. He stretches the tension that is a source of his richness of ideas to its extremes. He can do this because he isn't as aware of the conflict as he is of the power to unite inside himself whatever is different. "Ora et labora," as a formula for the desire for regularized interruption, means that we must carry contradiction as far as we can without weakening either of its poles if we want to find something new. The dynamic of being able to maintain extremely different positions without becoming unbalanced or splitting apart is usually called spirit. Hence, Benedict's recommendation has to do with to the spiritual prerequisite of the innovation process.

It is stressful to maintain divergent motivations. We generally tend to reconcile them quickly. In this way, leisure is justified as the need to relax, maintain functional efficiency, or to better complete a stage of thought—hence, it is legitimized with arguments borrowed from the realm of rational purposes. And the work that makes its home there is portrayed as imparting meaning, liberating, or fulfilling

—endowed with characteristics that describe leisure. But leisure never exists for the sake of working, however much strength we gain from it. It is a life form in its own right. And in no way does work occasionally represent a special form of creative rest, although it can certainly lend meaning and satisfaction to existence. "Leisure is not justified as keeping the official as free from disturbances and deficits as possible; the important thing is that it keeps the official human" (Pieper). We find new things only if leisure does not degenerate into being the method of the innovation process.

■

Being able to live a human existence humanely means appreciating the ability to think and act creatively as a gift that requires patience; hence, the *second rule states: That which is new appears in the world when time is devoted to it. Creativity is always a compensation for boredom. The Benedictine "ora et labora" prevents leisure from turning a slow pace into a fixed attitude and gives the fast pace of life a resourceful rhythm.*

Many are quick with a reference to a slow pace being prerequisite for innovative thought today. This is the mirror image of an experience of time that oscillates between hectic and boredom, and uses the change in tempo as a tensile test. Since it is no longer a matter of many things being possible for modern humans, but rather of everything being possible for them, their sense of reality is stunted. Who should decide what is really important when in one night the stock market crashes in Tokyo, Boris Becker wins the U.S. Open in New York, between two and five o'clock the telephone rates are so low that you can dial in through the Internet, and the neighbor's apartment is being broken into? When the Döner Kebab and the Big Mac are jockeying for the first-place position among the favorite foods of the German people, the Catholic Church and the Jewish community both have their headquarters on the same street, and Le Corbusier chairs, Chinese vases, and desk lamps by top Italian designers are grouped together in one house? When no more true adventures beckon because acquaintances have long since traveled paths that are still foreign to us and told us about their experiences, so that we can only take refuge in a fantasy trip from which we have to return in time for our "regularly scheduled program"?

Boredom always settles in where the appreciation of value has been lost. To the extent that we are lacking in the judgment to differentiate between fundamental and urgent, or useful and necessary, time loses the ability to let us experience anything special. Boredom is the loss of value in terms of the conditions of time. If we could have everything and if we could be many different things, it no longer matters whether it happens now, later, or not at all. The "now or never," the emphasis of the decisive moment, is unknown to boredom. Because boredom is resistant to enthusiasm, it is very dangerous for the development of anything new; innovations only appear when we allow ourselves to be fascinated.

Nevertheless, boredom has contributed a great deal to the history of innovation. Idleness was never the source just of all vices, but it was often the source of a labor revolution. When the desire to experience has not yet been completely paralyzed, it has always been victorious and has even used boredom as an adversary to work against.

There are two key moments in which boredom affects us: when not enough is asked of us, or when too much is asked. Either way, we react with weariness. The first type of monotony is evident when our field of activity is much smaller than our potential ability. We need to vent the frustration we feel from the surplus possibilities we can't use. Appropriate incentive is needed here to better exhaust this excess of ability; it often leads us to imagine a wealth of new thoughts. The other type of dullness appears in conjunction with the unremitting necessity of having to decide anew. When nothing more is firm, when everything is at our disposal, we either leave things as they were or lose our orientation and succumb to the ultimately numbing delusion that we must try as many things as possible from the special offers of the "Supermarket of Kicks and Thrills." And there is no appetite for life.

■

"Ora et labora" makes a case for withstanding monotony and conveys the power to do so. It is a rule of moderation that effectively stems the naturally limitless phenomena that accompany creativity. If the Benedictine formula is followed, the readiness of potentially creative people to be diverted transforms into attentiveness. And monotony gains a broader horizon. However, that is the subject of the *third rule: That which is new appears in the world whenever space is made available for it. Creativity is always a result of intensified presence and can thrive if a space is created in which attentiveness can expand. The Benedictine "ora et labora" represents the minimal routine, the free space, as something which must be fought for at every turn.*

Laziness is not given to us. Paul Lafargue, Karl Marx's son-in-law, realized that, and used satire to criticize social relationships. How much greater the effort is to occupy a territory which is undisturbed by everyday demands, and which is scarcely won through one's not working. It is no coincidence that for a long time, the word for "work" reflected the negation of the contemplative life, not the inverse. Both the Greek *a-scholia* and the Latin *neg-otium,* meaning leisure, show how radically situations have changed. For the Greeks and in the Latin Middle Ages, work was still regarded as a human behavior that was separate from the condition of creative rest; contemplation, the consideration of the beautiful cosmos, was always the highest state of being. The situation is exactly reversed under present-day conditions: anyone who claims the right to leisure must reckon with the accusation of idleness.

It is the increased awareness of life that appears in leisure and that, in the discovery of new things and the exercise of our own creative powers, sets itself up as a desire to be part of something bigger, which tells us how our priorities must be arranged. Our creative dispositions are easy to hide or, in the worst case, to destroy. How much more worrisome it must be to develop them in times in which there is little space available for them. Creativity is more than individual ability. It grows from the systematic interplay of psychological readiness, social demands, economic incentives, intellectual talents, and a series of conditions that promote attentiveness. Most importantly, these include the desire to interrupt much of what routinely happens around us. Not until we begin to ask in places where answers have long since been exhaustive, to disrupt where solutions have become routine, to cut away where methods have been legitimized—not until then will we again be able to look up, listen, and take notice.

Vigilance is something that I must make a conscious decision about. It is an act of release from spaces in life that are occupied by the best-introduced and well-coordinated conventions and compromises. To open them again means to push the degree of attentiveness over the degree that is necessary for immediately coming to terms with daily activities. If we want to find something new, we must fully deal with our faculties of perception. Centers of creativity have always enjoyed a surplus of attentiveness: the schools of Athens in the fifth century and those in Florence in the fifteenth century, convents, cafés, Silicon Valley, or the Max Planck Institute. This has to do with the power that must be expended in order to develop new ideas. Neither in places where no effort is required, nor where it is constantly required, does innovation find just the right field of tension in which it can flourish.

It can again be seen how cleverly Benedict's rule is designed and how beneficial its plea for the proper measure is for the resourcefulness of the creative processes. As a maxim that stipulates no content, it corresponds to the creative process, which is neither caused nor made. New thoughts aren't developed the way new products are. No blueprints or demand profiles exist for them. The one thing that can be done with great effect is to reduce disruptive factors that deny attentiveness more than sufficient space. It all depends on the switch between wandering attentiveness and concentration on one thing, on handling a situation in such a way that it retains richness and doesn't lose depth, and in spite of all composure possesses enough enticement for variation.

Space and time are usually the most severely restricted. They are usually enclosed in a web of numbers that traps our attention in many respects. Schedules that are specified by precise times and locations characterize the organization of a world that increasingly withdraws its consciousness of perception in this way. But where processes are predefined, we lose track of anything that is new. Nothing surprising is ever encountered on the beaten path. As long as we only hurry routinely from one appointment to the next in the course of work, get through meetings as though we were on autopilot, and meet deadlines that almost bring our calendars to the point of exploding, we must admit that we are not responsible for our actions in the killing of creative potential, even if we are occasionally inclined to assume that the acts were intentional.

■

Time and space grids replace orientation and create firmly established models. Strictly followed, they impede innovation because—*fourth rule: That which is new appears in the world where orientation becomes questionable. Creativity is an act of reevaluating old values. The Benedictine "ora et labora" compels us to a*

continual reevaluation of our own thoughts and actions and re-
minds us of a proven tradition. It makes the crisis permanent with-
out letting it get out of hand.

When Ernst Curtius, director of the excavations in Olympia, was asked by William I during one of the renowned Friday night circles what was new from Olympia, the scholar was momentarily confused. He couldn't tell the emperor that the south wall of Myron's treasury had just been discovered and that several inscriptions had been found at the Leonidaion. So he deliberated and replied, "Does Your Majesty know what was old?" (Burckhardt).

Each innovation has an ambivalent relationship to tradition. Whether something is seen as new is determined mainly by what is considered current. Only when an idea or discovery is powerful enough to replace existing paradigms does it deserve to be called innovative. Even though it is the view of the old that first qualifies anything as new, it doesn't owe anything to this distinction: fresh thoughts, trends, revolutionary discoveries very often cause earlier things to be forgotten. Insofar as that which is new condemns its predecessor as old, a judgment is passed on it. The old is old because it has not had the power to survive. The old is always yesterday's new thing.

But that which is new is also always the old of tomorrow. It carries the reminders of temporariness with it, which manifest themselves in the paradox of that which is new standing on the foundation of the old. So there is nothing more grotesque than the cult around that which is new, which peaks in the belief that it is simultaneously the first, the last, and the ultimate. Seasonal fashions repeat this ritual every six months. Not because something is new, but rather because it is valuable—for an individual, an institution, or a society—does it count as innovation. In the demand to let creative thoughts to be tested through activity and vice versa, "ora et labora" is able to be a methodical criterion to not glorify a discovery too quickly. Not until its significance is known does the creative process flow into an innovation. "Innovation is therefore a reevaluation of values, a change of the position of individual things in regard to value limits" (Groys, p. 66). It is leisure, with its sense of the whole, that directs such shifts and transfers of meaning. Any innovation that deserves to be called as such, brings about a reorientation.

■

Reorientations often answer the unsolved problems of a past value hierarchy. They provide answers and pose questions never before conceived of. Hence, the *fifth rule: That which is new appears in the world where it is permissible for us not to have to answer all the urgent questions. Creativity thrives best in areas protected from questions. The Benedictine "ora et labora" advises those who follow it to find detours when the existing paths become too easy and too quickly accessible.*

There is a bias among the leaders of modern industry and in the workings of the community of intellectuals. It is crucial, they claim, that questions be answered directly, problems solved immediately, and needs satisfied quickly. This model of purpose-oriented thought is borrowed from natural processes, whose law can be formulated in a typical and ideal sense as follows: reaction follows on the heels of stimulus. This has a very positive connotation, since this is how life functions are maintained and how a diversity of forms is guaranteed.

However, human beings are characterized by having the option of delaying their response, of not replying suddenly. We can allow ourselves to do something "instead." Instead of dwelling on the meaning of the question about newness for the role of thought in life, we can interrupt the discussion, break it off. Since we are relatively free of the stimulus-reaction mechanism, we are in a position to withdraw from apparently urgent needs for good reasons. To put it another way, the human being is a hesitant being, a creature for whom hesitancy is essential. The human being waits, observes, and considers. This would be fatal in a truly natural state, or at least highly dangerous, as the fight or flight response applies, and abstention would be mercilessly punished. So how does it happen that such an indecisive creature has survived in the battle for existence?

Given that humankind is prone to hesitation and reflection, over time we have apparently developed abilities that have ensured our continued existence. Everything that characterizes humans originates from this waiting space—tools, language, logic, fantasy—in short, human culture. Culture only originates if we are patient. It results from the renunciation of quick answers, immediate solutions, and instant gratification.

The same thing applies to business cultures. But often the notion of efficiency has planted an ideal copied from the natural stimulus-reaction model and then applied it to our thought: we too should formulate the answers to our questions without reservation. We call this the joy of decision-making. Our notion of thought is that it creates the shortest distance between two points—between a problem and its solution, a need and its gratification, conflict and consensus. This is no place for dithering.

Again, it is "ora et labora" that, with reference to its roundabout way, is able to remind us that not everything can be understood according to the demand profile of the pressure of problem-solving. There are questions that must be handled so carefully that no possible answer is immediately available. Where that which is new is to be recognized, time, the experience of freedom, intricacy, doing without results, the courage to leave a problem unsolved for a change, is indispensable, even desirable. Upon closer examination, that which looks like laziness and idleness from the outside could turn out to be a precondition necessary for breaking through habits and ordinariness in favor of surprisingly unconventional insights into the way things work. If we want to make progress, we must hesitate.

There are nature reserves that provide an undisturbed environment for endangered flora and fauna; there should also be similar protected areas for questions, since they too are threatened by extinction due to the fact that our tendency to give answers far too quickly has been developed to the point of perfection. Questions are defeated if their echo is cut short by an answer; they lose their meaning and can no longer guarantee that the reply coincides with its own level. There are questions we must not answer. They must be endured. Without this hesitation, nothing new would ever be discovered. The American writer Thornton Wilder reported that the last words of his friend Gertrude Stein on her deathbed were, "What is the answer?"—and after a few moments of silence—"What is the question?" But that precisely *is* the question.

■

It is always easier to work on a problem. What is harder is finding the problem. There is a reason for this. *Sixth rule: That which is new appears in the world where free association is possible. Creativity is also always a test of patience. The Benedictine "ora et labora," as a formula for distancing ourselves from daily activities, requires searching for access to innovative ideas through rituals. Leisure must become a habit if the extraordinary is to develop from it.*

Thinking means contemplation of the unknown. The process of creation can be traced back to this simple principle. It would be banal in its simplicity if there weren't resistance everywhere preventing us from finding what we have not yet discovered. These obstacles themselves are imaginary and very creatively formed products of a soul that is tirelessly engaged in finding plausible arguments to prove that it would not be at all opportune to venture out into barely accessible terrain to look for something new. We must not forget that there are always a number of fears in encountering the truly unknown, which shoot down our resolve to not let anything stop us.

Thus, thinking in new ways means going against the claims to power of the old. The innovation process is always a war that almost invariably culminates in revolution. If that which is new also turns out to be better, it shows its aggressive side. Any new thing is strange at first, and like any strange thing, it is more likely to be the object of wonder, amazement, and inspection than love. A latent, threatening character emerges out of every discovery or invention. Beginnings are always periods of uncertainty.

Amid the fears of that which is new, consciousness of the old— of things that were proven and had long been successful—created a protective, defensive form of expression. The old is more than just the best-introduced way of dealing with individual, social, or economic life. It is more of a representation of psychological compromise, supported according to the classic model by mechanisms of repression and forgetfulness. Everything previously included under the leisure tradition of "ora et labora" relating to strategies promoting attentiveness must persistently battle this inhibitive, restrictive power. Benedict's rule undertakes an almost therapeutic task. The forced self-observation and the resulting discovery of our motives for impeding the new shed light on their method. Bringing these motives into consciousness makes it easier for us to be on guard against them.

Factors contributing to this inhibiting timidity include the fear of mistakes and the repression of this fear. Hardly any of us will confess that our hesitation in accepting the unknown is motivated and controlled by the desire to avoid mistakes or weakness in every case. On the contrary, failure is loudly proclaimed today as an early form of success; courage and risk are played off against defensive avoidance tactics. But language often reveals more than it says. The talk is soon of a "controlled" risk, and courage gives way to a practical cowardice that doesn't want to do anything wrong. It is the structurally determined inability to sense the direction of an endeavor that is based on the interplay of reason, of free association, that often gives doubters the feeling they are right. But where that which is new cannot justify itself yet—as in the middle of an innovation process—because it has yet to take firm shape, it cannot be right that those who claim to be right actually are.

■

Discovering the new is a battle, a test of patience with ourselves and with the opposition from the outside that the desire for surprise runs up against. This dispute over future-oriented views results in a high level of innovation. These views must be strong enough to assert themselves. *Seventh rule: That which is new appears in the world where we expect it, but rarely how we expect it. Creativity is an ability that is available to us only with limitations. The Benedictine "ora et labora" reminds us that the creative spirit participates in a movement that is larger than itself.*

It is a long-cherished belief that creativity is reserved primarily for the gods or God, while we creatures down below can at best only imitate what was prescribed from a higher vantage point. Only since human self-consciousness reached a previously undreamed-of importance in the Italian Renaissance has the ability to discover and create new things been one of the elementary characteristics of humanity. In the concept of the genius, the notion of a person especially blessed by the muses, this self-consciousness bloomed magnificently, but human self-mastery was still ironically and metaphorically denied as the source of creativity. We have seldom entrusted our own kind with conspicuously outstanding ideas and works. With extraordinary achievements forces beyond humanity always had to be involved. We know ourselves and understand who and what we're dealing with.

Neither has democratization changed this formerly divine privilege. In particularly successful processes that generate new things, there is a sense of the work being a foregone conclusion, as though we alone are not the subject of our own actions. Being absorbed in the task seems like a loss of self. In the ideal case, developments succeed, thoughts occur, and we produce products that we would never have considered ourselves capable of before. It is as though the director of the innovation drama is not an "I" but an "it." This impression may perhaps emerge because tension eases in the progression of recognition—tension that it was necessary to have built up to let curiosity get its right to satisfaction. This is always connected with the experience of happiness: demands and talents balance each other, the goal is suddenly clear, the sense of permanence is momentarily lost.

But this would be a facile explanation of the creative individual. Surprising insights are more than symptoms of a disintegration of tension in the psyche. Benedict's rule of "ora et labora" may be viewed as a warning not to interpret creative events too simply. The rule constitutes a silent acknowledgment that the ability to bring forth new things depends on conditions which are not exclusively under our control. When beginnings are to really make a difference—revolutionary discoveries, systems that have never existed before, machines without antecedents—the effort to attribute them to earlier developments is equal to the amazement over their failure. For the most part we feel wonder when we are confronted with innovations that we would have had to come to eventually, since they emerge so simply and logically from the pressure of the problem they have relieved. They are innovations that inexplicably haven't occurred to anyone yet. That which surprises is generally not far removed from what is at hand and usual. It is the result of what we can still think of in addition to what has already been thought. It is often not so much extraordinary as unusual.

Every beginning is veiled in mystery. This must not be seen as a late mystical capitulation in the presence of the true characteristics of the innovation process, nor does it release us from the effort of seeking regularities. On the contrary, it's always true that that which is not comprehended conceals the incomprehensible. Not everything can be carried over the threshold of consciousness; some things remain unknown. It is this polarity to which the Benedictine dictum points and includes in one breath finiteness, work, infinity, prayer. Innovation contains both effort—sometimes grim and sometimes lighter—and the patience to wait because, ultimately, we cannot force anything to happen. Nietzsche said that "The artist has an interest in our believing in sudden impulses, so-called inspirations, as though the idea of a work of art, poetry, or the fundamental thought of a philosophy descends from heaven like a beam of grace. In reality, the imagination of a good artist or thinker incessantly produces things that are good, mediocre, and bad, but his powers of judgment, finely honed and trained, discard, select, and link together. . . . All great human figures were great workers, tireless not only in invention, but also in discarding, seeing, redesigning, and ordering."

It shouldn't bother us that innovations leave unexplained elements behind. This incomprehensibility is only the other side of human freedom, our ability to begin something for no reason. Creativity has its own life-force that draws into itself when we try to grasp it and blossoms when we leave it alone. This benign neglect, which, in the context of asking how new things come into the world, is probably a higher behavioral concept than action, doesn't mean that we do nothing. Waiting can take effort, be it the arrival of something new that can disrupt the effort to let something be. Hence, this arrival has to do with freedom—the freedom to think, and the freedom to take what we think to heart. "It is the same with thoughts," writes Arthur Schopenhauer "as with people: we cannot always summon them whenever we want, but have to wait until they come."

Bibliography

Aristotle. *Nicomachian Ethics.* In *The Complete Works of Aristotle: The Revised Oxford Translation,* vol. 2. Princeton: Princeton University Press, 1984.

———. *On Sleep.* In *The Complete Works of Aristotle: The Revised Oxford Translation,* vol. 1. Princeton: Princeton University Press, 1984.

Benedict. St. *The Rule of Saint Benedict in English.* New York: Vintage Books, 1909.

Brodbeck, Karl-Heinz. *Entscheidung zur Kreativität.* Darmstadt: Wissenschaftliche Buchgesellschaft, 1995.

Burckhardt, Jacob. *The Greeks and Greek Civilization.* New York: St. Martin's, 1998.

Csikszentmihalyi, Mihaly. *Creativity: Flow and the Psychology of Discovery and Invention.* New York: HarperCollins, 1997.

Groys, Boris. *Über das Neue.* Munich: Hanser Verlag, 1992.

Diogenes Laertius. *Lives of Eminent Philosophers.* Loeb Classical Library, 184–85. Cambridge, Mass.: Harvard University Press, 1991.

Lafargue, Paul. *The Right to Be Lazy.* Ardmore, Pa.: Fifth Season Press, 1999.

Nietzsche, Friedrich. *Human, All Too Human: A Book for Free Spirits.* Texts in German Philosophy. Cambridge: Cambridge University Press, 1986.

Pieper, Josef. *Leisure, the Basis of Culture.* South Bend., Ind.: St. Augustine's Press, 1998.

Reheis, Fritz. *Die Kreativität der Langsamkeit: Neuer Wohlstand durch Entschleunigung.* Darmstadt: Wissenschaftliche Buchgesellschaft, 1996.

Schopenhauer, Arthur. *Parerga und Paralipomena: Short Philosophical Essays.* Rev. ed. New York: Oxford University Press, 2000.

22

Where Art Does Not Come Sweepin' down the Plains
An Interview with Mary Frates
Frederick G. Dillen

There's nothing new about the notion of encouraging the fine arts in society at large.

But where they've never been widely received or deeply appreciated, fostering those arts today demands flexibility and persistent innovation.

A not-for-profit private-and-state partnership, the Oklahoma Arts Institute brings fine arts at their highest level to a frontier state that is powerfully ambivalent about the arts. For two weeks every summer the institute invites the 300 auditioned-best high-school artists from around the state to live in their own isolated village of peers, where they receive free instruction in their respective disciplines (and exposure to other disciplines) from nationally recognized professionals in ballet and modern dance, creative writing, painting and drawing, photography, acting, film making, choral music, and the full range of orchestral music.

Then every autumn, over a sequence of several weekends, the

institute invites 400 schoolteachers, college educators, and professional and amateur artists from around the state, on a first-come first-served basis, to four-day advanced workshops in most of the artistic disciplines as well as folk arts.

By successfully combining these many elements and by fruitfully exercising its singular prominence as the champion of artistic excellence in its state, the Oklahoma Arts Institute has repeatedly broken new ground and continues to do so.

Mary Frates directed the launch of this unique vessel in 1977 with a three-day pilot program for 100 hastily recruited students in the 106-degree heat of a church camp outside Tahlequah in the Cherokee country of eastern Oklahoma. Mary continues to work 50-, 60-, and 70-hour weeks overseeing the institute's dissemination, nourishment, and harvest of fine arts for an Oklahoma she believes needs those arts. Hers is a populist belief, and her institute, despite its own fierce insistence on excellence, aims itself, in one way or another, at every student and ultimately every citizen. A tall woman with the carriage of a dancer and the presence of royalty, Mary enjoys negotiating extreme circumstances, whether glamorous or parochial, and she does so with assurance. A woman who dresses with classic elegance and who drives extraordinarily fast cars, Mary rarely theorizes about what she does. She gave this interview while hanging an inaugural exhibit for the new museum honoring the hundreds of victims of Oklahoma City's 1995 terrorist bombing.

We want to get at innovation in the Oklahoma Arts Institute. But let's begin at the beginning. Why the arts, Mary?

I grew up in Ponca City, Oklahoma, a town of 25,000, and my mother insisted on taking me to all the community concerts and on my taking ballet lessons for years. Her great dream was that I would become a ballet dancer, and I was terribly shy and had to take "expression," and it was all just awful. But it stuck. Now, this was a very nice town and not particularly rural, but it didn't have the cultural resources of Oklahoma City or Tulsa, and even in those places, of course there was only so much. The fact was that, for all but a small percentage of Oklahomans, the notion of the arts was an innovation in itself.

Then I went away to college in Washington, D.C., a very strict Catholic women's college where the only way you could get out— I mean the only way; they locked you in—was if you attended political or cultural events.

That was when I got my real exposure to the arts, and to politics for that matter. I became a Young Democrat and a Young Republican, and I went to every concert and every performance I could, and most of all I went to the National Gallery.

And getting out wasn't just a matter of youthful exuberance. I was one of two freshmen students from west of the Mississippi, and I may have been the only person in the whole college who had graduated from a large public high school. The rest of them were from eastern boarding schools or from overseas, and of course I was not well traveled either. I found myself in cultural cross fire between the preppies and the daughters of ruling families from places like India and Pakistan. I was so painfully shy and so totally a misfit that I can't remember speaking a word for six months. I longed to go home to the University of Oklahoma, where my friends were spending their time at parties instead of in solitary struggle with 20 class-hour semesters of theology and philosophy.

But I couldn't go home, so I went to the National Gallery and found beauty and history and the world. I had certainly been to symphonies and ballets, but I had never encountered anything like a world-class museum, and I spent as much of my time as I possibly could there. Something went off in my head. I'm a very visual person, and the museum was it for me. With that—along with spending every waking moment pursuing everything else as well in order to escape the college—I built a groundwork of sophistication about the arts. I became a fan. I knew there was a communion in great art that made me whole and that bound me in the best ways to the rest of the world. I knew, at the easiest level to speak about today, that if you tried you could embrace the terrible mysteries of something like AIDS through a play like *Angels in America.*

Discovery of such universal and age-old communion was new to me, and it still feels new, and it's at the heart of whatever newness the Oklahoma Arts Institute holds.

That's a wonderful, almost an archetypal, vision of a mother's mid-century, mid-American aspiration, and a lonely young woman's flight from college cloister into revelation. But other Oklahomans who have that sort of revelation don't usually come back to Oklahoma. How did you find your way to the Oklahoma Arts Institute?

I spent two years in Washington, but after the death of my father, I did come home and graduate from the University of Oklahoma. By then I didn't fit in there, either. I no longer dressed like anyone else. I missed Washington's cultural diversity. I missed the architecture. I missed the National Gallery.

I realized that the two years away had caught me at a turning point and changed me forever, and having realized that, I never imagined I would live in Oklahoma.

But I met a man who imagined that he would. So. I began working very hard at arts-in-education volunteer work in Oklahoma City, and then got a job with the JDR 3rd Fund, directing essentially the program I'd been developing to bring arts to Oklahoma City elementary schools. After five years of that job I concluded that making the arts a part of every child's education in the public schools was not something I could do. It just wore me out, and I decided to move to France.

Before I could get out of town, though, the head of the state arts council called to say he had three parents who wanted a summer arts camp for their children, something like Interlochen. Would I help? I said I'd give him six months, and then I was leaving for France. We spent most of those months planning with artists and educators from across the state and then called everyone we knew to dig up willing students and to beg $30,000 for a pilot program.

And for three days that summer we had a pure community of students and faculty in every artistic discipline. I loved it. The students loved it. They were good, too. We'd had no real sense of whether they would be, and we made a difference with them in three days. It worked, and I thought here was a way I could help my state and keep my sanity: the Oklahoma Arts Institute. I was probably wrong about the sanity, but in any case I never did make it to France.

Interlochen is the arts academy and camp that was then still officially called the National High School Orchestra Camp. At that time it was primarily oriented toward music and took paying students from all over the country. Is that right? And it was a model?

Yes, and it was certainly an inspiration. But I didn't go to Interlochen myself, and from the first we wanted to have all the arts represented equally and we wanted to draw our students only from Oklahoma, free of tuition, which I think was quite innovative, especially then. Really, though, we didn't think about other places. We just did it here.

With state funding?

From the first we were a public-private partnership, which was innovative as well. And this also meant that over the years we've had to collect a lot of private funds. But the state has always been an important part of the partnership, financially and otherwise. Oklahoma is unique in that there aren't all the layers to keep you from doing things. There was a governor's cultural conference that year, and we got our idea put at the top of the agenda. Governor David Boren thought it was a great idea and gave us five thousand dollars. That doesn't sound like much now, and didn't sound like so much then either, but it put us in business. And Boren (later U.S. senator and now president of the University of Oklahoma) became a very important friend to the institute.

Of course the other side of the coin in a state like Oklahoma, where you can knock on the governor's door and walk in, is that once you get official blessing and maybe a little money to do something, especially something in the arts, then you're out there all alone. There wasn't enough arts support then, and there isn't much now. If you want to do something, you can do it, but you'd better believe you're on your own. With every step you take, you innovate.

Your first camp took place in Tahlequah, but the institute's home for its summer camp and its fall workshops has long been Quartz Mountain. In fact, most people think of Quartz Mountain as emblematic of the institute. How did that come about?

The day after we left that first camp at Tahlequah, three Girl Scouts were brutally murdered right near where we'd been, and we realized they could have been our students.

Well, the state tourism department had a derelict resort lodge in a state park in the far southwest corner of the state. It was absolutely isolated, and we could make it secure. So we looked at it. And we wanted the landscape. It's a lake and a rocky outcrop that does truly seem a mountain by the time you get to it, with eagles and rattlesnakes and bobcats, there in the dry, empty run of plains. It was also the ceremonial home of the Kiowa. They welcomed us, and we liked the connection to those plains warriors, to a people who had come to Oklahoma not by the Trail of Tears but down from the Yellowstone of their own volition to find this Quartz Mountain.

The lodge itself was another story. Every time someone turned on a hairdryer, the lights went out, and that was just the beginning. Still, we brought in 200 kids for two weeks our first year after Tahlequah, and it nearly broke us. But we stayed afloat, and Quartz Mountain became not just a practical home but the physical heart of the institute.

People who know Oklahoma know that the Trail of Tears refers to the forced migration of the Cherokee, Choctaw, and Chickasaw tribes from the South Atlantic states to a relocation of great hardship in Indian Territory, as Oklahoma was called before statehood. Many other tribes and parts of tribes were driven to Indian Territory as well. You began the institute in the seat of the Cherokee Nation and moved to Kiowa country. How important is the Native American connection to the institute?

Our Native American relationships have always been crucial. The first faculty member we chose in our first year was Maria Tallchief, the prima ballerina *assoluta* for whom Ballanchine choreographed *The Firebird.* Choosing Maria was important for two reasons. First, it announced that we had nothing to do with mediocrity, that we stood for only the highest caliber of instruction and learning in the arts. The second reason was that Maria was Native American.

I wish I could say that at the time we were clever enough to know all about what was politically correct, but we weren't. We just knew it was terribly important for Native Americans to be part of the institute, then and in the future. And they have been. All five of the Native American prima ballerinas, including Maria's sister Marjorie, taught with us. So have the painter Fritz Scholder and N. Scott Momaday the writer, and they come back again and again. And the Kiowa ceremonials are part of every season at Quartz Mountain. We're very fortunate in this. When you make things up as you go along, you make some mistakes, but this was something we got right.

The institute grew quickly from the first three-day pilot to the point where you were serving 200 and then 300 kids, and then over 400 teachers, with permanent offices in Oklahoma City, a permanent home for your camp, and workshops at Quartz Mountain. Were management skills a problem?

From the first we had to knock on a lot of doors to raise money, and one of the first doors I knocked on was Phillips Petroleum's. They not only gave us money, they took me under their wing and tried to educate me, with some success, about running things as a business. They also turned me over to their publicity and image people, who had us advertising in the *New Yorker* and the *National Geographic* before we had desks in our office so that we would have a profile to take to the schools, the legislature, and donors.

What might have been even more important than a profile we could sell was that we created an image of ourselves that we wanted to live into, an image that we did live into.

Phillips gave us those services as in-kind donations, and continued to give them and to try to organize me. And after Phillips had to tighten its belt, other corporations, like Southwestern Bell, helped in the same way—with cash, with invaluable in-kind donations, and yes, with the management skills. We still had to do the work; we were always understaffed and underfunded, but we did have help, and most of the time we had the sense to accept it.

You've had fine Native American instructors. Who are the rest of your instructors, and where have they come from?

They've come from all over the country. Wonderful photographers like Paul Caponigro from the Southwest, people like actor Richard Thomas from the performing arts community on the West Coast. From the east, the poet Donald Hall was among our first instructors and returned often. The actress Jane Alexander, who comes back regularly. JoAnn Akalitis, who was artistic director of the Public Theater in New York at the time she came. The artist Robert Zakanitch. Edward Payson Call from the Guthrie Theater in Minneapolis.

We have panels of Oklahoma artists and educators for each of the arts, and these panels propose whom we might choose as instructors. If I think of someone, I propose him or her as well. Not everyone is famous, but all of them have distinguished credentials and extraordinary ability to communicate their skills. And they come despite the fact that we can pay very little. Because the money has never ever been easy. I tell them that they will love the kids and that they'll make an incredible difference, and they come. Now I've become intimidated about calling some of these people. I call them anyway, but when we started, I didn't have the sense to be intimidated; I just called anyone I wanted. If I admired their work, I picked up the phone. That's one of the benefits of doing things for the first time: you don't know any better.

What about the students?

From the beginning we wanted to get it done with the best kids, and that's what has happened. We audition all over the state, and the good kids do want to come to us, so they show up for the auditions. Then they all come to Quartz Mountain for two weeks on full scholarship and live in a dynamic community of other young artists from every discipline. The state pays half the total cost of about $2,000 per student for the two weeks, and we solicit matching funds for the other half from the private sector. Then we pay rent to the state for the use of Quartz Mountain. It's a very good deal for the state. And it's a wonderful thing for the students.

Many of the instrumental students play in marching bands and have never sat in an orchestra. They go home transformed. They receive scholarship offers from statewide colleges because the colleges know that these are the best kids. Some of them go on to the

Ivy League or colleges of that quality. More than a few of them make their way as professional artists. Almost all of them stay actively in touch as a part of our family and participate in the arts wherever they are. All say we've changed their lives.

You didn't start out working with teachers, but now they're a big part of your focus. When did you start giving your workshops for teachers?

We started reaching out to the teachers after we'd been working with high school students for ten years. This was another innovation, a natural and probably inevitable one. Also an important one.

The teachers found their students coming back from the institute transformed, and they wanted to see what was going on. They wanted to be able to do the same thing in their own classrooms. They wanted their own transformation, too, of course. And we wanted them to have it. Not as teachers, but as students themselves, getting the best possible instruction in the arts from fine professional artists.

It fulfills them in all sorts of ways, and it gives us a far greater reach into the schools and toward the kids who will never get to the institute—also toward the kids who will never care about the institute, which will always be most of them. So we can hope, after all, to eventually make the arts a part, even if only glancingly, of every child's education.

And beyond that, training teachers takes some of the pressure off us with the state legislature for the high cost per student when we can take so few students and have to refuse so many.

That sounds like politics. Are politics a necessary part of the public-private partnership? Do you need to stay in the good graces of the state legislature?

We work on it every day. We get a tiny proportion of the state budget, and the arts are at the bottom of almost everyone's priorities, but if we want to stay in business, you'd better believe we try to find students from every district in proportion to that district's population.

I once got a call from a man who was then chairman of the Appropriations Committee of the state House of Representatives. He wanted to know if we'd ever taken a student from his district. I checked it out, and I called him back and said we needed to talk. I went to his office and told him we never had taken a student from his district and that that was going to change immediately. Then I had to find a qualified student down there. I found him through David Boren, who was a United States senator by then. He'd heard what we needed, and he called me as he was going in to chair the Senate Intelligence Committee hearings on the Iran-Contra arms sales. He told me about a trumpet player down in Spiro, a boy whose brother he had sponsored to West Point. "He plays a mean trumpet," the senator said. "Go get him."

That's one of the more interesting recruiting stories, but Senator Boren knew the institute couldn't survive if we put ourselves on the wrong side of the chairman of the Appropriations Committee.

Naturally, I got in the car and drove to Spiro and told the principal of the high school I wanted his students for the Arts Institute. He said that there could only be one kid, and I said, yes, the trumpet player. Then, so the student wouldn't feel uncomfortably singled out, the principal called an assembly and announced auditions for the institute. Since the principal also announced that anyone auditioning could skip class, I ended up auditioning the whole school. But it was only 60 kids, and we got our trumpet player, and the Oklahoma House of Representatives kept on delivering votes for us.

This level of politics may seem to be innovation in a minor key, but it's always there in the arts. It's always new with every circumstance, and it's always critical.

What if there hadn't been a trumpet player?

You do what you have to do to get where you're going. I've taken for myself some authority for choosing the bottom 5 percent of audition selections in order to give geographic and racial diversity to our programs. If we really need a student from here or from there, I can sometimes see that we get one if they have decent audition scores.

But it was also about the time we admitted the trumpet player that we started the programs for teachers. If we can't find qualified students from a district, we can go there and recruit for teachers. We don't audition the teachers; we accept them on a first-come first-served basis.

You do what you have to do, and you make it work for you. You get to know your governors, and regardless of their politics, you work with them. You learn, in the long term, that governors come and governors go, but the legislature is always there.

The lodge at Quartz Mountain burned down in 1995. When I first heard about that, I was afraid that it might be the end of the institute.

Sometimes keeping an innovative enterprise going can seem like the hardest job. Yes, that was a big blow. But really, we had been patching the place to keep it standing since our first year, so it didn't take long for us to understand the fire as a kind of blessing. Not that it was easy, even aside from raising the money for a new building, finding temporary quarters back in Tahlequah, and then at the University of Oklahoma with David Boren's patronage again.

While the fire was still burning, a state senator from the Quartz Mountain area called to urge me to keep the institute there and rebuild. I had to tell him that I would do that only if he would promise to protect the four million dollars we had already raised with a state bond for a new performance hall, because I knew other legislators would run at that performance hall money when they thought we were down. And they did run at it.

Then the president pro tem of the state senate called and said he wanted to see me, and I went in expecting him to insist we relocate the institute to his district. But that actually turned out to be another blessing. He only wanted to be sure we got the best possible facility, and he had the name of an architect for us. This was an architect who had designed the River Walk in San Antonio and who also had sent a son to the institute. The architect was very eager to work with us because of the good we had done his boy. He designed our new complex at Quartz Mountain, and it's everything we ever wanted.

That's a happy story. You have a larger community out around the state.

Circles and circles of community. The current students and past students, faculty, teachers, legislators, corporate and individual sponsors, the Kiowa, our neighbors in Lawton and Altus.

Mark Singer, who has taught at the institute and who writes for the *New Yorker,* some time ago was standing in Greenwich Village wearing his institute T-shirt and saw another T-shirt go past across the street.

Well, we're not taking over the world, but we're out there. We're doing it, and we're making a difference in Oklahoma.

The arts are always going to be a battle here, every day, but our community is alive, and we make a point of keeping it alive. Because it keeps us alive. We stay in touch with everybody at least four times a year, with exhibitions and concerts and catalogs, with reunions and field trips, with thank-you notes from current students to their legislators, you name it.

How about you? You've been doing this a long time now. Are you still learning through the institute?

I still love the arts, and I'm fascinated with the ideas of the new artists we bring to Oklahoma. I still love the kids. And sometimes the world teaches you whether you want to learn or not. The fire at Quartz Mountain taught us. And most of all, of course, the bombing taught us.

That was the 1995 terrorist attack on the Alfred P. Murrah Building, the federal agencies building in Oklahoma City. One hundred and sixty-eight people died in the attack, and many more were injured.

Yes. I thought we'd had the biggest shock we would ever have when Quartz Mountain burned down, and then a few months later the bombing happened. It was a national event, but here in Oklahoma it was much more than that. In Oklahoma City, where the institute has its year-round headquarters, virtually everyone in town knew somebody lost in the bombing, and many people lost friends, relatives, and loved ones.

The institute had to help, and we knew it. There were few other arts groups able to respond constructively, and the actress Jane Alexander, who was then head of the National Endowment for the Arts, called from Washington asking us to do something. Local ministers called us.

We decided to do what we knew how to do, which was hold workshops.

We did a job we were practiced at, but it was also utterly new for the situation. This is the kind of innovative action you'd hope the Oklahoma Arts Institute would be able to take.

We invited all the survivors and everyone who had lost family, any of them who wanted to come, to a long weekend of workshops six months after the bombing. Not for therapy. Just to come together and work, to make art. There was resistance to it within the institute because there would be all sorts of people who might not understand what we did—people who weren't artists, for goodness sake—but we did it. I called together practicing artists from across the country, a first-rate faculty, and not one person turned me down.

One hundred and forty survivors came—adults, teens, and children. We had workshops in poetry and essay, in memory boxes, masks, quilting, and Native American basket making. The people who came, many of whom were children and most of whom had never had anything to do with art, made art of the highest order, passionately eloquent poems and essays, memory boxes of heartbreaking beauty. They danced. They sang. It was not therapy, but it was healing. It made a difference. We saved lives.

We had mental health counselors in all the workshops, as participants, not observers, but it wasn't the people taking the workshops who needed counseling. It was the staff and faculty who every night had to regroup and pull themselves together, because the circumstances and the work were so powerful. It is one of the most important things we've ever done, and all of us were transformed. So yes, I'm still learning, and so is the institute.

And this exhibit you're hanging today is the work from those workshops?

Yes. When the workshops were done and we realized how powerful the work was, we assembled it into a show that hung in the main entry of the capitol for six months and then toured around the state. Now the curators of the memorial museum here at the site of the bombing want the work up for their opening, so I'm learning all over again.

What's next?

This spring we open the rebuilt Quartz Mountain as Oklahoma's Arts and Conference Center. From the beginning we imagined a true arts park, and in a few months we'll have one. Between now and then I have to deal with new management at the tourism department to make sure the concept of a state arts and conference center is honored and we don't fall back to business as usual for a resort, which means primarily golf courses and water skiing. I will knock on the governor's door this week. I'll get to know the new speaker of the house. I'll call on our old friends in the legislature. You would think after all these years that the arts would be understood as Quartz Mountain's greatest asset, but the battle begins again every day. Politics: the small sustaining innovations. But the new arts and conference center gives us a platform for new possibilities on a larger scale. How we use that will tell us if we still are truly innovative.

What about the cars, Mary? Is there a connection between your inclination to innovation and your affinity for fast cars?

I love good design, and I admire good engineering. I've never thought about it. I guess I like going fast. I like being in motion and making decisions, decisions that matter, quickly. I'm at home with that. It's not quite the same thing, but I'm also comfortable with confusion and with making decisions in that kind of motion. Coming through new territory at high speed and reacting quickly.

And with a fast car, obviously, I can go meet the new speaker of the house in his district, do what has to be done there, and get back to business here.

More
and
Too Much

23

Increase and Arrival
On the Finiteness of Progress
Gerhard Schulze

The Thesis

One of my friends, a tax consultant, dreamed for years of leaving his career and becoming an artist. Eventually he bought a barn, which he converted to a studio at great expense. After a long time, the studio was perfectly equipped; the artistic work could begin. But then something happened: my friend sat in his barn, empty of all inspiration, and became more and more despairing. Completely disillusioned, he returned to his original profession.

My thesis is that only once in the history of humanity can there be a period of innovation as extensive as the one we are presently experiencing. We are approaching the end of this phase; the studio is ready. In contrast to my friend, however, we can't go back from whence we came. We have no choice but to gradually shift the focus of our thoughts and actions: from the construction of the vast realm of possibility that surrounds us to actually living within it, from innovation to stabilization, from thought that is oriented toward what could be to thought that is oriented toward what is.

The "Increase Game"

During most of history, humanity has lived virtually without progress. Innovation was limited to the invention of simple tools, which have scarcely changed over many millennia. But in our time, we have to ask if there is any product at all that is *not* regarded as temporary. It is obvious that we live in a culture overflowing with innovation. Everything we produce is subject to the proviso of being replaced by something better.

Whether one regards this development as positive or negative is of no importance in regard to its progression. The natural sciences, technology, economy, politics, the educational system, people in work processes, and consumers are united in a context of action which has long been independent. In the following paragraphs, I will refer to this context of action as an *"increase game."* What I mean by this is an interrelated, worldwide network among actors who follow one and the same logic in their actions: the logic of increase. No matter how different the goals of the various actors are, the logic of increase enables their actions to be connected to one another, and links them to a gigantic social structure.

In the center of each of the countless variations on the logic of increase is an increase scale that allows specific conceivable events to be arranged in a ranked series. It includes things such as work productivity, the gross national product, standard of living, efficiency of machines, storage capacity of chips, the range of observations explained by a theoretical model, technical qualifications, the yield from agricultural areas, and increases in the number of possibilities enabled by inventions. However, a logic of increase is only formed when the participants think about the increase scale with which they are occupied in a very specific manner: they imagine this scale as *open above;* they assign the scale a *linear value,* in which the next-higher condition is always seen as "better"; they construct a *knowledge of increase* that enables them to go from one level to the next-higher one. Examples of this knowledge of increase include experiments in the natural sciences, knowledge of economic rationalizations, and consumer knowledge of the product world. The chronological model of the logic of increase is linear; people think of their history as essentially endless progressive steps on paths of increase.

Since its start at the beginning of the nineteenth century, the increase game has displayed an increasingly strong undertow. Anyone who tries to avoid it gets sucked into it, unless he lives at the expense of others, who participate that much more intensely in the increase game. The increase game is culminating in the current period of globalization. Individual and collective wills are completely insignificant in today's turbulent intensification.

The idea still in circulation is that our needs drive this development. These needs, it is said, challenge us to continuously expand the horizon of possibility that surrounds us, so that we can each tailor the world to fit our body a little more precisely. But now many new products are being introduced that one must first invent the need for, and consumers frequently must be snared by expensive advertising campaigns. It appears that the chronological sequence of needs and products is reversing. More and more often, the product comes first, and then at some point, one hopes, a need surfaces.

This reversal of needs and products shows us that the increase game no longer draws its social energy from the clearly perceived needs of everyday life and unfulfilled desires that fed it in the beginning. So what *does* power it? My thesis: its own *orientation*. The increase game tells us what to do. It supplies plans of action to the product developers, the researchers, the selective consumers, the businesses striving for competitive advantages, the politicians battling for advantages in location. It provides us all with a mutual direction. It allows us national and international understanding on objective grounds. It is the social glue that holds the world together.

What Do We Do When the Goal Has Been Reached?

It might seem a bit disconcerting for me to jump from these comprehensive considerations to a small device for daily use—the electric razor. But the one has a great deal to do with the other: the razor is a visible point for the crystallization of thoughts about the whole. It is possible that, in its present-day form, it can even provide us with information on the future of progress.

For decades, the performance of razors was tested by using objective measuring procedures. Among other techniques was one in which the weight of the hairs shaved per unit of time was recorded. What is noteworthy is that the shaving performance of the units tested hasn't increased for years. What's been going on? Have the researchers and the technicians and the product developers failed? Not likely. The iron hand of the market ensures success. It is much more likely that this path of increase has come to an end. Development of the razor has been played to the hilt. It is impossible to shave more closely than completely smooth, which razors can already do.

The way "innovation" is currently discussed in politics and business carries a downright metaphysical undertone: the belief that progress can continue forever. Granted, the essence of metaphysics is based on the belief that it cannot be definitively disproved. But the razor gives us a moment's pause. It still provides us with one example of a *finite* path of increase. We are plagued by an unsettling foreboding. Could the increase game actually end sometime?

Yet we immediately soothe ourselves again: it is only the basic use, the performance of the razor, that can no longer be increased. What is to prevent us from equipping the razor with additional functions beyond the bare basics and gaining an increase in this regard? For example, a digital clock could be built in, or a radio receiver with a connection for headphones, a shaving-water dispenser. Perhaps the service life or storage capacity of the batteries could be extended. And of course the design can be changed over and over again. Still, one doubt still remains: aside from the fact that it is doubtful whether the consumer actually wants any of these added features, there is probably an end to the "parallel increase path" as well.

Only the design, the aesthetics, can be excused from these considerations, not because aesthetics can be increased infinitely, but precisely because they *cannot* be increased at all. In this realm there is only the "different," not the "better"—otherwise Mozart would be better than Bach, Beethoven better than Mozart, Schumann better than Beethoven, and so on. Unlike the game of aesthetics, art, design, fashion, and entertainment, the increase game is organized by the principle of *progress in the objective sense*. It turns such increases into an idea about which we can reach an agreement, for example, through measuring procedures like those used to test products. Questions of taste are a whole different issue. To this extent it can be said that the first glimmers of a post–"increase game era" occurred at the end of the 1960s with the emergence of the "experience society." What was expressed at that time appears today in terms of cultural and sociological implications as the beginning of a "self-conscious consciousness of self." The triumphant entrance of a life philosophy thus began, whose essence is to define the subject as the measure of all things: "I do whatever pleases me."

There is a certain intellectual appeal in generalizing the finiteness of progress as demonstrated by the example of the razor. Anyone who wants to be consistent in dealing with the concept of innovation must also apply the concept retroactively. But an "innovation of an innovation" would cancel itself out. If the model of the razor can be generalized, the guiding force of this canceling out would be none other than the innovation itself. Through the gradual accomplishment of all conceivable tasks, it eventually works itself out of existence. The only thing left is variation, the endless playing out of predefined possibilities, but not innovation in the sense of expansion of the realm of possibilities.

Empiricism Instead of Utopianism

Next is the matter of allowing these thoughts at all, without simultaneously squelching them with cries of "What rubbish!" Controversy is often a sign of fear, and indeed the thought of it is somewhat unsettling. The contemporary social world is integrated above all via the medium of the objective increase of possibility. So this social world would have to collapse, countless people would be unemployed, economic organizations would fail, universities and research facilities would close, and the prevailing orientation system as we know it would crumble.

However, we would completely miss the point of this model of the end of the increase game if we wanted to oppose it with such fears. It is not a matter of a *suggestion,* but rather of an *empirical assertion.* It is necessary to emphasize this because in the past few years and decades, the talk has consistently been about the end of growth, although in a completely different sense than here, namely, as a cultural critique and moral challenge. The Club of Rome, the environmental movement, the technology skeptics, critics of consumerism, the diagnosticians of cultural failure, all talk in imperatives: Stop! Give that up! If it's feasible, omit it! This may be to their credit, but in view of the enormous undertow of the increase game, it will not have any effect. The thesis that the history of innovation is finite makes no claim; it describes a future that will be ours regardless of whether it suits us or not.

The discussion of ethics in the post-metaphysical age, demanding the return to old values, requiring businesses to be altruistic and employees to be self-sacrificing, planning utopias, setting up a "program to save the planet earth," and so on: all of these things at most result in the breaking down of psychic tensions. The increase game gives the impression of an "attractor" in chaos theory. We are trapped in a worldwide system structure and can't do anything to change it, either by protesting or appealing for help or rebelling. Globalization has greatly limited the playing field open to countries to absorb the social costs of this system structure; the increase of scarcity at the end of the increase game takes it one step further. Of course there is no cause for fatalism; there are still different options, as is shown by comparing the United States, the Federal Republic of Germany, and the Netherlands in the second half of the 1990s. With these options, however, it is a matter of social variants within the increase game, not beyond it. No one can really stop this process; one day it will simply be "played out."

Granted, this thesis is uncertain and speculative. But the reverse is also true: the antithesis of the *infinity* of innovation is also only a supposition, even though it is always mentioned as though it were a certainty. Let us therefore investigate the reasons for this.

Theory of Finite Information Resources

My main point can be summarized in one statement: the increase game is based on finite *information resources.* By "information resources," I mean cognitive conditions that must be met if people or institutions are going to practice an action-oriented logic of increase. I will shortly go into more detail, but first I want to try briefly to make this main point more accessible in its abstract form.

When we hear the term "information resources" for the first time, we first think of types of information that can be stored and then recalled at any time. The whole increase game is based on such "knowledge of increase." One of many examples is the methodology used in experiments in the natural sciences. How can this information ever be exhausted? It can be reproduced ad infinitum. A certainty: no reasonable person can doubt this. However, aside from the knowledge that is held to be true, there are also conditions for information that actually can be *exhausted.*

The history of geography serves as an illustration of this. For a long time, geography was a highly innovative science. But by the turn of the century, there was no denying that the end was at hand, since the last unidentified spots on the map had been filled in with the exploration of Antarctica. Because we essentially knew everything that could be known, the increase phase was over for geography. An information resource of geographical progress was indisputably conquered: *ignorance.*

I confess that it at first seems confusing to categorize ignorance as an information resource, but that is exactly the point. When one doesn't know something, it is precisely *because* of this ignorance that one knows what must be done. One mobilizes methodical knowledge, background knowledge about the target area, and creativity in order to attack ignorance. Knowledge increases through this process, but only as long as a supply of unknown things is available.

Let us now take a detailed look at the finite information resources of the increase game. There are four classes of information resources: usage deficits, supply of goals, objectivity of success, and undiscovered invariants. What do these terms mean?

Usage Deficits

As long as a razor doesn't provide the smoothest, most perfect shave imaginable, it has a *usage deficit.* This may be uncomfortable for the user, but the product developers are jubilant, because there is still something for them do. Once they have finally achieved the ideal usage, the shoe is on the other foot. Now it is the user who is jubilant while the product developers must search for a new task, since one of their information resources has been eliminated: the usage deficit. As long as there is a difference between the usage ideal and the actual level of performance achieved, there exists a usage deficit. Usage ideals are defined for all products, from screwdrivers to vacuum cleaners to data-storage units, and the products evolve over what is sometimes a millennium-long path of increase toward them.

Take the example of the data-storage unit. One of the usage ideals here is the conservation of as much information as possible in the smallest amount of space possible. A direct line runs from ancient cave paintings to the microchip. It is generally well known that the technology in this area has been advancing by leaps and bounds over the last decade or so. Innovations continue to race forward, but certainly not forever. There is a theoretical upper limit to storage capacity, which will "soon" be reached, compared to the vast period of time comprising previous product history. In a foreseeable amount of time, the usage deficit information resource will be used up once and for all. There will simply be nothing left to do, at least in this regard.

Supply of Goals

This much can be said: there are certainly enough other goals. If we have reached one, we can always apply our energy for innovation to another one that isn't too far removed. This is exactly what is repeatedly evident in the course of cultural history. As soon as a problem is solved, we throw ourselves into new jobs. We are like Reinhold Messner. Right after he had climbed the first 8,000-meter peak, he tackled the second, and so on. But in 1986, after the fourteenth one, this particular continuation was at an end, since there are only fourteen mountain peaks higher than 8,000 meters. True, the coasts and the poles remain extreme goals, but this supply is limited as well. Now transfer this notion to the future of the global increase game. Must we not prepare ourselves for a decrease in still-unachieved goals? Our repertoire of needs is limited, even if we interpret the term "needs" broadly. Our humanity provides us with an anthropologically limited supply of goals that appear to be reasonable, at least in regard to products that should have a specific use.

Objectivity of Success

Isn't it true, however, that people come up with the strangest ideas? Even when everything that is technically feasible is made, our fantasies, emotions, and desire to experience ensure that we remain seemingly inexhaustible generators of new goals. There is always something we want that we don't have. We want to be loved, see beautiful things, experience ecstasy, lose ourselves in creativity, taste exquisite flavors, have the feeling of being completely understood by someone, and be happy. All these examples are directed toward an area of goals, the location of which must be sought *in the person him- or herself.* Even if we have accomplished all the external things, there is much left to do internally. Very often it is the people who are most well-off financially who are the most dissatisfied. Subjectively defined goals are difficult to achieve and they change constantly, contradict one another, and alternate in an uninterrupted sequence, so that we cannot honestly say exactly when all the work has been accomplished.

This is exactly what has happened in the course of recent cultural history. In postwar Germany, a pattern of transformation developed that appeared for the first time in the cultural history of the United States and in the meantime has become a global pattern: transformation of the survivor society to the experience society. In the experience society, more and more work flows into activities that have something to do with subjectively defined goals. A vast consumer-goods industry has formed, whose items are increasingly less in demand for their objective usage and increasingly more in demand for their experiential value.

In the meantime, however, the belief that subjective happiness can be increased systematically, much the way the performance of a vacuum cleaner is improved, has turned out to be based on an illusion. People are gradually realizing that the search for happiness, in the sense of it being a perception rather than any type of material product, cannot be organized as an increase game in the usual way. The *objectivity of success* information resource is missing.

Supply of Invariants

This final class of information resources is perhaps best understood if one recalls the basic gist of technological history. In the seventeenth century, an easily remembered formula was introduced for this idea: "outwitting nature with its own means." But what do these means consist of? The answer is unambiguous: in *invariants*. All previous technological progress is based on the exploitation of our knowledge of invariants, which we encompass with various terms for the opposite of chaos: "natural laws," "structures," "probabilities." Without invariants, every attempt to shift the realm of human possibility even the tiniest bit would be doomed to failure. The inverse applies: with every newly discovered invariant, a broad field of usage possibilities crops up. Think of the diverse exploitation of the theory of relativity, from atom technology to space travel, as an example of how the discovery of invariants can trigger innovation.

But will this always continue? Most natural scientists believe the path of knowledge is infinite. But how do they know they are right? John Horgan's thesis of a gradual end to science is at least as plausible. The supply of invariants accessible to us from our supply of knowledge is limited. We are approaching the end of this supply in equal proportion to the increase in globally mobilized research efforts. All in all, the fate of geography anticipates the fate of natural science.

Interim Balance

Information resources are becoming exhausted for the social world of increase. Usage deficits decrease, supplies of goals and invariants disappear, the objectivity of success recedes. Exhaustion of information resources encompasses all the major areas of life involved in the increase game: economics, technology, natural science, work, education, consumption, politics. We have already reached the end of certain paths of increase, yet there are others with still plenty of room for exploration. It isn't a matter of one individual path of increase, but rather the totality of all the paths. My thesis concerns the *mixed relationship of closed and open paths of increase in global society.* Within this mixed relationship, the number of closed paths of increase is rapidly rising.

But our energy for increase, which we have trained, organized, and methodically refined for centuries, does not lessen. Researchers, business consultants, product developers, marketing specialists, growth-oriented economic theorists, consumers who are constantly striving for more, and politicians proclaiming prosperity are all crowding their way into the diminishing area of what can still be increased, thereby exhausting the still-remaining information resources all the more quickly—a self-accelerating process, an increase of increase.

The end of the social world of increase will not come as the result of decisions, consciousness, and deeds shining with heroic ethics. We will do everything possible to prevent this end; we will bet everything to be able to continue playing the old game, and this will cause it to end that much sooner.

Nowhere was the twilight of the increase game more clearly evident at the end of the twentieth century than in the labor market of the most developed countries. The rationalization of production, as can be seen in the history of agriculture, industrial work, and now the service industry, is not an unending process. It advances with dwindling usage limits until few are in the position to produce more goods than large sections of the population could earlier.

After the rationalization of the service industry, however, no new receptacle will be available in which the enormous mass of excess manpower can be contained in order for the increase game to be continued on a new level. Anticipation of the "information society," now common in everyday thought, is linked precisely with this hope. Yet the more one manages knowledge in accordance with the logic of the increase game, the more the game accelerates, and the sooner it ends. Only human services that cannot be rationalized seem to be inexhaustible: care, nurture, communication, consciousness issues. Leo Nefiodow hoped for a new, long-term upswing, a "sixth Kondratieff." Perhaps this is correct, but the economy of the increase game will no longer be suited to a social world characterized by such activities.

Four Objections

The *first* objection to this line of thought is that it is speculative. It is certainly relevant, but it is just like the prevailing assumption that the increase game is an infinite process. It seems to me, however, that which theory one prefers is not merely a matter of taste. The thesis of the finiteness of specific information resources is not to be tossed aside; it enables the version represented here to appear more plausible in contrast.

A *second* criticism is related to the tremendous room for development still presently open after more than two hundred years of history in research, industry, and technology. In actuality it would be rash to see the rationalization of production at an end. The same applies to a whole series of future technologies, such as photovoltaics, medical technology, materials technology, environmental technology, information technology, biotechnology, and robotics. And who would assert that the history of medicine, for example, has already reached the same stage as geography at the beginning of the twenti-eth century? I would counter the following: there is undoubtedly al-ways vast room for growth in the increase game, but this is not even an issue in the thesis concerning the end of the increase game. I refer sim-ply to an increasingly quick increase in the number of closed paths of increase in the *mixed relationship* of open and closed lines of develop-ment. The consequence will be that what can still be increased will continue to increase at an increasingly rapid rate to the end.

A *third* argument can bring up the ecological challenge. It can be argued that through the increase game, we are setting ourselves up for more and more environmental problems. If one takes the in-formation resources theory seriously, however, it means that the game can continue because from the viewpoint of the logic of in-crease, as strange as it may sound, problems are actually welcomed: they "improve" the low supply of goals and "provide" us with new usage deficits. This criticism is actually a matter of the appropriate application of the theory presented here. But the application doesn't go far enough, because the theory further states that the ecologically produced information resources are *finite*. Environmental technol-ogy even now is in full swing. The ecological problems will provide one last grace period for the increase game, since they can only be managed via the increase game. However, it will emerge that this type of management is limited by time. The environmentally inten-sive period of social history will come to an end, just like the peri-ods of agriculture, industrialization, and the massive service industry. And even in the environmentally intensive period, the management of ecological challenges will not be remotely capable of exploiting all the human energy released.

A *fourth* objection remains: even in the rich nations, social dif-ferences are rapidly increasing. The number of people who live in rel-ative poverty continues to grow. Actually, this is the situation all over the world. The majority of people live under conditions which the well-situated minority would find inconceivable for itself. Doesn't it border on cynicism to speak of the end of the increase game in view of these facts? Don't the figures published in the 1996 United Nations *Human Development Report* indicate vast uncharted territories in the increase game that must first be depleted before any real thought can be given to the time after the increase game has ended?

I can partially agree with this criticism, although I don't believe that it contradicts the thesis of the end of the increase game. Why? Primarily two reasons: because of the speed that globalization has attained in the meantime, and because of the crisis of demand breaking out on account of the end of the increase game. I will expound briefly on both.

Globalization and the Crisis of Demand

In the context of these considerations, globalization is interesting primarily in one regard: for a short time now, the increase game has been in the limelight all over the world, wherever national governments are doing the groundwork for it. The example of Korea shows how quickly a region can find the connection on a high level. We will find more and more areas of the world hurrying along the increase game path in increasingly shorter periods of time from beginning to end, the same path that took Western Europe around two hundred years. As in the case of ecological threats, there are threats of international inequality that represent an information resource for the increase game, but which will prove the finiteness of the resource.

However, this in no way means that inequality will disappear. On the contrary, at first it will continue to increase, not only internationally but intranationally as well. This phenomenon is a direct result of the logic of the increase game. In the social world of increase, work is also subject to the effect of the logic of increase.

The market ensures that there is an incentive for the working

class always to adapt to new, increased production scenarios, to qual-
ify for jobs that have undergone a transformation, and to intensify
work performance. In the social world of increase, work is by far the
most important source of financial income. It is certainly a cost factor
for employers; they are under relentless pressure to increase work
productivity. Again and again they have had impressive success, and
again and again, the labor markets of entire industries have collapsed,
painfully forcing workers to adapt. However, all this ultimately paid
off, since the products that used to be so labor-intensive to produce
can now be manufactured easily; the labor force has thus been freed
for the production of goods that previously were unavailable or
scarce.

However, at the end of the increase game, the following
happens: rationalization of production pushes into a new order of
magnitude, which actually provides fewer new possibilities for employment of the newly released workforce. Because of the connection between work and income, the social class of the needy grows.
This causes demand to recede, which in turn increases rationalization pressure and reduces financial income received for work. Here
the increase game hits a limit other than the one of information resources. A problem arises that cannot be handled by the logic of increase because the problem is caused by the logic of increase itself.
The information resource "scarcity" might be present, but we fail to
get at it because we ourselves are in the way.

From the World of Progress to the World of Circulation

To which social world should we adjust? How will the economy
function? How will business operate? These and many other questions are by no means mere inquiries into a future that is still so distant that this type of speculation is a waste of time. This future, the

time following the increase game, is already on the way. We must come to terms with a lack of synchronicity. While the increase game is still gaining intensity in many areas, there are areas in which it has already ended. The question of how we can expect to live in a post-increase game period is here, now, and it will soon be even more important.

From the world of progress to the world of circulation: the fundamental transformation looming in front of us could be characterized in these terms. The two worlds are different from each other both objectively and subjectively.

For the *world of progress,* from an objective viewpoint there is constant expansion of the realm of possibility; all economic matters, science, politics, individual consumption, the professional world, education—everything hinges on it. It is paradoxical that innovation is the most important element of tradition in the world of progress—or to be more precise, the type of innovation that can be objectively interpreted as increase. People have grown as accustomed to innovation as our ancestral cultures were accustomed to their centuries-old rituals. Subjectively, the world of progress is defined by the spirit of *what-could-be.* Nothing is as highly valued as innovations that allow us to do more than we could before: produce more, save or transfer more data, combine more functions into one device, subsume more empirical data in one new scientific paradigm, save resources—increase has a thousand facets.

The *world of circulation* is certainly not a world devoid of change, but changes here have a predominantly horizontal character. Instead of "more," the ruling category is "different." There are areas of life in which this has long been the case, such as fashion, music, literature, and art. Differences cannot be arranged in an objectively comprehensible sequence; scales of increase cannot be defined. In the world of circulation, the limits of possibility shift only marginally. There are certainly increases here and there, but their significance is no longer sufficient to make them major elements of the social world. The interwoven rules and routines on which everyday life is based are directed not toward expansion of the realm of possibility, but rather on the time spent within the given realm of possibility. Subjectively, the "what-could-be" mentality has moved over to make way for the "what-is" mentality. For us, this comes down to settling into a situation and "blooming where we are planted."

The term "world of circulation" could be misunderstood. The expression simply means that the people of this world must come to terms with *periodicity* on a larger scale than people in the world of progress. The increase game's linear consciousness of time in regard to an open, unrestricted future is in the background; a cyclical consciousness of time is in the foreground. In the world of circulation, we search for lasting harmonization among many different rhythms that pulse at different frequencies: human, vegetative, seasonal rhythms in asynchronous form all over the world; life-cycles of products from the moment of manufacture, through the warranty period, until the time when the product is thrown away; material circulation; day and night, summer and winter in conjunction with energy conservation. When the increase game is over, people's primary goal in their dealing with the physical world will no longer be "outwitting" it, but a long-term, calculable coexistence that is as free from disruption as possible. The principle of this closed circle and its harmonization with countless other circles will give everyday life a new character and enable the formation of a new economic system.

In this economic system, a consciousness of the value of *approximation* will replace the currently prevalent consciousness of the value of *increase.* The product world is intellectually mature; basic product ideas change only slightly. People no longer assume that a given product is merely the forerunner of a much better version yet to come. What can and does still change is the design and symbolic value of products—the result is otherwise a kind of secularized Platonism: product ideals are more and more frequently defined in the sphere of what has already been achieved, because we increasingly doubt that we will be able to advance very much more into the sphere of what has not already been achieved.

There are already examples of this type of economy, such as food (insofar as it is to be "good" food), or the art of musical interpretation. Good food and good music are certainly not easy to produce; they have their price, the same as high-quality furniture, houses, clothing, machines, factories, and means of transportation. But the paths of increase that lead to ideal quality are introduced as *finite* from the very beginning. The open increase mentality of the present economy, of science, technology, politics, and consumption, with its focus on the unlimited, is being displaced by notions of the arrival at ideals; one could also say, humankind's arrival at itself.

The Approaching End of the Increase Game

It was never my intent to connect the juxtaposition of these two worlds with a valuation or with the requirement that we ultimately switch from the world of progress to the world of circulation. The world of progress had and still has its place; it catapulted us into an objective situation that enabled more and more people at least to pose questions about happiness, without being completely preoccupied by simply surviving. And what about value judgments in this context, regardless of whether they are critical of culture or optimistic? If it comes to the judgment call that we have had enough of the increase game, it is much too powerful for us to simply choose to shut it off.

Only two events can end the game. One would be an ecological collapse. If I have not taken this into consideration before now, it is primarily because I think we will probably respond more and more strongly to the ecological challenge and ultimately overcome it, with the means of the increase game. This assumption seems plausible to me because the ecological challenge contributes an enormous, by no means nearly exhausted incentive for continuing the increase game. To express it paradoxically, the scarcity of natural resources creates new information resources for the world of progress. The second event that could end the increase game follows gradually from the logic of the game itself. It is *endogenous* and consists in the exhaustion of its information resources.

The conversion from one world to the other is certainly not instantaneous; it evolves over the course of decades. Yet even now, there are indications that we are in the transitional phase, even though the increase game has never seemed as powerful as it does now. One indication is the decrease in work, which even the rosiest employment figures cannot conceal. A second indication is the increase of products that haven't really changed for a long time except in their design—products that have been developed to their end. A third indication is the enormous increase in the importance of "happiness" in magazines, on talk shows, in conversations, in the psycho-boom, in self-reflection. The intensification of discourse on happiness in the 1990s will later be perceived as the sign of a collective learning process, as a turning point from the mentality of what-could-be to the mentality of what-is.

Collective Learning

In actuality, this is all a matter of a collective learning process. But are collective learning processes even possible? The increase game is probably the most impressive example of one. Industrialization was a gradual exposition, the increase game's present-day globalization is the interim test, and overcoming the ecological challenge is the final exam. Then we put it into practice: existence in a realm of possibility that has largely been fully developed. There is painful irony in the fact that we can no longer continue to live with the competence at increasing that we worked so hard to achieve. Learning the increase game gradually reduces the motivation to learn. Once we finally learn the lesson, we hardly need it anymore. The task is now to learn something completely different, namely to *be,* a chapter not found among the topics of our past history of collective learning, but one which is inevitably coming toward us.

Bibliography

Braun, C.-F. von. *The Innovation War.* Upper Saddle River, N.J.: Prentice Hall, 1997.

Horgan, J. *The End of Science: Facing the Limits of Knowledge in the Twilight of the Scientific Age.* Reading, Mass., 1996.

Martin, H.-P., and H. Schumann. *The Global Trap: Globalization and the Assault on Democracy and Prosperity.* New York: Zed Books, 1997.

Nefiodow, L. A. *Der Sechste Kondratieff: Wege zur Produktivität und Vollbeschäftigung im Zeitalter der Information.* Sankt Augustin: Rhein-Siek Verlag, 1996.

UNDP (United Nations Development Program). *Human Development Report.* New York, 1996.

24

Innovation and Global Responsibility

Stephan Schmidheiny

In the past few years, businesses have experienced and benefited in different ways from new liberties. The collapse of the Soviet empire and the then-evident failure of economies under government and central control have led to an opening and revival of markets in many parts of the world. Vast areas of potential that were inaccessible in the past have opened for internationally active businesses in Eastern Europe and developing countries. Electronic communication has enabled these possibilities to be exploited via a completely new type and intensity of global business management. The improvement and reduced costs of mobility both of people and of goods provide new opportunities for global division of labor, and a convergence of demand observed in many products and services creates the opportunity to provide a range of standardized products all over the world.

These new dimensions of freedom for companies, together with technological progress, have resulted in a significant acceleration in economic development, which has gone so far that today's successful company manager increasingly places more value on how quickly the new processes can be brought up to speed and implemented than on the size of the company. Speed, not size, determines beauty.

When developments and innovations in the technical and economic realm proceed at an increasingly rapid pace, alert citizens begin to question with growing concern whether these processes are still socially controlled or even controllable. Is it practical and feasible for our society and the government institutions acting on its behalf to monitor processes of business innovation for their compatibility with basic ethical standards? Or do the modern dynamics of innovation create uncontrolled loopholes by simply overwhelming the practical possibilities of government control with their breakneck pace?

In addition to the speed of innovation processes, globalization is another cause for concern in that businesses could escape government controls, and consequently social oversight, since politics and legislation and application of the law are still the primary responsibilities of national governments, even in this age of globalization. There is little that nation-states can do to control international activities compared with dynamic and powerful companies. Politics is rather helpless in the face of a development that can result in a critical social polarization: those who have the desire and means know how to profit from globalization, while those who lack the requisite education, mobility, capital, and technology find that their standard of living is increasingly threatened by global competition. If the political forces that led to a balance between the haves and have-nots in the past can no longer prevail, then lowered living standards constitute a threat to social peace.

The question is therefore posed from different perspectives: Where and how can the new dimensions of freedom and dynamics of innovation that have been found and claimed by companies involved in the global economy be given direction, and how can and should limits be set? Those who are disturbed by the fashionable overemphasis on "shareholder value" skeptically claim that companies focus only on maximizing profits rather than on human values, and demand that society and the government must therefore be prepared to control innovations and, if necessary, to stop them if ethical standards are violated. Economic leaders argue that the progress of human civilization is expressed in every innovation, and that the general interest is thereby served. Liberal representatives of the market economy maintain that every freedom correlates to a responsibility that must be exercised by those who take advantage of the freedom. And representatives of all views are agreed that not everything should be made that can be made. An object lesson is provided in the current topic of genetic alteration of plants, animals, and, ultimately, the human genotype.

With the demand for the distinction between what is feasible and what is allowable, not only the individual economic subjects are addressed, but also the economic system and rules defining it. Must the players involved in the market economy be required to subordinate their profit orientation not only to legal regulations but to basic ethical precepts as well, and can they do this? Is it conceivable or possible to impose critical self-control on them in regard to their activities and especially their innovations, and can this type of obligation be enforced for those who don't choose to follow it? Who sets the standards? Which authority determines what is generally binding? How does society express itself when these new duties overtax the established political mechanisms and the responsible government authorities?

There are obviously more questions than there are answers, and what answers there are differ according to viewpoint and personal interest. People for whom any relevant measure can and ultimately must be expressed as a monetary value, and who are convinced that the invisible hand of the market will therefore take all relevant values properly into account, will have trouble with the idea that there are nonmonetary values in addition to monetary ones.

However, if development must not be allowed to proceed un-controlled, and effective government controls are not guaranteed, then the question inevitably becomes one of new control mechanisms. The demand for personal responsibility for entities that, un-controlled, are allowed to pursue their own interests because they are uncontrollable seems either idealistic or fatalistic. However, it is increasingly clear that in a modern, highly complex industrial society, this regulation is becoming an indispensable instrument of control.

To take responsibility means to evaluate and decide among different competing interests. Value judgments based on ethical standards are critical to this process. People, who are creatures of habit and set in their ways, often have amazingly great difficulties with the apparent complexities of decisions that must be evaluated using "only" ethically based standards. But it is precisely on this level, which departs from purely rational points of view—which are by no means any less real—that the actual task of understanding personal responsibility begins.

The demand for personal responsibility increases in dimensions of the highest complexity, not only when a decision must be made between two divergent current interests, but also when it involves considering and evaluating the interests of future generations, as is the case with the ethical command to maintain a vital and productive environment. Economic activity and businesses consume resources and pollute the environment with their emissions and waste. They must adhere to legal restrictions and conditions that have become progressively more demanding in the past few years. Have these businesses fulfilled their responsibility to the environment if they have maintained the legal standards? Does their economically competitive market position give them the right to optimize their own interests by doing the bare minimum required by law? Or are they obligated by ethical standards to act on their own responsibility and take the initiative in shaping their own economic activities so that the environment and resources are protected as much as possible, so that their contribution will be part of a lasting development that will allow future generations to satisfy their needs?

I assume that the majority of citizens in industrialized nations today are prepared to assume a degree of responsibility that exceeds the legal minimum in order to avoid current and future environmental destruction. But I also see evidence that only a minority of manufacturers and consumers of economic services are prepared to live concretely and consistently according to the demands this responsibility engenders. Modern democracy and the market economy must learn to live with this contradiction. It is usually repressed from the consciousness but can break out with explosive force, as with the Shell–Brent Spar case, where the official approval process was handled properly, but then public pressure, provoked by the media, completely repudiated the result of this process and forced the company to take personal responsibility and reach a different decision, despite its legitimate approval. It must be assumed that the leadership of global business would learn from an experience such as this that respect of the legal system is not always enough, and that personal discretion and responsibility play an increasingly important role in decision making.

That only a minority chooses to consciously assume personal responsibility in everyday economic decisions must not be used as an argument for abandoning the principle. On the contrary, it is an indication of the presence of an as-yet untapped potential for regulating economic events. With the widespread demands on government, we are standing on the threshold of a social learning process that must first bring the individual closer to the proper usage of his or her civil liberties and the responsibilities connected to them. It is important that there are many successful competitors among those who lead the way as innovators in this learning process, since experience tells us that economic success is the most convincing argument and encourages emulation.

The rules of the game are not the only things that change in regard to increased personal responsibility. The group of players that defines social values and represents collective interests also grows. Earlier, society acted primarily through government bodies. Legislation and the administration and application of justice were the tried and true mechanisms. But in the new world system, new powers are emerging that are effective supplements to government or, in some cases, its replacement. In economic jargon, we call the players who embody such powers the *stakeholders* of the company. They represent different interests than the *shareholders* in regard to the company, such as the interests of future generations. These interest groups frequently base their claims not on government regulations or legalities, but on generally applicable ethical and moral standards. They pursue their task with increasingly professional methods and are supported in this pursuit by the media, which create the link to political authorities via public opinion, and are thereby able to introduce concrete sanctions if the need arises. In this sense, *stakeholder* representatives supervise whether the company recognizes its own personal responsibility and puts it into practice.

This type of influence by third parties in the meantime has become known to many business managers through personal experience. Unresolved questions regarding the legal legitimacy of these players and the occasional abuse of their positions cannot eliminate these new social powers. It is therefore in a company's own interest to work together with these players in some appropriate fashion in order to become familiar with what they want and take into consideration the results of their decisions. This can lead to growing awareness of business-related personal responsibility, which benefits all participating parties. It is the innovative businesses that know that the impetus for successful innovation very often comes not from the "appropriate authority," but from people who critically analyze old and existing products, who can recognize and establish connections between divergent interests, and who are ready to pit their convictions against resistance and prevailing opinions.

In this sense, we coined the term "eco-efficiency" on the occasion of the 1992 environmental summit in Rio.[1] The principle of eco-efficiency has provided business with a positive access to the topic of environment. In the past this topic was viewed from a purely economic view as largely negative. Eco-efficiency acknowledges a better future and principially favors progress according to the motto, "Better is the enemy of good." The essential point is that progress toward things which last longer means that as many people as possible have the chance to benefit from this progress, and progress in the direction of eco-efficiency also benefits business economically.

The latter is already the case to a certain extent in many industries, since, as a result of rapidly rising wage costs, optimization of work was the number-one priority, and efficiency in the use of raw materials and energy played a weak second fiddle by comparison. From this emerges a considerable potential to catch up. For this potential to be optimized, however, the economic conditions must be correspondingly further developed. It basically comes down to the so-called "internalization" of environmental costs, which were previously not understood and have therefore been borne unknowingly by the general public or will be passed on to future generations. If environmental costs are progressively internalized, and the price of raw materials, goods, and services comes to express not only the narrowly defined economic reality but also the ecological reality, then eco-efficiency will become a profitable principle for the environment as well as for human society and business.

Society is in dire need of an environmentally compatible economy and environmentally supportive growth. Eco-efficiency, defined as the ongoing quest for progress that protects resources, is steering the dynamics of business innovation in this direction. Companies that have correctly interpreted the signs of the times and recognize sustainability as one of the fundamental challenges of human civilization, will, in their own interest, seek out new competitive advantages from precisely this challenge. They have a rational self-interest in finding innovative ways to fulfill their environmental responsibility. Hopefully, representatives of the various stakeholders will exert their influence on the economy and business in such a way that the process of innovation will not be hindered but rather propelled toward eco-efficiency.

Note

1.   See my book *Changing Course: Executive Summary: A Global Business Perspective on Development and the Environment* (Cambridge: MIT Press, 1992).

25

The Logical Progression of Dreams and Ideas
An Interview with William McDonough

Christopher Tilghman

William McDonough is the founding principal of William McDonough + Partners, a full-service architectural practice in Charlottesville, Virginia, and co-founder of McDonough Braungart Design Chemistry, a materials and process development firm, also based in Charlottesville. The only individual recipient of the nation's highest environmental award, The Presidential Award for Sustainable Development, and named a Hero of the Planet by *Time* magazine, McDonough is the recognized national leader in ecologically effective design and sustainable development. With his business partner, Michael Braungart, he is committed to developing and disseminating new paradigms of sustainability for a modern world.

I met with Bill McDonough for two hours in his comfortable, somewhat ramshackle office in an old brick factory building in downtown Charlottesville. He had fit me in the day before he was to fly to Davos, Switzerland, to address the World Economic Forum

Interview, a gathering of the chief executive officers and chairmen of the largest corporations in the world. At the same time, confirmation hearings were being called to order in Washington, D.C., for the purpose of discussing the appointment as secretary of the interior of a person regarded with frank dismay by most environmentalists. In the context of this extraordinary forum for McDonough's views, on the one hand, and this apparent hostility toward them on the other, I asked him to assess the current political and public take on environmental issues and principles.

In the long term, nature will do what nature does. We're just dust aggregated into sentient beings. As we look at the history of the planet, we'll come and go. In that context, it really doesn't matter what happens in the political realm. No matter what is happening in Washington, design protocols are actually shifting, based on timeless common sense. And in a strange, perhaps perverse way, an interior secretary who looks at the natural environment as simply a resource to be taken and plundered puts us on firmer ground. For the environmental community this situation may be better than having a guardian who purports to be on top of these things, which then lets everyone relax and makes the activists slow down. Everyone cheered when Bill Clinton and Al Gore took over, but did the Clinton administration make the environment its highest priority? Absolutely not.

What, then, is the role of political activism? Is there indeed a place for environmental radicalism?

I want the world to function in a way that is both more fair and more profitable and more ecologically intelligent, which means that any extreme position is a dangerous thing: Nazism, fascism, sexism . . . any "ism" has to be questioned as possibly too radical to be generally helpful and useful, because it is ignoring something else if it takes an extreme position. But should that extreme position exist? Yes. It must. It represents a certain part of the condition that needs to be recognized in a vigorous and fierce way. Nevertheless, for us, operating from an isolated "ism" is simply too radical. It's not our job to be that kind of radical. What we realize is that capitalism and socialism are both two-dimensional agendas that have been missing the third ism, which is "ecologism." We're trying to find a balance in this triangle of "isms."

What does a system look like that's in balance? In short, what is your vision for sustainability in the future? How does it look to you from here?

It's not going back to nature. That's for sure. It's celebrating nature's abundance and intellectual, cultural expression. We celebrate the prospect of ecologically intelligent products that either return safely to the soil or back to industry, forever. In this way, we can celebrate consumption because it creates more life, it creates jobs—and we like people to have jobs, to be able to buy things for themselves and for their families. We celebrate plastic. We celebrate good synthetic materials because we know that they are critical to the earth's survival. If everyone wore 100 percent cotton and Birkenstocks, the planet would dry up and we would run out of cork in seconds. The idea that we would all "go back to nature" is unrealistic. You can't do it, and it's a completely foolish notion with six billion souls on the planet. We celebrate the abundance of creativity and we also add in an astonishingly important component of humility. We may be wrong.

Putting aside the humble disclaimer, how do we get there? How can we turn this vision into reality?

Our strategy is to seek new paradigms and protocols, and then to inform commerce—the business world—of the things that can be instantly profitable. We're very understanding of the need of commerce as an entity to be profitable. Commerce is defined by being profitable. If we remove their short-term profitability, we remove one of their foundation stones and they will collapse—especially today, when you don't have family-run companies that can look at legacy periods. Instead, like all of us, commerce is now looking at quarterly returns. Even the most benign leader of a shareholder organization at this point is required to respond to the quarterly pressure. We honor that, but we put it in the context of the larger agenda so that we might redesign the entire process. So we're focused on the commercial zone. Profitability is not bad: it is essential. Good things are profitable.

There is a sense of balance and synthesis that runs through much of your writing and speaking. I'm wondering whether it is a strategy for action, or whether it is really a critical element in the way you perceive true innovation.

Balance is critical to the way I think of innovation. It does a series of things. First, innovation must honor each radical position, which means it operates as a translation system, a language that communicates strongly held ideas. I remember meeting with the late environmentalist David Brower after he had read our Hannover Principles, and he said it was remarkable that he and I could talk and completely understand each other, and that I could in turn talk to a CEO and completely understand him, but that David Brower and a CEO wouldn't understand a word each other said. Innovation, for me, speaks of a role that helps to make common sense out of strong environmental, capitalistic, and social positions, which is a very unusual and useful translation zone.

So how does this translation foster creative new modes of thought? It removes people's fear, the fear of engaging in a new protocol. We go to people on the business side and say to them, "We understand you're in business to make money and there's nothing wrong with that." To a radical environmentalist I can say, "I completely understand the need to preserve wilderness. I agree with you completely."

I say to them that we can achieve both of their results by taking human artifice and encapsulating it in the biological and technical cycles so that the human impact on the planet is a coherent one that we can comprehend and understand and design into, which allows us to leave the rest of the world viable. Without doing it, without sequestering our activity in our defined area, we *will* destroy the rest of the world.

Can you give us an example?

You're sitting in your house and you're worried about termites. You should be worried about termites: they'll eat your house down. What you do today, under the current paradigm, is you poison the land, which means you've just poisoned your children, yourself, your pets, too. This is a strategy of using brute force of either a physical or chemical nature to say to the termite, "I destroy you and your habitat. Don't get within two hundred feet of my house. I have declared war on you." Of course, you've declared war on everything else—trees, for example. What's the better way to deal with termites? We actually design buildings where the termites are told, "This is the human zone. Here's the line." We make a physical line and say, "This is our nest. Not for you. Your nest is over there. Here's me. There's you." It turns out we can do this gently and elegantly using fungi.

So you realize the paradigm shift. The whole landscape shifts if you honor a different strategy. Everything can move to a place where we achieve our commercial purpose and keep people busy, but we don't need to destroy the world at the same time. You don't need to poison the land within two hundred feet of your house just to get this worked out. In the larger context, humans need to understand where they are and let the rest of the world continue to thrive on its own terms.

Back to the question of balance as a principle of innovation. I can see from what you say that it makes you effective . . .

No. Watch what happens. All of a sudden I can no longer accept the status quo. Because the status quo is one that is destructive. The present paradigm of design is this: take from the world whatever it offers to us in a cradle-to-grave flow cycle. Whatever you're designing —termite control, a house, a car—the modern instruction appears to be that if brute force doesn't work, you're not using enough of it. So add more chemicals. Add more gasoline. If you have a building in Rangoon that is uncomfortable, add more energy. The fact that this building is causing nitrogen to disperse willy-nilly, the fact that it is causing global warming, is not part of the question. This idea of understanding distant effects is new.

So, instead of saying that innovation is thinking "out of the box," you're saying you should be more deeply in the box. If you're outside the box, can you really understand the forces that have created it?

I'm asking a more fundamental question. Why a box? What box? Whether you're in the box or out of the box is not the question. It's like growth/no growth. The current debate between the environmentalists and the new administration is reduced to this overly simple equation. The commercial actors are saying we have to have growth because it is the engine of commerce, and they're right. Then you have the environmentalists saying you have to stop growth because growth is destroying the world. It's an idiotic conversation. Is growth bad in a tree? Is it bad in children? That's a box. The real question is: *What* do you want to grow . . . and how?

That's the first question, and there is no box around it. There's nothing but the human imagination around it. Do you want to grow prosperity or poverty? Health or sickness? Intelligence or stupidity? If every case of leukemia has the effect of creating eleven jobs, is that how we want to increase employment? So is it good that we pollute and give people cancer? It's a fundamental question. I was talking to a major petroleum company and I asked them what business they were in. They said, candidly, "We don't know." Well, I said, from an environmental perspective, you're in the carbon-releasing business. The question is, is it really your strategy to cause this tragedy? Is that your intent? Is that the box?

How does our era of high-speed change foster innovation? Does it demand it, or simply reward it?

I look at the issue of change on a very personal basis. I look at the people running these companies and I see so much stress forced by change. It's no wonder that they don't engage the larger issues; they have to deal with changes that have happened that day in an important but infinitely small aspect of their operations. Change is something business people see microscopically. What we're trying to do is to help them look at change macroscopically. We suggest that the better way to deal with the small issues is to deal with the larger issues. If you're focusing without a macroscope, then you don't know where you are in the universe, in the culture. All you know is next week's stock ticker.

Your celebrated article in the October 1998 Atlantic Monthly, *"The Next Industrial Revolution," really turned a lot of the discussion about the environment on its head. In it, you argued that ecoefficiency, the standard bearer of ecological consciousness for the last 20 years, was merely a way of polluting at a slower rate. The real answer was a radical shift to what you called ecoeffectiveness. Can you tell us a little about the effects of this publication?*

It's driving a lot of people crazy. We have corporate people coming to us, managers of sustainability in a company, telling us they have done what they were supposed to do, they have all these programs for ecoefficiency that have saved all these millions of dollars, and then you guys come along and tell me I have been following a completely misdirected strategy. You're telling me all I've done is make the existing paradigm more profitable.

But the truth is, efficiency is not innovation. That's a false goal of innovation. Efficiency has no value per se. From a philosophical perspective efficiency is valueless. There is nothing inherently positive or ethical about it. Nazis were efficient. In other words, if you're doing the wrong thing, efficiency is pernicious. My partner, Michael Braungart, points out that the truly efficient dinner is a pill and a glass of red wine. Imagine Mozart being efficient. Hit the piano with a 2×4, all the notes at once. Done. A sonata.

The simple truth is that the industrial system we have now is largely wrong, and efficiency only perpetuates it. If we say to Mitsubishi, "You must make twice as many boxes out of the trees in Indonesia," they may be more efficient, but it doesn't change the story. Good-bye Indonesia. Efficiency doesn't change the underlying program. That's where the innovation comes in. Innovation in this case is the simple insight that we really shouldn't be making boxes out of trees. What's the right story for packaging? What should it be made of? What is the ecologically effective way to make packaging? That's the question.

Who is asking that question these days, besides you and a few of your colleagues?

Clients like Bill Ford, that's who. We have many more like him, wonderful people and organizations to work with. Clients who will open the door in a company and say, "Go out there. Be with my people. See what happens." Once clients recognize that they can engage us, and track their careers around our strategies, things begin to happen that are very interesting.

You have been retained by the Ford Motor Company to assist it in reengineering one of the largest and oldest industrial sites on earth, the Ford River Rouge Center. Would you describe how some of the thinking we have been discussing is manifesting itself in the project so far?

We're doing a hundred separate projects with Ford. Perhaps ten of them are at the Rouge plant. We're doing fabrics, interiors, manufacturing protocols, adhesives, paint, coatings.

You're allowed to speak publicly about all this? Most clients are a little more averse to publicity, aren't they?

Ford has done something truly remarkable. They have said to us that they don't want ownership, they want leadership. All the ideas and all the materials we come up with in the automobile industry are going to be made available to everybody. As soon as we have our work done, and we understand that what we have come up with seems really to be a good next step, we put them out there. Like polyesters for upholstery and car interiors that don't include carcinogenic residues from catalytic reactions. We're currently working with the chemical industry creating polyesters that are simply delightful polymers, safe for all generations, a terrific synthetic human material, designed to be in closed cycles. What actually does get into the biological cycle is not simply free of contaminants, but is nutrition. For example, as the fabric abrades and I breathe in the fibers, they are good for me. It's a very exciting thing.

What took the chemical industry so long? Why does it need you, and people like you, to come along and show the way?

We just begin with a radically different set of principles. For example, we think every product made should be tested against drug standards developed for children. What happens if your child chews on a doll's head? If the toy company says dolls were never designed to be chewed upon, they've never seen a child. So why are there endocrine disrupters in the polymers of a child's toy? The point is, this toy can be seen as a drug for children, and should be tested that way. We think the same logic applies not just to toys but to every product on the market. It's never really been thought of that way, and now that we think that way, we tell the companies we work with, and they say, "Of course. Why didn't we think of that?" The people running these operations are not unprincipled and they're not idiots—they just haven't been operating under a set of principles.

If you as an innovator had to choose between asking great questions and implementing great answers, which would you choose?

I can't choose. It depends on what we're trying to do at the time. Maybe the best way to put it is that innovation means you can't do one without the other, questions and answers. For example, when I ask an oil company, "What business are you in?" there is a critical pause. Any business manager understands that this is a fundamental business question that only they can answer. But they must answer the question and they must get it right, because ultimately it is the thing that will drive their business. So for me to ask that isn't being contentious, it's opening the door to innovation. It's a good opening because they understand that the only constant in the world of commerce is high-speed change, and that how they answered the question last week may well be different from how they answer it this week.

Then how about the answers? If the right questions can open the doors, what is the room people now get to enter?

The invention, fabricating the answers, implementing the solutions, is actually the delightful part of life. I think everyone on the planet should have this much fun. That's the reason I work with Michael Braungart. He's the smartest person I have ever met and he and I seem to have a certain chemistry. He, in fact, is a chemist. He can help us actually make things, these fabrics, all the products and places I have described. That's the fun.

You have described elsewhere a relationship with your partner that all of us would kill for, a mutual fueling of ideas. How critical is having such a relationship in your role as an innovator?

Michael and I are committed to working together for the rest of our lives, and our most delightful condition is when we are inventing. We are structuring our businesses so that they operate first as legitimate operations that serve clients and customers, but also so that they operate in ways that bring us together. That give us as much time as possible to simply dream up new things. Innovations aren't momentary flashes while you're sitting in a marketing meeting. They're something you work for, give time to.

Can you describe a modus of dreaming that seems to yield practical results? We've all sat around a table for occasions of "brainstorming," and actually spent most of the time thinking about lunch. What principles can you share about how you structure and shape these sessions of dreams?

Michael was once asked by another interviewer why he didn't work with anyone else but me in this kind of project. His answer was that when he worked with others and proposed an interesting idea, the response was usually, "What an interesting idea!" He said that when he works with me, I say, "Well, if we do that, then why not do this as well?" And then he says, "And then we could do that." And then after a few minutes we may look at the string of ideas we have just generated and conclude that they're all nonsense. Except that maybe the problem was that we took a slight wrong turn halfway back, and if we go back there and begin again, we might really have something. We exchange ideas at a fierce rate because we're not afraid of being wrong.

But we have clients, you see. All of this idea generation occurs in the context of specific challenges that force us to focus. It's just that we have principles that force us to look at the big and the small, as I already said. We have to speculate on the energy and flows for the whole planet in order to understand how our small design might fit within that picture. We constantly reflect on the wider philosophic frame in order to attend to these microscopic issues and problems.

How does creativity of such a high order as you are describing work in a collaborative environment? I understand how this process of creative dreaming works between you and your partner, but how do you communicate it to the troops in such a way that they can act on it?

We tell stories. Back in the early days when he and Norbert Weiner were coining the term "cybernetics," Gregory Bateson constructed a little fable for his book *Mind and Nature*. He says a man went to a computer and said, "Tell me, computer, when do you think computers will begin to think like humans?" There was a long pause, and then the computer said, "That reminds me of a story I once heard . . ." So humans all communicate best through stories, and that's what we do with our staffs. We tell a story of what we did with textiles and then ask what we should be doing with cars. Stories of what we did in the past work as models and protocols for new sets of innovations and solutions in the future.

You often tell stories about the more distant past, a time when there was more balance because humans had simply not devised tools that could cause so much harm. Part of innovating seems to be "innovating back."

The overlay of modern technology on ancient traditions is actually the most astonishingly obvious thing that has occurred during the process of industrialization. Look at architecture. The ancients had mass—stone which had the ability to store heat for the cold nights and coolness for the hot days—and they had resistance in the form of shingles, tents, things that resisted water and wind, insulation from the vagaries of nature. But the ancients loved transparency; luminosity was their hope for the transcendent building, the cathedral with its stained glass. They understood our psychic connection to illumination. In benign climates this was easy: a window, a hole in the wall. Modern architecture now has the large sheet of glass, something that both illuminates and resists. In ancient terms glass is magic. But what has happened? Ironically, we have lost our connection to, and understanding of, the sun. I gave a talk to 10,000 architects in 1993 at McCormick Place in Chicago, and I asked how many of them knew how to find true south. Only a few people raised their hands. We're sealed behind glass and cut off. We're trapped in sealed gas chambers that we call office buildings. So yes, we can "innovate back," past our age of brute-force applications of energy, past this use of glass that, ironically, is used to cut us off from that for which we, as humans, have such a deep yearning.

Who are your heroes? What personal inspirations from the past?

Gandhi, for one. Martin Luther King. Nelson Mandela. They understood the need for dreaming. They understood the usefulness of storytelling. And they were nonviolent. I'm so nonviolent in my thinking that I would take up the sword to defend nonviolence, but the sword would be one of persuasion, of passion. A perhaps more obscure hero is Sir Albert Howard, the British agronomist who was initially sent by the Crown to Africa and, later, to India to explain to the native cultures what Western agriculture was all about. When he got there he realized his mission was going to be quite different. His story is in his wonderful book, *An Agricultural Testament.* What he realized was, "It's the bacteria, stupid." Brute-force chemical approaches and steel blades were doing nothing that the planet hadn't figured out billions of years ago.

How did this happen for you? You grew up in the Far East and have spoken of the culture shock you felt as a child coming here to this land of waste. I'm wondering where along the line, as an adult, you realized that you could not solve problems by simply doing better, but that you had to do it by doing different. How do you account for that?

Two things. First, I studied under Bauhaus masters in college, and I took in their notion that the world could be reimagined. That was the Bauhaus principle, and you can make your peace or not with their hubris. Yet the fundamental charge stayed with me. And then, as a graduate student at Yale, I built the first solar house in Ireland. It was an accident. I'd been in Paris working at the Le Corbusier Foundation in 1974, cataloging his early drawings, and saw his heroic intentions manifested by drawings he had made when he was my age. But I had girlfriend problems in Paris, or actually, girlfriend's father problems. So I went to Ireland on the way home because my excursion ticket took me through. While I was there I met my first client, the glassblower Simon Pearce, and through him I became part of the old William Morris crowd—the potters and furniture makers who were still there practicing in the Arts and Crafts tradition. One of these potters asked me to build her a house. With Le Corbusier in my head, and in the midst of all these extraordinarily creative people, the ordinary wouldn't do. So what I built was a solar-heated house. It's an ancient idea really. I have been following the logical progression of dreams and ideas ever since.

26

Always Faster? More? Newer? Better?

Christoph-Friedrich v. Braun

The Compulsion to Grow

Growth—the magic word of our time. Idolized and cursed, measure of success and dire portent, source of well-being and root of all evil. We fear world population growth and yet bless the birth of children in our own country. Productivity improvements and sales increases, deterioration of the ozone layer and soil erosion, old-age benefits and alienated generations—it all stems from, is based on, and is a necessary and inevitable symptom of the growth process.

Growth is built into the system. "That which does not grow is dead" (which, by the way, is an erroneous statement in reference to nature; the life forms that live the longest grow the slowest). The dictate of monetary interest is based on growth of capital. A starting amount of 100 marks must be managed to yield more than 100 marks. And because the productivity of manufacturing and services increases over time, growth is necessary to exploit these newly freed-up capacities.

But what happens when growth hits its limits, when markets are saturated or grow more slowly, when the charm of the new wears off? Populations can grow only when at least one of two conditions is fulfilled: either more means are available to them, or the means that are already provided are extended. Up to now, history has shown that both conditions were always feasible within certain limits. The same applies to corporate sales. They can only grow if existing markets allow it or if new markets can be tapped. Only in the past 20 years have doubts arisen about whether it must be this way for all time.

When it was a matter of hungry markets with high purchase power, as in postwar Europe, or Southeast Asia during the past 10 years, growth as a rule was no problem, even without intensive marketing. Demand was great enough to absorb everything manufacturers could provide. This is no longer the case. Many markets are saturated. If every household already has one or even two TVs, and the number of households doesn't grow, it becomes harder and harder to maintain increases in the sale of TVs. The demand is gone, except for satisfying replacement needs. Hence, the only solution is to find new markets for TVs.

Other factors beyond market saturation can limit growth. The more overcrowded streets become with cars, the more unattractive driving, and consequently buying, a car becomes. Externally imposed conditions, taxes, or restrictions can also limit automobile usage long before every citizen has his or her own.

The general compulsion to grow has little regard for limited markets or sales prospects. Motivational and value systems, praise and reward, are all directed toward more, faster, and bigger. When one source of growth dries up, another must be found. In principle, there are only five possibilities:

1. Higher market shares
2. New sales channels

3. New sales regions
4. Mergers
5. Innovations

Methods of Growth

Often enough, the possibilities listed above function quite well. There are countless examples of companies that have used one or more of them to make a comeback from a stagnant phase to a period of healthy, long-term growth. Yet every source of growth has its own characteristics and problems.

The task of gaining *market shares* in a stagnant market always runs into immediate resistance from the competition. The "purchase" of market shares through rebates, advertising campaigns, or other means can become expensive and result in disastrous price wars. The current situation in the German detergent market is indicative of this in that there is no longer any growth potential because the population, though well supplied, is stagnant or even declining. The battle for advertising space and TV airtime among the industry giants is apparent everywhere.

Alternative sales channels, i.e., finding new ways to reach customers, first requires the existence and the knowledge of such channels. Very often there are potential conflicts with existing distribution channels. A company whose previous success was based on the shipping of products, for example, or on sales being processed through middlemen will shoot itself in the foot if it suddenly opens its own stores. Kodak would be ill advised to open its own chain of photo stores in which competitive products by Fuji and Agfa were not sold. Not only would the company have to fear the wrath of the established photo business, there would also be internal organizational resistance and real as well as perceived reservations against the construction of an unfamiliar, unknown, and probably risky distribution track.

The third source of growth—*breaking out into new geographic regions,* especially in foreign countries—is also sometimes difficult. This is where adaptability kicks in. Many companies, German ones included, have mastered this art. But still the path toward the outside often leads to failure, whether because of political risks, differences in standards, cultures, and values, or because with increasing frequency, competitive industries that defend the home market with all available means have been established in other countries as well. The automobile industry is a prime example of this. In the 1950s, there were no more than 10 countries in which the world's automobiles were manufactured (excluding socialist countries). Today there are more than 50 active in this market, with various value-added levels, all wanting to export. New plants are being built everywhere, but the old ones are not being shut down. The global automotive production capacity was expected to have risen to 80 million by the year 2000, but demand would lag behind at 60 million. Even if the entire U.S. automotive industry were to be shut down, there would still be overcapacities in the world. The route to the outside is not always paved with gold.

Mergers, be they through takeovers, strategic alliances, partnerships, or other forms of cooperation, have been a preferred means of company growth since the 1980s. The volume from mergers and takeovers in the United States in 1995 alone reached $515 billion. Of all the growth methods, these are probably the fastest because, on paper at least, they allow the sales of the participating companies to be simply added up. However, numerous studies and statistics show horrible success ratios from takeovers. The consulting firm McKinsey, for example, reported that out of 116 major acquisitions tracked over an 11-year period, a total of only 23% regained their takeover costs. The same is true for alliances in which the participating companies maintain their respective independence. Experience shows that partnerships *can* be a highly effective means of growth, but only in rare cases in which predefined expectations are met. This stems chiefly from different company cultures, not having thorough, inside knowledge of the participating company in terms of common-alities, and different ideas regarding strategic alliance goals.

Which brings us to *innovation*. There are probably very few companies today that have not espoused this particular cause. Still, many of them don't exactly know what innovation really is. The term has existed in English since the fifteenth century. In German, it means generally the same today as then: the introduction or appli-cation of something new, a new idea, a new procedure or device that concerns not only the technical invention, but also its economic im-plementation.

A Brief History of Innovation

In earlier centuries, new things and ideas either appeared or failed to appear for the most part coincidentally. Innovations either hap-pened or didn't, depending on whether an inventor stumbled onto a good idea that he or someone else could market successfully. But nobody at that time had yet realized it was a matter of intentionally using it as a means to expedite company growth.

Edison, the inventor and genius, was the first to make this con-nection, as well as entrepreneurs like Siemens, Krupp and others shortly before the turn of the century. Until that time, emerging tech-nological progress and innovations were marveled at amidst the eu-phoria of industrialization, but nonetheless largely considered to be uncontrolled and uncontrollable occurrences—rather like the weather —which, in whatever form, were either present or weren't.

That the time was ripe for a new way of looking at things was ex-pressed by Werner von Siemens in 1883: "A country's industry will never gain a leading position and be able to maintain it if the country is not simultaneously at the very peak of scientific progress. *To bring this about* is the most effective means of elevating the industry."

In the 1930s, the economist and sociologist Joseph A. Schumpeter undertook a more precise analysis of the process by which new technologies are formed. Building on teachings of the marginal utilities school, he worked out a theory of economic development that was characterized particularly by the appearance of "dynamic companies" in which an increase in competition was brought about by means of *intentional* (i.e., not randomly "coincidental") innovations. This involved not only winners, but losers as well. And it was largely the determination of the company to beat out the competition —or the company's fear of losing—on which the dynamics of free markets depended.

The teachings of Schumpeter and other guiding intellectual forces were not only studied and grasped; their use today in the field is increasing. Innovations and their scope, their local usage, chronological introduction, and degree of improvement in regard to previous products are specifically used as strategic rules of competition. Enormous amounts of money are poured into the development of new products and processes. The Siemens company alone spends approximately 1 million marks *per hour* on research and development (R&D), including nights and weekends. Among the 25 Western industrialized countries that are members of the Organization for Economic Cooperation and Development OECD, the total cost is considerably higher than $1 billion per day. Over 70% of this total goes to industrial laboratories. Industries also finance a somewhat smaller amount—around 30%–50% per country. The rest is carried by the state, universities, and other nonprofit organizations. Only a relatively small amount of the total R&D expenditures (approximately 5%–10%) goes for nonspecific basic research.

Industrialized companies today mutually outbid each other in attempting to spend a larger portion of their profits to foster innovations. In internal benchmarking, R&D expenditures regularly serve as a gauge used by the most important competitors in determining their own R&D budget. The impression that a company is somehow lagging behind must be avoided at all costs, since this could be interpreted by the public or in the marketplace as too little preparedness or a general ineptitude in regard to innovation.

The International Technology Race

It's easy to understand today how things got to be this way. The first sign that we were headed toward competition for leadership positions in technology was probably the Russian atomic bomb in the late 1940s. Still, if an exact starting date were to be assigned to the international technology race, it would have to be October 4, 1957, when the first Russian satellite, *Sputnik,* completed an orbit around the earth. Already in the world wars it was evident to all participants that technology and the possibilities connected with it could determine the outcome of a war. The English fighter planes in the Battle of Britain, the German "super-weapon," and particularly the American atomic bombs on Hiroshima and Nagasaki forcefully drove this point home. However, the fact that the well-being of entire nations, even outside a raging war, would or should depend on technological skills did not become abundantly clear to the general public until the shadow of the Soviet Union suddenly loomed over the United States, leaving it outdistanced and vulnerable in terms of space exploration, rockets, and other space technologies. The response to "Sputnik Shock" between 1957 and 1967 was a doubling of U.S. R&D expenditures, to approximately $30 billion (in 1972 equivalents). Relative to the gross national product (GNP), this amount constituted a doubling, from 1.5% in 1957 to approximately 3% in 1964. As a gauge for comparison, at the end of World War II, American R&D efforts came to approximately $10 billion —less than 1% of the GNP.

The core of this enormous growth was the 1961 Apollo Moon Project announced by President Kennedy, for which virtually unlimited funds were available from the mid-1960s. No other highly developed countries even came close. In 1964, the American R&D

efforts totaled $24 billion—an amount that was approximately three times higher than those spent by England, France, West Germany, Japan, Canada, Holland, Italy, and Sweden combined. Of the approximately 770,000 engineers and scientists employed in these nine countries at that time, just under 500,000 were in the United States. The annual per capita expenditure for R&D in that year in the United States was approximately $111, as compared to $40 in England, which came in second in R&D funding at that time, followed by West Germany with $25, and $9 in Japan.

Naturally it did not escape the notice of companies in other industrialized nations that the growing U.S. research and development efforts not only made possible the construction of moon rockets, satellites, landing modules, and ground stations, but also indirectly helped promote technological advances in other areas, such as optics, medical and communications technology, data processing, material sciences, etc., where in the past there had always been competitive relationships. The idea that from such a technological backwardness, a subsequent economic and ultimately political backwardness could arise was broached by Jean-Jacques Servan-Schreiber in 1967 in his book *Le Défi américain* (The American Challenge). He warned that lack of sufficient technological efforts on the part of industrialized European nations would place them in danger of degenerating to an economic colony of the United States.

The book was a best-seller in many countries, even in Japan. It stimulated numerous political and economic considerations on the part of government and industry concerning what steps might be taken, with help from massive technological programs, to bring about a boom in Europe similar to what American companies had experienced through Apollo. Also worthy of consideration is the idea that the civilian program responsible for the English-French supersonic Concorde may have been a result of these efforts. Even though it became clear before the aircraft was built that it would never recover its own cost, there was still the hope of spin-off effects, as was the case with Apollo. The Soviets were of a like mind and began development of their own supersonic Tupolev 144, which was remarkably similar to the Concorde. At the same time in the United States, serious worries began to emerge that the Concorde could herald the end of American leadership in aviation; thus began the independent SST (Supersonic Transport) project, which would have surpassed the achievements of the Concorde in regard to range, speed, and passenger capacity by a wide margin, except that the project was suspended prior to its initial flight due to economic and ecological considerations.

With these and other similar efforts (German examples include the numerous federally promoted data-processing programs and the Transrapid maglev train), the international technology race was off to a hot start. Even if it didn't penetrate the general consciousness of the 1970s and 1980s, the real opposition had shifted from the Soviet Union to other highly industrialized nations, at least in regard to civilian technologies. In all the OECD countries, R&D budgets were continually increased in both the private and government sectors until the 1990s. It was not until after 1991 that the situation began to calm down somewhat, due to the economic restrictions in the three largest Western economies: the United States, Japan, and Germany.

Since the mid-90s, however, Japanese and American budgets have been on the rise again. In Germany, too, numerous voices are calling for such an increase. The reason: the general belief that economic growth in today's globally competitive arena requires the ability to place attractive, competitive innovations on the market.

Competitive Leveraging

Behind all this is the belief that in a market well-supplied with all the necessities of life, innovative growth can only take place if the consumer is ready either to pay for the attraction (and the cost) of new or more efficient products and technologies with higher prices, or—if prices remain the same, or drop—to change over earlier to an innovative offering. A simple example: I can either buy a new camera every five years and pay a higher price for all the technical improvements it has undergone in the meantime, or because of technological progress, I can do this after four or even three years, and pay the same or even a lower price. For the camera industry, both methods count as growth as far as the books are concerned.

But if a supplier wants to recoup the cost of his technical growth efforts not only via the price charged but also through an earlier realization of profit, timing becomes an important competitive factor. Every supplier must then attempt to gain an advantage over the competition—or, in other words, every supplier must try to provide specific technical performance features before all the other suppliers. This gives him a market position similar to a monopoly and greater freedom in setting price, which will last at least as long as it takes for the competition to come out with the same performance features.

Such a leadership position is naturally highly attractive. It is the foundation of the frequently described and often troublesome innovator's profit. If I can do something nobody else can do, I can demand the highest price for it the market will bear. The result is the high-tech competitive paradigm so prevalent everywhere today: whoever is quickest, whoever is first on the market, wins the race. Unconditionally, inevitably, guaranteed.

It is unfortunately different in practice. This is mostly because the competition in timing the introduction of new technologies and products in the meantime has become a generally used instrument of competition. Any company that is active to any extent in any industry characterized by innovation (which today means almost all industries, even forestry) wants to be faster than its competition. This is in accordance with a creed represented at all levels of government, science, and economy. Governments demand speed in their respective national industrial companies. These in turn define "time-to-market" as an explicit strategic goal. Academics write comprehensive textbooks on simultaneous engineering, linkage management, skunk works, patent strategies, conjoint analysis, technology transfer, and numerous other processes to accelerate innovation. Business consultants help business managers and R&D managers with the creation of technology portfolios for evaluation and acceleration of alternative technological investments, highly promising R&D orientations and decisions. And R&D managers ultimately see themselves confronted with requirements in line with increasingly short-term milestone reports, cost-time prognoses, acquisition and cancellation decisions, competitive analyses, and budget applications.

The Escalation of Acceleration

Problems arise primarily because the attempt to speed everything up has become an industry-wide phenomenon. *All* companies want to be faster than the others. *All* of them use more or less the same acceleration processes to be able to introduce the next generation of products just a little quicker than their competitors. And because all of them have the same technical and economic problems and the same technical and economic know-how, all of them provide the same markets with the same or similar products. This has several important consequences.

The amount of time between the first innovator and the second, third, or even later successors is getting smaller all the time. In the past, technological leaders enjoyed long-lasting positions, protected through patents or other types of procedures. For example, Xerox successfully defended its copier technology for years and was almost untouchable because of it. The same thing happened with Apple and its PC technology for most of the 1980s. Both companies had something that was effectively protected and that the competition, for whatever reason, could not duplicate. Such situations today are much more rare.

Technological leads that used to last for years and then months in the fast-paced electronics industry are now compressed to weeks, sometimes days. High technology itself has contributed to this phenomenon through the development of modern communications media, since information on scientific findings, technological breakthroughs, patent registrations, and new project plans can now be spread around the world literally at the speed of light.

In February 1995, for example, the Japanese electronics firm NEC announced the manufacture of the first experimental memory chip with a capacity of one gigabyte. Only two days later, Hitachi went public with the same announcement. Chemical companies come out with the same or similar substances within very short intervals. Automotive firms at the same trade fairs are repeatedly introducing new vehicle concepts that are identical to the competition's—recreational vehicles, vans, or other innovations that are practically indistinguishable from one another, which nobody was offering last year but which everyone is touting this year. Because all competitors know the same things, they all draw the same conclusions, which accordingly shortens the time during which the intellectual or technical leadership position could be rewarded with profits.

Not to be overlooked is the fact that it is often *not* the first supplier on the market who has the greatest long-term success, but instead the smart latecomer who sees how to avoid the mistakes made by early pioneers and who can then introduce a better, more complete version based on the same innovative idea. Home video recorders, permanent four-wheel drive, computer tomography, kidney lithotripsy, and many other new ideas from the past few years and decades are impressive examples of this.

Along with the effort to get new products on the market in quick succession comes a new factor: a general reduction in the product life cycle. This phenomenon has been frequently documented over the past 20 years. The time between the introduction of a new product and its obsolescence due to the introduction of a still-newer product is getting shorter and shorter. Fifty years ago, the supplier of a successful pharmaceutical could count on a market presence of around 25 years. This period of time now runs about eight years. This has little to do with the technological service life of products or appliances. On the contrary, it is precisely *because* the technology has been further developed that products tend to last a longer instead of a shorter time. For example, this text was written using a two-year-old, perfectly good computer, which was bought new, but is no longer available on the market. Refrigerators and washing machines easily last more than 10 or 15 years, cars are capable of driving the equivalent of four or five times around the earth, modern truck tires could handle 20 times around the earth and more, an average reflex camera can survive 1,000 rolls of film and produce private photographs quite well for a number of years. But so-called innovative products are still being placed on the market in increasingly quick succession.

The Speed Limit

For a time, this type of innovation policy may be reasonable and bear fruit. As long as consumers can be convinced that they have to have the newest, fastest, smallest, largest, brightest, or most astonishing, perhaps they can be enticed to acquire more before the previous product has quit working or reached its technical limits. But what happens when the technical newness of a product and also the continued increase in its performance ability begin to lose their appeal? This is often enough the case even now. Many computer users complain about the incomprehensibility and unusability of annual

software upgrades that continue to require higher-capacity computers. In addition to the purchase price of the hardware and software,
they must simultaneously contend with considerable conversion
and learning expenses before they are even able to use their innovative new acquisitions. Not only are the charts that list the best-
selling musical selections changing faster than ever, the media formats in which the music is recorded are changing rapidly as well.
The evolution from 78s to long-playing albums to cassettes to
compact discs to digital audio tape to minidiscs, etc., requires investment in new equipment and systems at increasingly shorter intervals, and the number of consumers who are willing to make these
investments is declining—particularly since the perceived benefit
or performance ability is less with each new generation of technology.

Further, it must be made clear that under such accelerated conditions, it is not the *duration* of the product's life cycle that brings
about growth, but rather the *shortening* of this duration. That which
is perceived as growth is basically not true market expansion, but
only the early realization of sales that would otherwise have occurred later. This type of growth can be maintained only as long as
suppliers can implement this shortened product duration and life cycle. Once the cycles quit shortening, "growth" caves in. The fact that
this must eventually happen is crystal clear, because there is a unique
lower limit for the duration of any product's life cycle: it cannot be
shorter than the sale of even one single item from a product generation. This leads to an interesting insight: if the ultimate goal of numerous production engineers and process developers of hitting the
proverbial jackpot is reached, a historic line of development comes
to an end. What then?

In addition, with the increasingly hectic turnover of innovations,
the actual or intended improvements between product generations decrease. Who can really hear whether the tone quality of a minidisc is

better than that of a CD? Is the new Golf really so much better than the old, or are there really just a few improvements here and there in the seating arrangement, curve-gripping performance, and exhaust values, which could be relativized by the higher price, more weight, or higher consumption? Companies in development-intensive industries today typically have several product generations simultaneously in the lab and on the design screen. Money has already been laid down for future products with predecessors and pre-predecessors that have not even been put on the market yet. The big automotive companies frequently work on up to four models at the same time. It is clear that they must adhere to limits regarding the extent of technological improvements integrated into the generation after the next, and the one after that, and so on. Because of competitive pressure regarding innovation, a supplier must often put more emphasis on being in position with a new product—*any* new product—at the right time than on presenting the consumer with a product that is truly improved. At any rate, it is often difficult under pressing time constraints to develop something responsibly to the end, which results in the product being forced into production before it is ready, as with, for example, the premature introduction of the (at that time still defective) Pentium chip by Intel. It is also not unusual for an innovation not to work in the environment for which it was intended. There are many examples that could be cited: new cameras don't fit old interchangeable lenses, new software is not compatible with the existing operating system, new kitchen appliances don't fit the same places the old ones occupied, etc. Frustration is steadily rising with poorly designed, defective, expensive innovations that are technology-friendly but not user-friendly.

Because of the continuous onslaught of new products, it can happen that a new product is obsolete before the customer has learned how to operate it properly or been able to pay it off. When a new product is introduced, appropriate support and service from the manufacturer for older products is then only grudgingly provided. It is rather blatantly suggested that the new product be acquired, after which the whole scenario can be repeated within a short time. It is precisely here that, because of the mass quantities of old products that are both installed and functioning, innovations must actually be introduced with the greatest care; too often the introduction is made with a careless disregard that pushes the purchase price into the background. Consumers have to put up with this all the time. It's no wonder that in the change-intensive PC industry and others like it, a distinct tiredness with innovation and a general mood of resistance is noticeably on the rise. Among users who, for better or for worse, are intent on the ergonomic, proper functioning of their investments for better or for worse, the rule of thumb is: "Don't buy anything that hasn't been on the market at least a year."

Innovation = Progress?

The general phenomenon that is evident behind such excesses in innovation is the widespread equating of technical change with technical progress. The result is that the word "innovation" has consistently positive overtones. It is deemed as something worthy of being cultivated, in the same boat as health, well-being, and a good reputation. It is accompanied by the belief that innovations are a cure-all for virtually all the ills of the world. They are thought to ensure national competitiveness and job security, offset expenses, guarantee growth, increase tax revenues, straighten out the environment, provide people with education, entertainment, health, creative and political freedom, and joyfully usher the entire planet into a wonderful future.

Unfortunately, this is not always the case. Here as everywhere else, it is possible to have too much of a good thing. Innovations that bypass actual needs, that only come about for their own sake, that fail to take natural aging and habituation processes into account, that are too hurriedly and incompletely produced, that don't sufficiently address all the operational requirements of the innovator and the market, that equate "new" with "significant improvement," and many other apparent and pseudo-innovations, waste a lot of money, both on the part of the supplier and the would-be consumer. They harm more than they help, and they ultimately get in the way of innovations that would be really useful and important. There are countless innovations in this latter category that would be warmly welcomed, even if they arrived on the market a bit later. Being the first on the market is not a guarantee of success, and being second doesn't have to be a death sentence; it is becoming increasingly clear that having the right innovation is much more desirable than simply having the fastest. Technology today offers many opportunities to change practically everything. Still, it is not the choice of what *can* be changed that continues to grow in importance, but instead what *should* be changed.

Contributors

John Barnie is the author of twelve collections of poetry, fiction and essays. He was a Lecturer at the University of Copenhagen from 1969 to 1982, and has been editor of *Planet, The Welsh Internationalist* since 1990. His latest book, *The Wine Bird,* was published by Gomer Press in 1998.

Gerd Binnig studied physics and has worked at the IBM Zurich Research Laboratory in Rüschlikon, Switzerland, and the University of Munich. He has garnered many awards, including the German Research Prize, the Otto Klung Prize, the Hewlett Packard Prize, the King Faisal Prize, and the Nobel Prize for Physics. Since 1990 he has sat on the board of Daimler Benz Holding and is currently at the IBM Zurich Research Laboratory.

Katja Blomberg studied art history in Freiburg i. Br. and in Hamburg. She lived for several years in Japan as an art critic before completing her academic training in Heidelberg. She lives in Aachen and works as a free correspondent, covering the Netherlands and Belgium, for the *Frankfurter Allgemeine Zeitung.*

Christoph-Friedrich v. Braun studied space law and technology management. He has worked as an engineering consultant at Dorsch Consult GmbH in Munich and then at Siemens AG in various capacities. Since 1990 he has worked as an independent consultant in Japanese affairs and technology and organization. He is the author of numerous publications, including *Der Innovationskrieg* (*The Innovation War,* 1994). Since April of 2001, he has been secretary general of a major foundation that focuses on the promotion of transdisciplinary thinking and methods.

William Forsythe studied classical dance in New York and joined the Joffreys Ensemble in 1967. In 1971 he joined the Stuttgart Ballet and also held guest positions as choreographer in Berlin, Munich, and the Netherlands. Since 1984 he has directed the Frankfurt Ballet and since 1996 also the Frankfurt Theater am Turm. His Frankfurt works, *Gänge, Impressing the Czar, Slingerland, Limb's Theorem, As a Garden in This Setting,* and *Eidos : Telos,* have brought him international fame.

Mary Frates, from 1970–1976, worked in Oklahoma City public schools with the Arts in Education program of one of the Rockefeller Foundations. In 1977, she helped found the Oklahoma Arts Institute, of which she remains president, and for which she produces the institute's prizewinning educational films. She serves on the boards of many arts and cultural institutions, has received the Governor's Arts Award for her service to Oklahoma, and in 1998, received an honorary doctorate from the University of Oklahoma.

Peter Greenaway studied at the Art College in Walthamstow and the British Film Institute. His first short film, *Train,* appeared in 1966. Since then, he has directed many films and is also active as a painter, author, and opera director, designs exhibitions, and illustrates books. He has received many awards for his works, including the Hugo Award and the IMZ Dance Screen Award.

Michael Hilti was born in Liechtenstein and studied management at the School of Economics in St. Gallen. In 1973 he joined Hilti AG, becoming a member of the board of directors in 1976. In 1990 he succeeded his father in the directorship of the company and since 1994 has also been chairman of the board of Hilti AG.

Tao Ho studied art, theology, and music as an undergraduate at Williams College and completed a master's degree in architecture from Harvard University. He worked for several years as personal assistant to Walter Gropius before founding Taoho design. He is cofounder of Great Earth Architects & Engineers International and president of the Hong Kong Institute of Architects. He works frequently as an adviser in Beijing and is a brand-name product designer for several companies.

John Kao studied psychiatry at Yale and Harvard Universities and business as Harvard Business School. He is also a trained concert pianist and film producer, founded a medical technology company, and lectures on the subject of creativity at Harvard University. He is academic director of the Management Innovation Executive Program at Stanford University and CEO of the Idea Factory in San Francisco.

Daniel O. Leemon is Executive Vice President and Chief Strategy Officer for The Charles Schwab Corporation. He and his staff are responsible for a variety of strategic opportunities and initiatives, including helping Schwab's line managers set the course for new opportunities and growth strategies. His group also develops the strategic direction for Schwab's corporate development and venture investing activities. Leemon came to Schwab in September 1995 from twelve years with The Boston Consulting Group.

Berthold Leibinger worked as a developmental engineer at Cincinnati Milling following his education in machine tooling. He has been with TRUMPF GmbH & Co. since 1961, first directing the construction division, then as technical director and partner, and in 1978 as CEO. He is chairman of the Council on Innovation for the provincial government of Baden-Württemberg and was a member of the Council for Research Technology and Innovation under Chancellor Helmut Kohl.

William McDonough is cofounder and principal of McDonough Braungart Design Chemistry, a product and systems development firm, and also the founding principal of William McDonough +

Partners, Architects and Planners, an internationally recognized design firm practicing ecologically, socially, and economically intelligent architecture and planning in the U.S. and abroad. William McDonough + Partners has been a leader in the sustainable development movement since 1977. He was named by *Time Magazine* in 1999 as a "Hero for the Planet," and in 1996 he became the first and only recipient of the Presidential Award for Sustainable Development, the U.S.'s highest environmental honor, presented by President Clinton.

Harry Mulisch had his work first published at the age of twenty, in *Elseviers Weekblad.* He worked as a reviewer and writer for several Dutch newspapers before assuming the editorship of the publication *Podium.* His works, including novels, stories, essays, plays, and poems, have earned many awards, including the Anne-Frank Prize, the P.C. Hooft Prize, the Constantijn Huygens Prize, and the Libris Prize, and have been translated into all major languages.

Bolko v. Oetinger studied political science in Berlin and holds an MBA from the Stanford Graduate School of Business. He has worked for the Boston Consulting Group, where he is now senior vice president and director of the Strategy Institute. He is coeditor of *Clausewitz on Strategy* (John Wiley & Sons, 2001).

Heinrich v. Pierer studied law and economics and joined Siemens AG's legal department in 1969. From 1977 to 1987 he held various commericial duties with Kraftwerk Union AG and in 1988 became the commercial head of the corporate sector of KWU. In 1989 he became a Board Member of Siemens AG. In 1992 he became its President and CEO.

Harold Prince was recipient of a National Medal of Arts for the year 2000 from President Clinton for a career spanning over 40 years, in which "he changed the nature of the American musical."

In addition to his numerous directing and producing credits, he serves as a trustee for the New York Public Library, and served on the National Council of the Arts of the NEA for six years. He has received twenty Tony Awards. He was a 1994 Kennedy Center Honoree.

Wolfgang Rihm studied composition and music theory in Cologne and Freiburg. Since 1985 he has been a professor of composition at the Karlsruhe Music Academy. His work, which has won many awards, has been the focus of concert series and retrospectives. He is artistic consultant for the Deutsche Oper in Berlin and for the Center for Art and Media Technology in Karlsruhe and sits on the governing board of the German Copyright Society.

Claus Otto Scharmer teaches managing change at the MIT Sloan School of Management and consults with leaders of Fortune 100 companies in Europe and North America. He copioneered and led the Global Studies Program, a virtual global university among twelve universities across five continents in 1989–90, for which he received the Initiative Prize by the Foundation of Industrial Research in 1991. He codirects with Peter Senge the research on leadership at the Society for Organizational Learning.

Stephan Schmidheiny studied jurisprudence in Zurich and Rome. He holds board memberships in a number of business enterprises as well as offices in the nonprofit sector. In 1990 he was named principal business advisor to the secretary general of the UN conference on Environment and Development, and he founded the Business Council for Sustainable Development. He is author of *Changing Course: A Global Business Perspective on Development.*

Gerhard Schulze teaches empirical social research at the University of Bamberg. His research focuses on cultural sociology. Professor Schulze is the author of several books, including the influential *Die Erlebnisgesellschaft: Kultursoziologie der Gegenwart.*

Peter M. Senge is director of the Society for Organizational Learning and formerly Director of the Center for Organizational Learning at the Sloan School of Management, MIT. He is the author of *The Fifth Discipline: The Art and Practice of the Learning Organization,* cited by the *Harvard Business Review* as one of the seminal management books of the past 75 years, and coauthor of two fieldbooks. He has lectured throughout the world, translating the abstract ideas of systems theory into tools for better understanding of economic and organizational change.

Ron Sommer received a doctorate in mathematics in 1971. In 1980, he joined the Sony electronics group and in 1986 became president of Sony Deutschland, then president and COO of Sony USA in 1990; in 1993, he took over the management of Sony Europa in the same function. Since 1995, he has been the Chairman of the Board of Deutsche Telekom AG. He received the Global Leadership Award by the American Institute for Contemporary German Studies at the Johns Hopkins University.

Roger Y. Tsien received his A.B. in chemistry and physics from Harvard in 1972, and his Ph.D. in physiology from Cambridge University in 1977. Since 1989, he has been an Investigator at the Howard Hughes Medical Institute and Professor in the Departments of Pharmacology and of Chemistry & Biochemistry at the University of California, San Diego. His honors include first prize in the Westinghouse Science Talent Search, the Artois-Baillet-Latour Health Prize, the Gairdner Foundation International Award, and the American Heart Association Basic Research Prize. He is a member of the National Academy of Sciences and a cofounder of two biotech companies, Aurora Biosciences and Senomyx.

Franz Emanuel Weinert was a professor of psychology at the University of Heidelberg from 1968 to 1981, then director of the Max-Planck Institute for psychological research, and held emeritus honors from both those institutions. From 1990 until his death in March

2001, he was vice president of the Max-Planck Society. His main areas of research focused on the psychology of human learning and cognitive development.

Jürgen Werner studied Catholic theology at the Jesuiten-Hochschule Sankt Georgen, then philosophy and German, acquiring a Ph.D. in philosophy in 1984. He worked as an editor at *Frankfurter Allgemeine Zeitung* until 1998, then worked as a freelance journalist and advisor. Werner is a professor at the University of Witten/ Herdecke, where he teaches philosophy and rhetoric. He holds workshops on rhetoric, ethics, and management and works as a coach for senior executives. His most recent publication is the book *Die sieben Todsünden: Einblicke in die Abgründe menschlicher Leidenschaft* (*The Seven Deadly Sins: Insights into the Blackest Depths of Human Passion*).

Todd Winkler, a composer with expertise in computer music, formerly taught at Oberlin College Conservatory and California Institute for the Arts. He is currently an assistant professor at Brown University, where he teaches courses in computer music and multimedia studies and directs the MacColl Studio for Electronic Music. In 1994, he established Brown's Multimedia Laboratory. He has pioneered new methods for integrating acoustic instruments with computer technology, writing software that allows a computer to create expressive music by responding intelligently to real-time musical gestures, phrasing and tempo. He has written a book based on his research, *Composing Interactive Music*.